# Program Evaluation

# Program Evaluation

*Forms and Approaches*

*International edition*

John M. Owen
with
Patricia J. Rogers

SAGE Publications
London • Thousand Oaks • New Delhi

First published 1999
by Allen & Unwin
9 Atchison Street
St Leonards NSW 1590
Australia

SAGE Publications Ltd
6 Bonhill Street
London EC2A 4PU

SAGE Publications Inc
2455 Teller Road
Thousand Oaks, California 91320

SAGE Publications India Pvt Ltd
32, M-Block Market
Greater Kailash – I
New Dehi 110 048

**British Library Cataloguing in Publication data**

A catalogue record for this book is
available from the British Library

ISBN 0 7619 6177 1 (hbk)
ISBN 0 7619 6178 X (pbk)

**Library of Congress catalog record available**

Typeset in 10.5/12 pt Sabon by DOCUPRO, Sydney
Printed by South Wind Production Ltd, Singapore

# Contents

# Figures and Tables

## FIGURES

## TABLES

# Acknowledgments

John Owen would like to acknowledge the support provided by The University of Melbourne, including leave from the University during the second half of 1997. During this time, John Ainley and Barry McGaw at the Australian Council for Educational Research, David Fetterman at Stanford University and Jim Sanders and Dan Stufflebeam at Western Michigan University made arrangements at their institutions that facilitated the development of this book.

Special thanks are due to Pamela Andrew and Beverly Showers, who provided intensive ongoing support during the research and writing phases. Marvin Alkin and Bruce Joyce also provided material assistance.

John would also like to thank his colleagues at the Centre for Program Evaluation at The University of Melbourne for their various contributions to his knowledge about evaluation, in particular Faye Lambert, Marion Brown, Neil Day, Rosalind Hurworth, Jenni Livingston and Gerald Elsworth. Finally, John would like to thank Patricia Rogers for her critical perspectives that helped get the book from a set of ideas to the publication stage.

Patricia Rogers would like to acknowledge the contribution of the fellows, staff and directors of the Harvard Project on Schooling and Children, Carol Weiss and the Spencer Foundation whose interdisciplinary fellowship program provided a stimulating environment in which to work on this project.

Patricia also extends thanks to Jerome Winston, Gerald Elsworth, Bob Williams and Gary Hough who continue to challenge and extend her thinking about evaluation.

# 1

# Evaluation Fundamentals

## INTRODUCTION

You may have picked up this book because of an interest or involvement in the planning and/or delivery of a policy or program. Perhaps you work in one of the 'helping professions', such as social welfare, health or education. Alternatively, you may have a management or leadership role in government, business or industry. In all of these areas, there has been a burgeoning interest in evaluation. More and more, people who have responsibility for the development and delivery of policies and programs are being asked to plan more carefully, reflect more critically and justify reasons for selected courses of action. This is the stuff of evaluation.

Evaluation is not an alien activity for most of us. We engage informally in evaluative activity in our everyday lives. What clothes to wear on a given day, whether the plans for the home renovations are satisfactory, how the new worker in the office is coping, whether our football team played well—these are all examples of everyday evaluation. For most of these examples, evaluation is informal—in other words, we often assemble information 'in our heads' based on a variety of sensory inputs, such as observation and our existing knowledge to make judgments about the issue under consideration. For example, an evaluation of how the new worker in the office is coping may rely on informal observations of performance and the opinions of others, including the worker.

This book provides a rich conceptual framework for anchoring your existing evaluation knowledge and practice. We have adopted an eclectic view of the field in order that you may also see new directions for evaluation work in your area of work or interest. Topics of current interest to the decision-maker, such as needs assessment, benchmarking and performance auditing, are placed within this framework.

Our concern here is to assist those with a brief to undertake evaluation work to create and use knowledge that bears on key policy and program-related decisions in the workplace. A key aspect of sound decision-making is having access to knowledge that can influence a decision. Especially in a time of reducing resources, there is an understandable pressure to use new knowledge wisely. We believe that well-conducted, focused investigations, undertaken by individuals and groups who have a sound understanding of what they are doing and why they are doing it, can provide a major contribution to decisions about policy and program provision.

Typical evaluation scenarios include the following:

1   A philanthropic agency has funded an after-school recreation program as part of an initiative to reduce juvenile crime. After several years, an evaluation is commissioned to see whether the program has been effective.
2   A new community centre is being planned. An analysis of the needs of the community, including population information, availability of other facilities and a feasibility study is put in train.
3   Weekly and monthly measures of performance of major programs administered by a state government department are mandated by the state treasury.

You may be aware that scenario 1 poses questions one associates with issues such as:

- How good is this program? and
- Did the program work?

However, we have known for some time that the information needs of policy-makers and program developers require approaches over and above those associated only with these issues, which relate to the determining the impact of a program. This was recognised at the 1995 International Evaluation Conference in Vancouver, where Michael Scriven, a major evaluation theorist, made a distinction between impact evaluation based on 'traditional' approaches, and the fact that practising evaluators had expanded their range of activities to address questions such as:

- What is needed?
- What are the components of this program and how do they relate to each other?
- What is happening in this program?
- How is the program performing on a continuous basis?
- How could we improve this program?
- How could we repeat the success of this program elsewhere?

An evaluation based on Scenario 2 or 3 would address some of these issues.

Evaluators now need to expand their repertoire to keep pace with evaluation needs within modern organisations and agencies. An expanded perspective has evaluators performing a range of tasks and undertaking various roles, including:

- negotiation and planning of evaluations;
- paying attention to dissemination of findings;
- attending to ethical considerations and codes of behaviour; and
- working interactively and internally with clients to achieve effective change.

For example, Preskill and her colleagues discuss most of these roles in the context of undertaking evaluation in learning organisations. In these circumstances, the evaluator is likely to fulfil these roles as an 'internal' evaluator (Preskill & Torres, 1996).

This expanded perspective of evaluation is supported by a group of evaluators with special concern for the influence of evaluation. In addition to Preskill, they include Michael Patton and David Fetterman in the United States, Elliot Stern in the United Kingdom, our own experiences in Australia (Owen, Lambert & Stringer, 1994) and those of others in a range of settings in the private and public sectors in different countries: see, for example, work in Canada by Rowe & Jacobs (1996).

Ernest House suggests that evaluation consists of:

> collecting data, including relevant variables and standards, resolving inconsistencies in the values, clarifying misunderstandings and misrepresentations, rectifying false facts and factual assumptions, distinguishing between wants and needs, identifying all relevant dimensions of merit, finding appropriate measures for these dimensions, weighting the dimensions, validating the standards, and arriving at an evaluative conclusion. (House, 1993)

Consistent with House, we would regard a needs assessment as an evaluation approach designed to assist with the development of a program. As we have implied, in a different circumstance, the goal of an evaluation might be to assess program impact.

We should also note that there is a range of 'objects' for an evaluation. The objects which are focused on in this book are policies and programs, often interventions of a social or educational nature. Evaluation theorists have coined the term 'evaluand' as a generic label to describe the object of an evaluation.

---

At this stage, you may feel the need for a working description of what we mean by evaluation. So we will describe evaluation as the processes of:

- negotiating an evaluation plan;
- collecting and analysing evidence to produce findings; and
- disseminating the findings to identified audiences for use in:

  - describing or understanding an evaluand; or
  - making judgments and/or decisions related to that evaluand.

---

## KNOWLEDGE PRODUCTS OF EVALUATION

From the description of evaluation in the box above, it is clear that the notion of *findings* is central. Findings encompass the following:

- *evidence*: the data which has been collected during the evaluation. This could be regarded as information;
- *conclusions*: the synthesis of data and information. These are the interpretations or meanings made through analysis. Conclusions result from analytical processes involving data display, data reduction and verification;
- *judgments*: in which values are placed on the conclusions. Criteria are applied to the conclusions stating that the program is 'good' or 'bad', or that the results are 'positive', 'in the direction desired' or 'below expectations';
- *recommendations*: these are suggested courses of action, advice to policy-makers, program managers or providers about what to do in the light of the evidence and conclusions.

The four dot points above may be regarded as a chain of 'knowledge products' of evaluation. One of the key issues in the planning and negotiation stage of a given evaluation is to decide which of these products will be delivered by the evaluators.

The box above shows that one use is to 'describe or understand' the evaluand. There are instances where an evaluation audience or client merely wants to know about the impact of a particular evaluand. In these cases, the knowledge products would consist of evidence and conclusions. Our view is that understanding an evaluand involves both the assembly of evidence and making conclusions based firmly on that evidence.

A more likely scenario is that the audience or client needs to make a decision related to the evaluand. One issue is whether the evaluator provides judgments and recommendations, in addition to findings and conclusions, to assist with that decision. Making recommendations is a more proactive step in terms of using an evaluation to encourage action rather than just providing conclusions.

It is, of course, possible that decision-makers may wish to be involved at some point in the knowledge product chain. There are many instances in which evaluators and decision-makers have worked cooperatively to draw conclusions and develop recommendations regarding the future direction of a given policy or program. Evaluation theorists differ in their opinions about this. Michael Scriven, for example, believes that it is essential for evaluators to be responsible solely for making evaluative judgments. However, most other contemporary evaluators acknowledge the contributions of others at key points in the evaluation knowledge production chain—for example, House (1986) sees the evaluator playing the part of an 'independent, incorruptible, wise counsellor' in evaluation decision-making.

There will therefore be variations from study to study in:

- the degree to which a given evaluation provides key knowledge products: evidence, conclusions, judgments and recommendations; and
- the degree to which audiences are involved in producing these knowledge products.

## THE LOGIC OF EVALUATION

The above discussion has set out the key components of the knowledge production chain in evaluation. But to what degree are they interdependent? For example, is there a fundamental basis for drawing conclusions and making judgments? To address these issues, we would like you to read the following extracts from a 'test report' on breakfast cereals, typical of those found in

*Consumer Reports* in the United States of America, or *Choice* magazine in Australia. The 'object' or evaluand here is a product, something that we buy to use or consume. Specifically, the extract describes the evaluation of a range of breakfast cereals. When reading this extract from *Choice*, keep thinking about the following issues:

- What is the underlying basis for selecting criteria for judging the worth of each breakfast cereal?
- What evidence was used and on the basis of what criteria was the judgment of worth made?
- What standards were applied and how were the conclusions reached and presented?
- Decision-making: you have been asked to recommend one brand of cereal to members of your household or to a friend. Which one will you choose?

**Example 1.1 Test report: evaluating breakfast cereals**

Most of us eat them, but just how healthy are they? We've assessed more than 80 breakfast cereals to find out which are the most nutritious, and compared them with other breakfast options.

Breakfast is probably the most important meal of the day, but it's generally the most neglected one. By morning, around ten hours have usually passed since you last ate, so your body is running low on fuel. You need to replenish your stores, or your performance will suffer.

Studies have shown that, by lunchtime, people who eat breakfast are functioning better than those who don't. Adults who haven't eaten breakfast are more likely to be involved in industrial accidents, and children who miss this meal suffer significant drops in concentration levels in the late morning.

Breakfast-eaters are also more likely to eat well throughout the rest of the day than those who give it a miss. If you meet your nutritional needs at the start of the day, you're less likely to binge on sweet or fatty snacks for morning tea. If you're trying to lose weight, there's another reason you shouldn't miss breakfast: studies have shown that, when you do, the body's metabolic rate remains lower for the rest of the day—and with a low metabolic rate, you burn fuel more slowly, so you're not shedding those kilos.

*The ideal breakfast*

It's also important to feed your body the right kind of fuel in the morning. The best breakfast is one which is high in complex carbohydrates. Once digested, carbohydrates are stored in the muscles and liver as glycogen, a convenient storage form of glucose which your body can then draw on throughout the day to fuel mental and physical activity.

Unprocessed cereals and grains—the starting point of breakfast cereals—fit this bill perfectly. They are high in complex carbohydrates, as well as being a good source of protein, fibre, vitamins and minerals. They also fit in with national dietary guidelines, in that they contain very little fat, sugar or salt.

But how nutritious are they after they've been processed, when things are often added to them or taken away? We looked at more than 80 breakfast cereals, assessing their nutritional profiles to find which are the most and the least nutritious.

There is an enormous range of breakfast cereal products so we weren't able to look at them all. Our selection includes those widely available in supermarkets and all the top sellers in the ready-to-eat segment of the market.

*What makes a good breakfast cereal?*

A nutritious breakfast cereal should be low in fat, sugar and salt, as well as high in complex carbohydrates and dietary fibre. Some of the processed cereals on the market have retained many of the nutritional virtues of the original whole grain. But many more have had fat, sugar and salt added to them. Some have also had other nutrients added to them, often ones which were naturally in the original grain but were lost during processing, like fibre and thiamine (vitamin B1).

All up, we found 30 cereals that are a good choice to eat for breakfast ; the data on these cereals is included in Table 1.1.

Figures given are those supplied by manufacturers in their nutrition panels. Numbers were rounded to the nearest whole number in order to place products into ranking categories—for example, 19.3 per cent was considered to be 19 per cent.

**Table 1.1  Characteristics of breakfast cereals**

| Brand/type (alphabetically within groups) | Category | Fibre (g/) | Fat (g/) | Sugars (g/) | Sodium (mg/) | Carbo (g/) | Energy (kj/cal/) |
|---|---|---|---|---|---|---|---|
| | | all = per 100g | | | | | |
| **Highly recommended (4% or less fat, 5% or less sugar, 7% or more fibre, 600 mg/100g or less sodium)** | | | | | | | |
| HOME BRAND Wheat Biscuits | Biscuit | 12.2 | 2.7 | 2.3 | 270 | 64.5 | 1380/330 |
| KELLOGG'S Mini-Wheats Whole Wheat | Shredded wheat | 9.3 | 2.6 | 0.9 | 3 | 77.1 | 1523/363 |
| KELLOGG'S Wholegrain Wheat Flakes | Wheat-based | 11.0 | 1.1 | 2.0 | 468 | 81.3 | 1437/382 |
| SANITARIUM Lite-bix | 'Light' | 12.0 | 2.7 | 1.2 | 20 | 62.0 | 1340/320 |
| SANITARIUM Puffed Wheat | Wheat-based | 7.5 | 2.6 | 1.0 | 17 | 71.0 | 1440/344 |
| SANITARIUM Weet-Bix | Biscuit | 12.2 | 2.7 | 2.3 | 270 | 64.5 | 1380/330 |
| UNCLE TOBYS Organic Vita-Brits | Biscuit | 12.4 | 1.4 | 1.8 | 400 | 65.6 | 1320/315 |
| UNCLE TOBYS Shredded Wheat | Shredded wheat | 13.2 | 1.2 | 2.0 | 8 | 82.0 | 1330/318 |
| UNCLE TOBYS Wheeties | Wheat-based | 10.1 | 1.4 | 2.5 | 340 | 69.8 | 1390/332 |
| **Recommended (9% or less fat, 19% or less sugar, 7% or more fibre, 600 mg/100g or less sodium)** | | | | | | | |
| GOODNESS Tropical Toasted Muesli | Toasted muesli | 7.4 | 8.7 | 15.4 | 9 | 51.5 | 1569/375 |
| KELLOGG'S Just Right | Combination | 9.3 | 1.4 | 18.2 | 295 | 65.0 | 1534/381 |
| KELLOGG'S Mini-Wheats Apricot | Shredded wheat | 11.9 | 1.1 | 16.4 | 26 | 66.5 | 1503/358 |
| KELLOGG'S Sustain | Sports | 7.5 | 2.9 | 15.0 | 112 | 67.8 | 1607/399 |
| LOWAN Australian Rolled Oats (A) | Rolled oats | 11.5 | 8.7 | 1.2 | 6.3 | 65.3 | 1624/388 |
| MORNING SUN Natural Apricot and Almond Muesli | Natural muesli | 17.6 | 8.3 | 17.8 | 32 | 51.4 | 1420/339 |
| THE OLD GRAIN MILL Australian Gold Classic Muesli | Natural muesli | 12.2 | 8.7 | 19.3 | 46 | 46.7 | 1610/385 |

| Brand/type (alphabetically within groups) | Category | Fibre (g/) | Fat (g/) | Sugars (g/) | Sodium (mg/) | Carbo (g/) | Energy (kj/cal/) |
|---|---|---|---|---|---|---|---|
| | | all = per 100g | | | | | |
| THE OLD GRAIN MILL Australian Gold Natural Muesli | Natural muesli | 11.9 | 6.3 | 17.5 | 66 | 56.5 | 1548/370 |
| SANITARIUM Bran Bix | Biscuit | 22.0 | 4.4 | 5.7 | 410 | 45.0 | 1180/280 |
| SANITARIUM Crunchy Bix | Biscuit | 7.7 | 5.5 | 13.0 | 320 | 58.7 | 16/380 |
| SANITARIUM Natural Muesli | Natural muesli | 7.1 | 5.1 | 18.6 | 124 | 44.0 | 1400/333 |
| SANITARIUM Weet-Bix plus Oat Bran | Biscuit | 11.6 | 4.8 | 7.3 | 250 | 54.7 | 1440/345 |
| UNCLE TOBY'S Crunchy Oat Bran | Bran | 15.0 | 5.8 | 16.6 | 240 | 51.2 | 1499/358 |
| UNCLE TOBYS Hi-Fibre Oats | Rolled oats | 12.9 | 9.0 | <1 | 5 | 58.3 | 1500/358 |
| UNCLE TOBYS Instant Porridge (A) | Rolled oats | 10.0 | 9.2 | 0.5 | <5 | 61.3 | 1530/366 |
| UNCLE TOBYS Muesli Flakes | Combination | 9.0 | 2.6 | 19.0 | 240 | 53.9 | 1390/332 |
| UNCLE TOBYS Natural Apricot & Almond Muesli | Natural muesli | 13.8 | 8.3 | 17.8 | 30 | 41.4 | 1420/339 |
| WEIGHT WATCHERS Fruit & Fibre Cereal | 'Light' | 11.8 | 2.5 | 18.5 | 170 | 60.0 | 1495/357 |
| WILLOW VALLEY Multi Bran | Bran | 36.3 | 9.3 | 12.8 | 122 | 57.4 | 1727/413 |
| OK (9% or less fat, 19% or less sugar, 3% to 6.5% fibre, 600 mg/100 g or less sodium) | | | | | | | |
| KELLOGG'S Puffed Wheat | Wheat-based | 6.0 | 2.3 | 1.1 | 3 | 78.1 | 1614/385 |
| KELLOGG'S Special K | 'Light' | 2.9 | 0.5 | 14.4 | 475 | 57.7 | 1436/379 |

Source:  Reprinted from CHOICE, January 1994 with the permission of the Australian Consumers' Association (ACA).

*How the cereals were rated*

Ideally, we would want a branded breakfast cereal to provide similar levels of nutrients to uncooked wholegrain cereals. We looked at the nutrient profiles of some of these raw cereals and used them as a starting point for developing a model for ranking the breakfast cereals. For details of the amounts of each nutrient in our 'highly recommended', 'recommended', 'OK' and 'not recommended' cereals, see below. A product had to meet our requirements for all four nutrients—fat, sugar, fibre and sodium—to get into a category.

1 *Fibre*. Fibre is an important part of the diet: it adds bulk which helps you to feel full and satisfied, and helps with the elimination of wastes from the body. Too little fibre in the diet leads to constipation, and has also been suggested as a contributory factor in some cancers, particularly of the breast and colon. To be highly recommended or recommended, a cereal had to contain 7 per cent or more fibre. To be 'OK' it had to have a least 3 per cent fibre; anything less than this meant the cereal was not recommended.

2 *Fat*. To be rated as highly recommended, a cereal had to contain 4 per cent or less fat; to be recommended or 'OK' it had to have 9 per cent or less. Packaged cereals which are more than 9 per cent fat were not recommended. Fat should be kept to a minimum in the diet. It's the most energy-dense nutrient, and excessive consumption is linked to diet-related conditions like obesity, heart disease, diabetes and some cancers. Generally, it's recommended that fat should contribute no more than 30 per cent of your total energy intake. However, infants, preschool children, underweight people, lactating women and those who do unusually heavy work may need more than this.

3 *Sugars*. Unprocessed cereals have a naturally low sugar content—less than the 5 per cent we considered the maximum for highly recommended products. This figure also takes into account the increase in sugar content that would occur through loss of moisture when the cereals are processed (which makes the nutrients more concentrated). For a cereal to be rated as recommended or 'OK', the amount of sugar had to be 19 per cent or

less. This represents the 5 per cent plus the equivalent of an extra teaspoon per serve. Anything over 19 per cent and the cereal fell into the 'not recommended' category. If you sprinkle much more than a teaspoon of sugar on to your bowl of some of these cereals, you could turn them into the equivalent of 'not recommended'.

4 *Sodium*. Sodium may be found in some breakfast cereals in the form of common salt (sodium chloride), sodium bicarbonate or other compounds. Current knowledge suggests that a high sodium intake is linked with the development of high blood pressure, stroke and coronary heart disease in susceptible people. Recent international studies have shown that salt added by food manufacturers makes up the bulk of most people's daily intake, so it is important to watch out for high-sodium cereals, particularly if you eat a lot of other processed foods.

Just how much salt is too much is not clear. The amount we chose for cereal to be recommended or 'OK'—600 mg or less of sodium per 100 g—is not overly strict. If a cereal contained 600 mg per 100 g, a 30 g serve would contribute one-fifth of the lower recommended dietary intake (RDI) of sodium. (The RDI for sodium is expressed as a range; we used the amount at the lower end of the range as our guide.)

*Findings*

Many of the cereals have a very short list of ingredients, indicating they are fairly close to their original, unprocessed counterparts in terms of nutritional characteristics. We split these 30 into 'highly recommended' and 'recommended' categories: the difference between these two groups was that, to be highly recommended, a cereal had to contain less fat and sugar. Overall, we based our evaluation on the amount of fibre the cereals contain (the more the better), and the amount of fat, sugar and salt (the less the better).

* *Fibre*: All the top 30 were a good source; the two that fell into the 'OK' category in our table contained less but were still a reasonable source.
* *Fat*: Oats naturally contain more fat than other 'raw' cereals; although the fat levels of oat-based cereals kept

them out of our 'highly recommended' category, they're still a good choice for breakfast.

- *Sugar*: Our nine highly recommended cereals had little or no added sugar. Some people might put more on them, but we rated them without extra sugar. Most of the others in the table contained more sugar than these nine—around a teaspoon more per serving than naturally occurs in whole grains. For some brands it was contributed by dried fruit, which has a health advantage over cane sugar as it contributes some extra fibre.
- *Sodium*: The top 30 contained only small amounts of sodium. Common salt is sodium chloride and it's the sodium that's considered the problem.

## Review

Let's go back to our questions, and your answers, with a view to 'pulling apart' the evaluation exercise. Later we will review this exercise using some concepts developed by evaluation theorists.

- What is the underlying basis for selecting criteria for judging the worth of each breakfast cereal?

It is clear that *Choice* set up their criteria assuming that a nutritious breakfast is a 'good' breakfast. They believe that such a breakfast is important to give you a 'good start' to the day and to sustain you through the day. Additionally, they claim that a nutritious breakfast is also one which will help you stay away from snacks that cause you to put on weight. In a nutshell, the evaluators placed a high value on nutrition to set up their criteria.

- What evidence was used and on the basis of what criteria was the judgment of worth made?

The value position of the evaluator was translated into the selection of the characteristics of the breakfast cereals consistent with them being nutritious. These characteristics are: fibre, fat, sugar and sodium. These were turned into variables or criteria, and data were collected on each of these. In addition, data on complex carbohydrates and energy provision were also collected. The evaluator was able to access these data from the cereal packets. Note that a cereal was more likely to be recommended if it was higher on fibre and lower on the other three criteria.

Acceptable levels needed to regard a given cereal as 'good'

were derived from the nutrient profiles of uncooked (raw) cereals. Note that, for each of the four criteria, this *external* frame of reference provides the criterion for ranking the cereals and ultimately placing them in categories.

- What standards were applied and how were the conclusions reached and presented?

For each of these criteria, a standard was set in order for a cereal to be 'highly recommended'—for example, the criteria for fat content was 4 per cent. Different standards were employed for the 'recommended' category.

- Decision-making: you have been asked to recommend one brand of cereal to members of your household or to a friend. Which one will you choose?

The evaluator has gone as far as categorising the cereals and pointing out nine which are highly recommended. But for this last aspect of our case study, it is now over to you—or, in context, the readers of the article. Ultimately the choice of which product to buy will depend on the reader's decision-making. Choosing one cereal from those highly recommended may depend on which one of the criteria is more important to the reader—for example, there may be a preference for the cereal with the lowest sodium level, independent of the levels of the other variables. It could also be that a reader may choose on the basis of energy provision—selecting the cereal within the highly recommended category that is highest on energy provision.

## EXTRAPOLATING TO A PROGRAM EVALUATION

The above discussion provides us with a basis for understanding what is referred to as the *logic of evaluation*. This is a logic which is consistent with making a judgment about the worth of the object under review.

The logic of evaluation is of particular importance to evaluations which are concerned with determining *impact*. Evaluations of this nature generally have a summative role—that is, they report on what the program has achieved and should be undertaken on programs that are settled or stabilised. As many readers are likely to have an immediate interest in impact evaluations, we devote the remainder of this chapter to issues relating to the logic of evaluation.

Fournier (1995) summarises what we have just done above very nicely when she describes the logic of evaluation as follows:

- *Establishing criteria*
  - On what dimensions must the evaluand do well?
- *Constructing standards*
  - How well should the evaluand perform?
- *Measuring performance and comparing with standards*
  - How well did the evaluand perform?
- *Synthesising and integrating evidence into a judgment of worth*
  - What is the worth of the evaluand?

It should be noted that theoretical evaluators use the term 'worth' to indicate the *extrinsic* value of an evaluand within a given context. This in contrast to its *intrinsic* value, or merit. The worth of the cereals in this case might be regarded within decision-making about the most appropriate foods for people who are undertaking an extended nutritional regime.

Fournier notes that this is logic accepted by theorists. However, what count as criteria, what evidence is invoked, and how information is synthesised can vary across different approaches within evaluation practice. She also notes that the logic can be applied with different fields, by which she means product evaluation, program evaluation, policy evaluation and personnel evaluation (the last we would prefer to label as 'assessment' or 'appraisal'). The generality of the logic is its strength: it gives us a base from which we can delve into different approaches to evaluation practice.

While the logic of evaluation seems cut and dried, the reality is that, in practical evaluations, the evaluator must make a series of interrelated decisions in order to make a judgment of worth. Take the cereals case study above. In setting up the criteria, the evaluators made it clear that their value position was that breakfasts should be nutritious. In good evaluations, values which frame the remainder of the evaluation should be made explicit; however, in practice those who have analysed evaluation practice have found that this is rarely the case (Kirkhart & Ruffolo, 1993). Making the value base explicit is important because the conclusions follow from the value position taken, and those for whom the evaluation is intended must be aware of the value system which has undergirded the evaluation.

In Example 1.1, if we had adopted a value position that we would choose the cereals that young children prefer to eat for breakfast, the recommendation list would almost certainly have been different. This would have had implications for the remainder of the evaluative process—the collection and analysis of data and the making of judgments. Instead of fibre and salt content, the data collection would probably have been based on levels of satisfaction that children reported from eating different cereals! The standard might be a point on the upper end of a 'delicious' scale.

There are some points that should be noted about making the judgment of worth. Scriven (1971) behoves us make a 'simple' judgment about an evaluand:

> It's [the evaluator's] task to try very hard to condense all that mass of data into one word: good or bad. Sometimes this is really impossible, but all too often the failure to do so is simply a cop-out disguised as or rationalised as objectivity.

It is clear that the evaluation in Example 1.1 is really a refinement of Scriven's position. Each cereal has been allocated to one of three categories: highly recommended, recommended or OK.

It should also be noted that this evaluation provides data on many evaluands (cereals). This is consistent with situations in program evaluation where decision-makers need findings about the parallel delivery of a program offered at different sites.

In summary, the logic of evaluation as a basis for thinking about evaluation practice cannot be overstated. One issue that arises is whose values or value frame will be used if we are required to make a judgment about a given evaluand? You can see that the selection of this frame is vital. When different value positions are held among the stakeholders—those who have an interest in the evaluand—a great deal can hang on the choice of the value perspective chosen. This has implications for practice and represents a challenge for evaluators to handle this diversity of views when negotiating and planning the evaluation (see Chapter 4).

## EXPLICIT OR IMPLICIT LOGIC

Choosing criteria and setting standards by which an evaluand can be judged acceptable is obviously key to decision-making. As we implied in Example 1.1, criteria and standards must come from somewhere. Owen & Downtown (1990) evaluated a large-scale conference for educational consultants. An objective of the evaluation was to assess the impact on participants of the conference, that was designed to provide them with information for their day-to-day work in schools. Conference organisers wished to gauge participant reactions to key sessions of the conference and to the quality of the conference overall.

The major form of data collection was a structured questionnaire. All participants were given time at the end of the conference to complete it, after the evaluators had emphasised the importance of the feedback data. A page of the questionnaire is included as Figure 1.1.

### Figure 1.1   Conference evaluation: excerpt from questionnaire

*Session 2: Science & Technology Policy Directions and Initiatives*

Thinking about this session, to what extent:

- has your knowledge of the rationale and operation of this policy/initiative increased as a result of attending this workshop?

  not at all        a little          some            a lot              a great deal

- has your understanding of how the policy/initiative fits into the overall scheme of science/technology education in the state increased?

  not at all        a little          some            a lot              a great deal

- were the underlying professional development principles made clear in the presentation of the policy/initiative?

  not at all        a little          some            a lot              a great deal

- could you (or were you able to) explain the major features of the policy/initiative to a consultant who did not attend the session?

  not at all        a little          some            reasonably         comprehensively

- are you confident of being able to follow up on the policy/initiative if the need arises in your work?

  not at all        a little          somewhat         a lot              a great deal

- Do you have additional questions about the policy/initiative which need to be answered before you could use the information in your work? If so, jot them down below.

  _____

  _____

  _____

Data were coded, analysed and presented in tables as part of a written report. The findings for sessions 1–4 of the conference are reproduced as Table 1.2.

The four criteria in Table 1.2 were important for judging the conference from the point of view of the organisers. We chose to present evidence on these criteria in terms of the percentage of respondents who responded on the highest two points on the five-point scale, for example 'a lot' and 'a great deal'.

To establish the effectiveness of each session, we inspected the

**Table 1.2  Comparative impact on participants: sessions 1–4**

| | 1 | 2 | 3 | 4 |
|---|---|---|---|---|
| | Trends in Professional Development | Science/ Technology Policy Directions | Maths/ Technology Policy Directions | Regional Initiatives in Sm &I |
| Increased knowledge of the rationale and operation of projects within theme | 58 | 61 | 63 | 80 |
| Increased understanding of how policy/initiative fits into overall state scheme | – | 39 | 51 | – |
| Clarity of underlying professional development principles | 79 | 36 | 51 | 68 |
| Ability to explain the major features to a colleague | 91 | 72 | 64 | 86 |
| Willing/confident to follow up on the project | 68 | 49 | 58 | 71 |

*Note:*  Each figure in the table is the percentage of participants responding to the item on the highest two points of a five-point scale (generally 'a lot' and 'a great deal').

findings, as set out in Table 1.2, in conjunction with the clients for the evaluation, the conference organisers. It was clear that the organisers looked for patterns of responses for particular sessions and, as could be expected, they regarded sessions 1 and 4 as 'more successful'. All analyses were comparative; there was little discussion as to whether any individual session was successful in its own right. This was almost certainly due to the fact that neither evaluators nor the audience considered the level of response needed for an individual session to be judged as successful in advance of the data collection. That is, standards were *not set 'up-front'*. One plausible standard was that, unless two-thirds of respondents (66 per cent) responded favourably on *all* criteria, a session would not be regarded as 'worthy'. On this basis, only session 4 would be regarded as worthy and the conference could be regarded as a failure.

When the findings were actually presented, the organisers decided that the conference as a whole had gone well. We surmise that the conference organisers arrived at a standard that was less demanding than the one we have just mentioned, and furthermore that the standard—far from being set out formally—was implicit and shared by those concerned. In practice, many evaluations actually operate on a more informal interpretation of the logic of evaluation, a finding backed up elsewhere (Fournier, 1995).

The application of the logic of evaluation to real settings involves the evaluator, client or some other stakeholder holding a view about the worth of a given program based on a defensible empirical enquiry. However, as a program needs to have been implemented, or 'in place', for such a judgment to be made, evaluations which are based on the logic of evaluation must lag behind program development, and are thus retrospective in nature. The logic of evaluation thus applies to situations which call for an assessment with a summation or summative role for evaluation.

## WHO MAKES THE EVALUATIVE JUDGMENT?

Judgments about the worth of a given program should be made on the basis of the evidence provided. The evidence can be of a qualitative or quantitative nature, or a combination of both. A study designed to assess the worth of a major educational policy, titled the Curriculum and Standards Framework (CSF), used largely qualitative data obtained from schools by observation, interview and document analysis. The focus of the study was its impact on school practice and thus concentrated on the implementation of the policy across a school system.

The client for the findings was the education committee of a state-level Board of Studies, for which a final report was assembled. The findings were presented as a discussion based on five objectives of the CSF. The reporting strategy was to lay out a summary of information and conclusions, and allow members of the committee to make their own judgments about the worth of the policy. This was done with a recognition that different members of the committee and other readers would have different opinions of the relative importance of each of the objectives of the CSF. In this example, the evaluators:

- encouraged clients—in this case a committee—to make a judgment of worth;
- explicitly introduced the notion of values to the clients in the evaluation report.

A copy of the first page of this report is presented in Example 1.2.

In this case, the report formed the basis of a vigorous debate about the net impact of the CSF policy at committee level (Owen, Meyer & Livingston, 1996). This example has implications for the negotiation of an evaluation. As we have noted earlier, clients and evaluators should determine, in advance of any evidence-

18

## Example 1.2 Evaluating the Curriculum and Standards Framework (CSF)

*First page of final evaluation report*

[Note that we have not included details of references here.]

A key aspect of evaluation is making a judgment of the worth of the policy or program under review. Kirkhart and Ruffolo believe that it is important to be explicit about the criteria being used to determine worth. There is also an associated issue of who makes the necessary judgments. While the onus of judgment is often on the evaluator, stakeholders are sometimes in a better position to determine the value of a given program.

*Synthesis of the evaluation findings*

Below, we lay out the more salient conclusions from the case studies, so that an evaluative judgment can be made. While we are prepared to make conclusions we prefer to leave the *final* judgment of the impact of the CSF to the readers of this report. This is an acknowledgment of the fact that value judgments are relative. That is, what one stakeholder might value is likely to differ from the values of another stakeholder.

The conclusions are organised around five themes. We believe that these themes provide a valid framework for making evaluative judgments. They were derived from the early stated policy documentation from the time the CSF was released to schools. As such, they are explicit and independent of any one person's view of what the CSF should achieve. The themes also incorporate the facets about which the primary stakeholders expressed an interest.

The themes are:

- Adaptation at School Level;
- Selecting and Arranging the Curriculum;
- Assessment and Reporting;
- Accountability to the Community and to the System; and
- Policy–School Level Interaction.

In making a judgment about the worth of a program, there is a tendency to reduce the judgment to a single finding, to say that the object being evaluated is 'OK' or 'not much good'. Taking a line from the evaluation of products, some evaluators have urged that a single judgment can be made about educational programs. Our view is that the real world is more complex, and that most policies or programs need to be considered on several dimensions. This is the position taken here. Judgments could be made for each theme on the basis of the summary presented. If a final single judgment of the worth of the CSF is to be made, it will depend on a stakeholder's valuing of the relative importance of the policy themes.

gathering, who is to make a judgment about the worth of the program under review. In some instances, the client of an evaluation is more than happy to let the evaluator do so. But in other cases, the client prefers to take on this responsibility. The fact is that, in studies which use the logic of evaluation, some judgment of worth must be made by someone.

## CONCLUSION

We have introduced two major ideas in this chapter. The first is a working description of what evaluation means with consequent implications for what evaluators do. Evaluators need to be involved in a range of tasks associated with:

- negotiating an evaluation plan;
- collecting and analysing evidence to produce evaluation findings; and
- dissemination to identified audiences for use in
- understanding an evaluand or making judgments and decisions about that evaluand.

The second major idea in this chapter relates to what we mean by evaluation findings and the notion of a knowledge production chain. Within this chain we have examined how key elements in the chain link together in certain circumstances, creating a logic of evaluation. As we have said, the logic has been discussed with reference to impact evaluations. The extent to which this logic relates to other approaches to evaluation can be broached only after these approaches are outlined. This is a major objective of this book.

## REFERENCES

Australian Consumers' Association (1994). 'Test report: Breakfast Cereal'. *Choice*, January

Fournier, D.M. (1995). 'Establishing Evaluative Conclusions: A Distinction between General and Working Logic'. *New Directions for Program Evaluation*, 68 (Winter 1995), pp. 15–32.

House, E.R. (1986). 'Drawing Evaluative Conclusions'. *Evaluation Practice*, 7 (3), pp. 35–9.

——(1993). *Professional Evaluation: Social Impact and Political Consequences*. Thousand Oaks, CA: Sage.

Kirkhart, K.E. & Ruffolo, M.C. (1993). 'Value Bases of Case Management'. *Evaluation and Program Planning*, 16, pp. 55–65.

Owen, J.M. & Downtown A.P. (1990). *Towards Effective Conference Design*. Melbourne: Centre for Program Evaluation, The University of Melbourne.

Owen, J.M., Lambert, F.C. & Stringer, W. S. (1994). 'Acquiring Knowledge of Implementation and Change: Essential for Program Evaluators?'. *Knowledge: Creation, Diffusion, Utilization*, 15 (3), pp. 273–94.

Owen, J.M., Meyer, H. & Livingston, J. (1996). *School Responses to the Curriculum and Standards Framework*. Carlton, Vic: Victorian Board of Studies.

Preskill, H. & Torres, R.T. (1996). 'From Evaluation to Evaluative Enquiry for Organisational Learning'. Paper presented at the annual meeting of the American Evaluation Association, Atlanta, GA, November.

Rowe, W. & Jacobs, N. (1996). 'Principles and Practice of Organisationally Independent Evolution'. Unpublished paper. Personal Communication.

Scriven, M. (1971). 'Evaluating Educational Programs'. In F. G. Caro (ed.), *Readings in Evaluation Research*. New York: Russell Sage Foundation.

# 2

## The Nature of Interventions: What We Evaluate

### INTRODUCTION

In Chapter 1, we introduced a working description of evaluation and the logic of evaluation. This introduction indicated that evaluation is a well-established field of study, with contributions by theorists and practitioners in many countries throughout the world. There are well-established canons of practice and evaluators have their own journals and conferences which give evaluation the status of a profession. Agencies and organisations which commission evaluations have been prepared to allocate funds and other resources to support these studies. Evaluation activities are frequently of interest to the general public as well as to stakeholders. A lay observer might be justified in asking why there has been such a growth in the status of evaluation, and how in fact evaluation assists in improving the social condition.

One response is that evaluation is complementary to, and supportive of, the development and provision of effective and responsive social, educational and other like interventions or evaluands. All programmatic interventions cost money and resources. In a democratic society, it is incumbent on providers to ensure that policies, support and administrative programs and other resources designed to improve the social condition are as effective and efficient as possible. This means responsive program planning, attention to implementation and checking to see that program intentions have been translated into outcomes. Evaluation has a potential role at all stages of program provision.

22

The need for effective and efficient program planning exists within the context of governments from the four corners of the world providing services in a time of economic constraint, and an increased concern among the citizenry that money be spent wisely. One particular concern is that funds allocated to disadvantaged community groups are actually spent 'on the ground' in ways that directly benefit those for whom they have been earmarked. For example, in countries such as the United States and Australia, there has been concern that the funds designed to provide health and welfare support for native Americans and Australian Aborigines respectively have been used inefficiently, on poorly conceived interventions which have made little impact of the general wellbeing of the recipients.

Shadish et al. (1991) suggest that studies of social and educational interventions should attend to three aspects of evaluands:

- their internal structure and functioning;
- constraints that shape design and delivery; and
- societal factors that influence the development of evaluands, how evaluands themselves change over time and how, in turn, the evaluand contributes to social change.

Taken together, these aspects concern both program design and implementation and the links between the evaluand and the context in which it is set. This reminds us that social and educational interventions do not exist in a vacuum, and that evaluators need to be mindful of the influence of context when planning studies and providing advice to policy and program developers.

There is often uncertainty about the meaning of some terms used to describe different objects or evaluands. We need to have a common working understanding of types of interventions and associated concepts, so that a common 'evaluator language' can be built up which will serve as a sound base for exploration of key issues. So the next section is devoted to coming to grips with some shared definitions. A more meaningful discussion can then be advanced about ways in which evaluation can be used to develop, review or improve an evaluand.

It is also important that the evaluator and others interested in the findings of an evaluation are clear about the object or evaluand of a given evaluation. While this seems trite, experience shows that being absolutely unambiguous about the *what* of evaluation is essential if the evaluation is to go forward to answer other fundamental questions, such as why the evaluation is being conducted.

## OBJECTS OF AN EVALUATION

Objects for an evaluation can be classified into the following categories:

- programs;
- policies;
- organisations;
- products; and
- individuals.

Each of these is discussed in turn below.

### Programs

Smith (1989) defines a program as:

> [a] set of planned activities directed toward bringing about specified change(s) in an identified and identifiable audience.

This suggests that a program has two essential components:

- a documented plan; and
- action consistent with the information contained in the plan.

**Figure 2.1    Program components**

Formal evaluation language speaks of a 'theory of action' or a program logic which specifies causal linkages between various components of implementation, and between them and one or more outcomes. There is an assumption that those responsible for program planning have sufficient knowledge of the phenomenon to codify these causal linkages in ways that can be disseminated to those with an interest in the impact of the program—for example, program deliverers and those who may benefit from the program, who could be thought of as program clients. In other words, selected activities, presented in a given sequence, should produce desired effects on the participants.

Many programs are described as *social interventions*. They are provided to the community by government or social service agencies, on the basis of 'non-market' criteria, in areas such as welfare, health and education. A review of social interventions

24

suggests that we need to extend the definition of a program to encompass a more extensive range of program interventions. At one level, we can distinguish between programs designed to produce an end result by influencing behaviour, and those which are designed to satisfy a need by providing a product or a service.

Extending this distinction and incorporating the contributions of Funnell & Lenne (1989), five specific types of intervention can be identified as follows:

- *educational programs*, which emphasise the acquisition of information, skills and attitudes (ISA) typically provided through formal learning settings by institutions such as schools, colleges and universities. Examples include:

  - a reading program at an adult education centre;
  - an in-house training program for child protection workers.

- *advisory programs*, such as communication and mass education programs for the public. The receptiveness of the target group is dependent not only on the quality of the intervention devised by the advisory group, but also on the credibility of those who have the responsibility to 'sell' the product. This is the motivation behind employing people with high profiles to encourage a change in the behaviour of the 'clients'. Examples include:
  - a health promotion program designed to improve the eating habits and general wellbeing of the citizens in a targeted region or city—for instance, a media campaign in which well-known football players are featured;
  - a publicity program encouraging people to visit a region or area of natural beauty, such as the Lakes District in England, or the Grand Tetons in the United States.

- *regulatory programs*, which try to influence behaviour to alleviate a problem through a process of deterrence. While the likelihood of incurring a penalty is believed to have an effect on behaviour, more recent studies suggest that the perceived risk of being detected is the more powerful influence. Examples include:

  - the implementation of measures to reduce the incidence of alcohol-induced accidents on the roads, such as the use of 'booze buses' and the enforcement of blood alcohol standards for drivers;
  - the enforcement of fishing regulations which deter professional fisherman or weekend anglers from taking fish

under a given size, with a view to ensuring an adequate supply of the species in the longer term.

- *case management programs*, where individual objectives are set for each case within an overall program framework. The case may be an individual or a group within an organisation. By implication, a plan must be developed for each case. Examples include:
    - a systematic set of rehabilitation procedures designed for an individual worker injured on the job;
    - the development and implementation of case plans for children needing foster care because of family dislocation.
- *product or service provision*. While it might seem simple to devise programs of this nature, the actual outcomes may be complex and this has implications for evaluation—for instance, for example the provision of services may be particularly subject to issues such as effectiveness for cost. Examples include:
    - the provision of meals and other forms of support for the elderly who are unable to fully fend for themselves while remaining within their own homes;
    - the installation of a power line to an isolated community in a valley not presently covered by the national electricity grid.

Some services may be used as an individual pleases, for example the use of facilities in a local park. Others may be available according to the status of the individual in a social system—for example, access to child-minding services may be only available to families with children in a given age range. Other services, such as meals for elderly citizens, may be made available as a result of the professional judgment of a social worker. Even for programs which directly provide a tangible product or service, there are consequences beyond the immediate outcomes of the programs themselves. For example, the installation of a power line may have economic, agricultural and human resource implications for the valley which should be considered prior to the decision to go ahead with the project. The program planner may need to anticipate these effects and to monitor the expected and unexpected outcomes of the intervention for the agent providing the program.

Different objectives and delivery across the five types of program implies that different evaluative methods are needed for the evaluator working across all types. Among other skills (to be discussed later), the evaluator needs a range of data-collection and analysis skills to cope with this diverse array of analyses appropriate within and between program types.

## Program levels

Programs can be planned and presented at several levels.

The broadest is the *mega* level—the level of the office of the head of a government department or boardroom of a private company. This is often described as the *corporate level*. At this level, planning is likely to be in terms of overall economic or social impact. The second level is *macro* planning, which may be the responsibility of divisions, regions or branches of an organisation. The third level is the *micro* level, with the responsibility of work units or individuals within an organisation. The degree and emphasis on planning at each of these levels varies from organisation to organisation. The motor vehicle industry is a case where different arrangements have been noted in planning across levels. Whereas American car firms have adopted a top-down planning style, there has been far more emphasis on worker participation in Japan and Sweden, which have encouraged greater job satisfaction and economic performance (Thurow, 1986).

The level of a program is generally important to the design of an evaluation, largely because stakeholders generally have different concerns at each level. Evaluators must be sensitive to these needs when designing evaluations that are responsive to needs of clients at each level.

> **Example 2.1 Levels of development and the evaluation agendas of stakeholders**
>
> A training course has been developed for people wishing to work in the area of intellectual disability. The curriculum has been produced by a central curriculum agency and is being taught in sixteen Technical and Further Education (TAFE) colleges across an education system. Within this context, different evaluation agendas can be imagined which are related to decisions about the course. For example:
>
> - *Mega level:* The system-level authority may wish to know whether the course, assessed over all colleges, and over a period of time, is providing adequate graduates to staff intellectual disability centres. This evaluation may be motivated by a need to inform the government's Treasury Department about the cost benefit of the program.

- *Macro level*: The curriculum agency may wish to know whether the curriculum is actually providing graduates with the skills needed to perform on the job. This evaluation may be motivated by a need to revise the curriculum.
- *Micro level*: Staff responsible for the course in one of the colleges may be unhappy with the way they are delivering the course. This evaluation may be motivated by a wish to finetune the delivery to make the teaching more effective and to use staff time more efficiently.

Different questions need to be answered at each level. A combination of the level and the concerns of audiences at each level implies that the agenda of evaluative enquiry would be different in each case.

A manifestation of the planning process is the creation of a program. Moving from planning to program development means converting value choices into concrete directions for action by choosing from among alternatives and allocating resources to achieve defined goals.

### Specificity of program plans

Expectations about the specificity of program documentation, and hence prescriptions for action, vary. We have seen that programs can be classed along two dimensions, according to:

- level (mega, macro, micro); and
- type (educational, advisory, regulatory, case management, service/product provision).

This provides a three-by-five matrix within which to classify an intervention about which you have some interest. This may be helpful if you are asked to think about undertaking an evaluation, because locating a given program in such a matrix almost certainly will reduce the possible decisions about how the evaluation will proceed.

As a rule, as one moves from the mega to the micro level, the specificity of planning increases. While a regional or school district science program may be written in general terms (macro/educational) a six-week science curriculum unit is likely to be more detailed (micro/educational). A question which arises is: what level of detail is adequate in order for those involved to know what the program is really about?

Leithwood suggests that a curriculum unit would be ade-

28

quately specified if the program plan contained coherent information on the following dimensions:

- platform;
- objectives;
- student entry behaviours;
- assessment tools and procedures;
- instructional materials;
- learner experiences;
- teaching strategies;
- content; and
- time or length of the unit.

Most of these dimensions can be readily understood by educators and even lay people. The possible exception is 'platform'. Leithwood (1981) defines platform as:

> patterns of implicit and explicit beliefs and assumptions accepted as the bases about what to include in and exclude from a curriculum . . . Such platforms are the product of interactions between a developer's value systems on the one hand, and information about society, culture, learners, the learning process and the nature of knowledge on the other.

The inclusion of platform or a rationale in the program specification reinforces what was said before: that programs do not exist in a vacuum, but are a response to a variety of influences, including that of perceived need in a given context.

Not all programs need the degree of specification suggested by Leithwood. For example, a planned intervention designed to save homes and gardens due to floods caused by the El Niño effect in Costa Rica or San Diego—which could be classified as a macro/service provision program—may require little more than a rationale, a set of intentions (goals or objectives), details about resource requirements and a statement of how the program is to proceed. Some program plans may also incorporate an evaluative component—for example, criteria or indicators, and standards for monitoring program implementation and impact. This reinforces what we said in the introduction to this chapter: we should view evaluative enquiry as something that is not divorced from program provision.

In practice, we find that even these minimum requirements are often not met, that many operating programs have no statement which attempts to outline the essential features of the intervention. Program planners seem to have difficulty in developing program logic, links between ends and means, and causes and effects. A major issue in program logic is the development of meaningful goals.

Our experience is that writing specific goals up front is very difficult. The 'real' goals of a program often emerge during the 'first round' or trialling of a program. A realistic approach to specifying goals is therefore to work backwards from what developers see as plausible program achievements as the basis for setting the program's true goals. In Chapter 10, on Clarificative Evaluation, we expand some of these ideas.

Now that we have some idea of what is meant by a program, several possibilities arise as to the focus and issues for an evaluation of a specific program. One possibility is the degree of internal consistency between the program plan and action. A key issue could be the extent to which the implementation is consistent with the plan for implementation. The evaluation would also need to identify problems, if any, associated with the effective delivery of the program. Alternatively, one might ask about the extent to which the outcomes were consistent with the program goals.

Understanding what is meant by a program in a generic sense enables us to focus in on the evaluand, the object under evaluative review. We can see that the program could be considered as the evaluand if we wanted to know whether it was effective. It could be, however, that the evaluators are asked to focus on one component of the program. For example, invoking the Leithwood framework, the science department in a school might want answers to the following questions about the implementation of the program:

- Are the teaching strategies working?
- Is the time allocated to this program long enough?

In this case, the evaluation focuses on two components of the program: teaching strategies and time allocation. This helps focus the evaluation and means that the evaluator can devote evaluation resources to the components of concern to the decision-makers.

In summary, a program must have some direction. At a minimum, there must be a plan in the head of someone associated with program delivery. Writing this down invariably helps, because the act of writing helps the developer(s) to think about program logic. Documenting what is to happen or has happened also makes the program public, an essential condition to justify the resources devoted to program planning and implementation.

## Policies

A second set of objects or evaluands to which the principles outlined in this book can be applied are those described as *policies*. Like the term 'program', it is difficult to find a satisfactory definition of 'policy' in the evaluation literature. Bauer (1968) suggests that:

> various labels are applied to decisions and actions we take, depending in general on the breadth of their implications. If they are trivial and repetitive and demand little cognition, they may be called routine actions. If they are somewhat more complex, have wider ramifications, and demand more thought, we may refer to them as tactical decisions. For those which have the widest ramifications and the longest time perspective, and which generally require the most information and contemplation, we tend to reserve the term 'policy'.

Difficulty about the use of the term 'policy' is evident among those involved in policy in the public sector. Looking at the development of policy across institutions such as the US Congress, state legislatures and a higher education accreditation board in the United States, Guba (1984) developed the following eight perspectives. Policy is:

- an assertion of intents or goals;
- a governing body's 'standing decisions' by which it regulates, controls, promotes, services and otherwise influences matters within its sphere of authority;
- a guide to discretionary action;
- a strategy undertaken to solve or ameliorate some problem;
- behaviour sanctioned formally through authoritative decisions, or informally through expectations and acceptance, and established over time;
- a norm of conduct, characterised by consistency and regularity, in some substantive action area;
- the output of the policy-making system: the cumulative effect of all the actions, decisions and behaviours of the millions of people who work in bureaucracies. It occurs, takes place and is made at every point in the policy cycle, from agenda-setting to policy impact. As such, policy is an analytical category;
- the impact of the policy-making and policy-implementing system as it is experienced by the client.

Kahn (1969) suggests that policies are 'standing plans'. Policies are guides to future decision-making that are intended to shape those decisions. Decisions must be consistent with a goal, an integral part of the policy documentation. A policy is a general

31

guide to action, an overarching statement which includes a goal and guiding principles for an intervention. According to Guba and Kahn, policy documentation thus has some characteristics in common with program plans—for example, the inclusion of goals. However, policy documents are more general than those for a program—for example, they are less likely to specify the means by which the ends are to be attained. This implies that a policy provides general directions for action, but in itself does not prescribe a course of action. We expect that, in many organisations, programs would be developed which are consistent with the direction of the policy in a given area of concern. For example, a government's policy about welfare housing might translate into different programs (action) in different locations. In effect, policy is at least once removed from specifications of action, so evaluations designed to determine the effects of policy must take this into account.

Another distinction between policy and programs lies in the organisational responsibility for their development. Policies tend to be the domain of mega and macro level planners, those at 'the centre' of the operations of an organisation. Programs might also be developed centrally, but often the responsibility for implementation lies with staff 'close to the ground'.

Two major investigatory activities related to policy have emerged in the social science literature. These are *policy analysis* and *policy research*.

- *Policy analysis* is concerned with issues such as giving an account of the development of a policy, the explication of choices which faced the policy-maker, and the assumptions made and values employed in making choices between alternatives. Much of what passes as policy analysis could be thought of as reflective, often done in retrospect, relying on secondary data, and directed towards an understanding of policy development *per se*, rather than towards the direct improvement of a specific policy initiative.

- *Policy research*—which, in the context of this book, might be renamed *policy evaluation*—involves the determination of the impact of policies on targets for the direct and timely use of those responsible for a policy intervention. Johnson (1975) suggests that policy research (evaluation) could operate in a range of modes from description of the impact of a policy, through explanation of why patterns of impact occur, to criticism of the policy direction. The systematic collection and analysis of data is seen as the first step to scientific criticism of policy. Coleman (1975) suggests that there has been too much emphasis on analysis compared with research and evaluation. He recommends that this imbalance should be corrected, implying that evaluative investigations have more potential than policy analysis in the improvement of policy delivery.

## Organisations

A third major object of evaluation is an organisation such as a corporation or a government department, or a logical sub-group within that organisation. The objective of an organisational evaluation might be to determine the impact of its mission, or the effectiveness of its processes and services, or a combination of these elements. Some organisations are so large that they are divided so that sections have responsibility for a major aspect or Program of the organisation's work.

---

### Example 2.2 Organisational Programs in community services

Until 1991, the government agency in Victoria, Australia responsible for social welfare was Community Services Victoria (CSV). Due to the size and complexity of its operations, CSV offered its services through six macro programs as follows:

- Community Support Program;
- Family and Children's Support Service Program;
- Alternative Accommodation and Care Program;
- Youth Services Program;
- Intellectual Disabilities Services Program;
- Health and Community Care Program.

The annual budgets for these Programs ranged from $27 million to $233 million in the financial year 1990/91. Each of these programs was delivered through a set of regional offices spread across the state.

---

Programs such as those in Example 2.2 are sometimes referred to as 'Big P' programs. In some organisations, the term 'Division', rather than 'Program' is used. A mission statement is often developed for the work of a Division or Program, including objectives, either implicitly or explicitly stated.

It is interesting to note that the Division of Prisons was responsible for specific interventions or programs as defined earlier.

However, the majority of implementation within the Division was in the day-to-day administration of prisons across the state.

> **Example 2.3 Divisions as Programs**
>
> An Office of Corrections divided its operations into Divisions, one of which was the Division of Prisons. An analysis of the operational plan of the Division of Prisons revealed that its mission was to:
>
> * manage and administer the sentence proposed by the courts;
> * provide sufficient security to minimise danger of offenders inflicting harm on themselves, other inmates, staff or the public;
> * meet humane, medical and health care needs of offenders;
> * assist offenders to develop and adopt acceptable behaviour patterns;
> * assist offenders to become responsible citizens through education, training, social development and work experience.

Programs or Divisions are obviously at the mega end of our distinction between levels of program planning and delivery. They are different from 'little p' programs in that it is more difficult to describe the ends–means and cause–effect relationships by which the outcomes are delivered—in other words, it is more difficult to describe the underlying *program logic*.

Day & Owen (1990) assisted this Office of Corrections to develop monitoring indicators of the impact of this Program. This was in response to a need for Office of Corrections management to have access to information to account for the funds spent on their Program. At the time, there was a heavy emphasis on developing and using appropriate outcome measures by government agencies, generally in the form of a series of indicators of performance. Despite this, it is difficult to find exemplary cases where Program performance measures are routinely used in 'big P' Program evaluation. There is obviously a need for more training and ongoing support if the notion of management evaluation of 'big P' Programs is to become institutionalised.

There are clear links between policy development and program provision. Shadish et al. (1991: 107) describe the situation in the United States in the following way:

Policy expresses intentions about the kind of executive and legislative actions that have priority. Policy gives guiding assumptions and goals for many programs, and may be formally codified or informally expressed by policy makers in speeches, agendas, or expressions of support or opposition. Programs are administrative umbrellas for distributing funds under a policy. Programs rarely turn over entirely . . . They are mostly changeable at the margins, so a summative evaluation of a program will rarely if ever result in a complete program replacement . . . Programs are not homogeneous. They consist of locally implemented projects where service delivery occurs . . . Projects can differ widely in character within the same program, because they are implemented under a national tradition of local control, service providers have discretion in the services they implement and needs and demands change from place to place and over time at the same place. Like programs, projects have great staying power.

It is clear that the closest concept to our 'little p' program in Shadish's terms is the notion of a 'project'. However, an important distinction is that 'little p' programs in, say, the Australian or British contexts do not necessarily have to fit under a broader umbrella—that is, they do not have to be part of a 'big P' program as Shadish and his co-writers assert. This may have to do with the nature of public-sector funding in different countries. For example, in Australia it is not uncommon for funding support to be sought by or provided directly to local agencies to develop and trial a small-scale program without reference to a larger administrative umbrella. In effect, there is more often a direct link between policy and 'small p' program provision. This reminds us of the assertion made at the beginning of this chapter that program provision needs to be understood within the social and political context. In this case, there are obviously national level differences which impinge on how social and educational policy and programs are delivered.

## Products

Another class of objects of evaluation consists of—*products*, for example, a software computer package, or a technical manual used in on-the-job training. We have come across the evaluation of a product in Example 1.1 in Chapter 1. You will have noted that the approach taken there was to provide comparative data on a set of criteria, and then to use these data to make recommendations about the 'best buy'. This approach can also be used to make decisions about the adoption of resources—for example, the choice of a given textbook for use in a specific educational program. In this case, it is important that the criteria used take into account the needs of the students and the nature of the curriculum within which the text will be used.

Michael Scriven, a noted contributor to evaluation theory over the past 20 years, has used product evaluation as a model by which the logic of evaluation can be invoked and transferred to program evaluation. However, as we saw in Chapter 1, the extrapolation from product to program evaluation requires the evaluator to take into account the context of program provision, and other factors which generally makes program evaluation a far more complex activity.

## Individuals

We have come to accept the need for information about the performance of individuals to be collected and used within our society. The most prevalent terms now in use are *performance assessment* or *performance appraisal*, and there is currently considerable emphasis on the application of these principles in government services. Assessment is generally used when we are talking about the achievement of students, and appraisal is often associated with the performance of staff in an organisation.

Much attention has been given in recent times to the development of valid and reliable assessment procedures. Key features in the reform of assessment and appraisal include:

- the conceptual separation of assessment from testing and the encouragement by authorities of an assessment rather than a testing culture;
- an increased understanding of the various uses and reporting of assessment (diagnosis/grading) and implications for the ways in which data about individuals are assembled;
- a concern for more valid methods of assessing the actual achievements of individuals;
- an enhanced role for instructor observation and judgment in the assessment of competencies;
- the development of innovative ways of setting up assessment frameworks—for example, student profiles which enable the progress of students to be indicated.

These are key issues in setting up acceptable performance assessment regimes for use in assessment and appraisal systems.

As indicated above, evidence of attainment can be used to rank order or grade individuals for purposes of certification or selection—for example, across the school–college interface, or as the basis for employment. Assessment can also be used as a basis for individual diagnosis and improvement.

As well, assessment information can be used in conjunction with program or policy evaluation, particularly studies of impact. Typically, we are interested to determine whether the program makes a difference to the performance or attainment of those for whom it is intended. If this information is used to make decisions *about the program*, then this is seen as a legitimate part of program evaluation.

However, if the emphasis in collecting information about individuals is to decide on aspects such as promotion, reallocation or firing, the process is more appropriately thought of as assessment or performance appraisal. This is a most important distinction which must be understood by budding program evaluators. While there is currently strong interest in assessment and appraisal, they are not taken up in any detail in this book.

## REFERENCES

Bauer R.A. (1968). 'The Study of Policy Formation'. In R.A. Bauer & K.J. Gergen (eds), *The Study of Policy Formation* London: The Free Press.

Coleman J.S. (1975). 'Problems in Conceptualization and Measurement in Studying Policy Impacts'. In K.M. Dolbeare (ed.), *Public Policy Evaluation: Sage Yearbook on Politics and Public Policy*. Beverly Hills, CA: Sage, pp. 19–40.

Day N.A. & Owen J.M. (1990). *Performance Indicators in Custodial and Community Based Programs*. Melbourne: The Centre for Program Evaluation, The University of Melbourne.

Funnell S. & Lenne B. (1989). 'A Typology of Public Sector Programs'. Paper presented at the Annual Meeting of the American Evaluation Association, November. San Francisco.

Guba E.G. (1984). 'The Impact of Various Definitions of Policy on the Nature and Outcomes of Policy Analysis'. Annual Meeting of the American Educational Research Association. New Orleans, LA, pp. Session 24.15.

Johnson R.W. (1975). 'Research Objectives for Policy Analysis'. In K.M. Dolbeare (ed.), *Public Policy Evaluation: Sage Yearbook in Politics and Public Policy*. Beverly Hills, CA: Sage, pp. 75–92.

Kahn A.J. (1969). *Theory and Practice of Social Planning*. New York: Russell Sage Foundation.

Leithwood K. (1981). 'Dimensions of Curriculum Innovation'. *Journal of Curriculum Studies*, 13, 26–37.

Shadish W.R., Cook T.D. & Leviton L.C. (1991). *Foundations of Program Evaluation*. Newbury Park: Sage.

Smith M.F. (1989). *Evaluability Assessment A Practical Approach*. Norwell: MA Kluwer.

Thurow L. (1986). *Management in Crisis*. Sydney: Australian Broadcasting Commission.

# 3

# Focusing Evaluation: Evaluation Forms and Approaches

## INTRODUCTION

In Chapter 2, we examined the range of possible objects or evaluands that could be investigated within an evaluation study. Identifying the object answers the 'what' question for a given evaluation. The 'what' issue is a basic one when thinking about the evaluation of interventions. But when thinking conceptually about the ways in which evaluation can provide leverage and help decision-makers, the 'why' question is the most important. By focusing on and providing answers to the 'why' question, it is possible to develop and turn effective evaluation plans into well-focused fieldwork and dissemination.

As Day (1991) has pointed out, guidelines for choosing appropriate models and methods based on the 'why' question appear to be missing from most evaluation textbooks. To remedy this, we posit a 'meta-model', consisting of five *evaluation forms*, each with a defining orientation and a focus on a set of common issues, which provide guidance for the planning and conduct of investigations.

If you have undertaken a formal evaluation subject in a university or college, or read about evaluation, you will be aware that a range of 'models' already exist, which have been developed from practice. We will use the term *evaluation Approaches* when discussing these 'models'. For example, three Approaches to determining program impact have been labelled as:

- objectives-based;
- needs-based; and
- goal-free evaluation.

The notions of Forms and Approaches provide an epistemological framework for understanding the breadth of evaluation. For each Form there is a cluster of existing, mostly well-known Approaches which have elements in common. The Forms, taken together, point to a wide range of roles for evaluation. This framework is consistent with the recent view of a noted evaluator that the 'world of evaluation has grown larger than the boundaries of formative and summative evaluation, though this distinction remains important and useful' (Patton, 1996). So let us examine each of the Forms. At this stage, we wish merely to connect them to evaluation Approaches. Later, we expand the framework by providing guidance for undertaking evaluation work consistent with the orientation of each Form. The frameworks in these chapters are designed to provide you with more practical directions for the conduct of real evaluations in the field.

## THE 'WHY' QUESTION AND EVALUATION FORMS

Evaluation can be classified conceptually into five categories, or Forms. These have been labelled as follows:

- Proactive;
- Clarificative;
- Interactive;
- Monitoring; and
- Impact.

Below and in Table 3.1, we set out the basic tenets of each evaluation form, including the following aspects:
- purpose or orientation of an evaluation consistent with the form;
- typical issues which are consistent with each purpose;
- major approaches taken from a social science or management perspective.

The third of these points needs an additional comment. It is widely accepted that social scientists, and in particular those connected with the field of education, have dominated advanced thinking about the work of the evaluator's profession.[1] However, there have also been considerable contributions to practice from the management/accounting perspective. That both 'cultures' have something to say about the conduct of evaluation in the workplace is evident

---

[1] For example, the major theoretical text on evaluation, Shadish et al. (1991), analyses the work of seven major 'first wave' evaluators. Of the seven, only one, Joseph Wholey, provides what might be labelled a business or management perspective to evaluation. Of the others, Stake, Weiss, and Cronbach had or have strong links to education.

to anyone who has attended conferences or meetings of professional associations of evaluators held in North America,
Australasia or Europe. Yet, up until now, textbooks in evaluation
and more esoteric works have failed to integrate the thinking
about evaluation which has and continues to emerge from the two
cultures. Here we have made an attempt to integrate perspectives
from the two cultures where it makes sense to provide a more
holistic and inclusive perspective.

## Proactive evaluation (Form A)

### Purpose or orientation

Evaluation within this Form takes place before a program is
designed. It assists program planners to make decisions about
what type of program is needed. The major purpose is to provide
input to decisions about how best to develop a program in
advance of the planning stage. Proactive evaluation places the
evaluator as an adviser, providing evidence about what is known
about policy development, what format of program is needed or
how an organisation may be changed to make it more effective.
For example, proactive evaluation may provide leaders with 'just
in time' advice for making key decisions which affect the future
or even survival of an organisation.

### Typical issues

Issues about which an evaluator might be engaged include the
following:

- Is there a need for the program?
- What do we know about this problem that the program will
  address?
- What is recognised as best practice in this area?
- Has there been other attempts to find solutions to this prob-
  lem?
- What does the relevant research or conventional wisdom tell
  us about this problem?
- What do we know about the problem that the program will
  address?
- What could we find out from external sources to rejuvenate
  an existing policy or program?

### Major Approaches

Approaches which are consistent with this Form include:
- *needs assessment* or *needs analysis*. This is probably the best

41

known Approach within this Form, and a strong body of theory and practice has been developed around the practice of needs assessment. In the past, the evaluation community has perceived needs assessment to be something different from conventional evaluation practice, mainly because needs assessment precedes the development of a program. As the name implies, needs assessment involves assessing the degree to which the projected program can respond to a perceived want or need among the community for which the program is intended.

- *research review*. This approach involves the synthesis of what is known about the problem from what is sometimes described as 'funded knowledge'—that developed through research and other scholarly enquiry. This generally involves the use of library facilities and ways of focusing the review on the most relevant literature. The research review is an opportunity for the aggregated work of pure and applied research to impact on social and educational planning. As such, evaluation of this nature bridges the gap between the work of the research community and practitioners.

- *review of best practice*, and the *creation of benchmarks*. In particular, there is an emphasis on selecting and studying exemplary practice which has relevance to the problem that needs to be addressed. The use of the term benchmark comes from a management perspective, and the trend for business to model their activities on leaders in their field. This has been followed by similar developments in the public sector. It should be noted that the selection and analysis of how exemplary or 'lighthouse' agencies run their businesses is fundamental to the benchmarking activity, but is not the whole story. The creation of benchmarks must be followed by implementation of processes that will deliver more effective and efficient outcomes.

Of the three Approaches discussed here, needs assessment and research review emanate from a social science perspective, while review of best practice has a strong place in the management literature. Proactive evaluation will be discussed in greater detail in Chapter 9.

## Clarificative evaluation (Form B)

*Purpose or orientation*

Evaluation within this Form concentrates on clarifying the internal structure and functioning of a program or policy. This is sometimes described as the *theory* or *logic* of a program.[2] It refers to the causal mechanisms which are understood to link program activities with intended outcomes. The need to outline or define the logic arises when a program has not been fully specified or described, even though it is in operation. This can occur when there is pressure for developers to implement an intervention without an opportunity to think through its underlying structure and rationale, or when those responsible for delivering a program are in conflict over aspects of its design, such as program intentions. Another possibility is that, even though program staff are implementing the program in some way, there is confusion about how the program should ideally be implemented. All these situations call for a *Clarificative evaluation*. In this Form of evaluative investigation, the evaluator works with policy or program staff. Alternatively, program clarification can be carried out by program staff themselves. The feature that distinguishes program planning from Clarificative evaluation is that, in the latter, the collection and analysis of data are essential. This generally involves the use of interview, observation and document analysis.

### Typical issues

Issues about which an evaluator might be engaged include the following:

- What are the intended outcomes of this program and how is the program designed to achieve them?
- What is the underlying rationale for this program?
- What program elements or structures need to be modified to maximise program potential to achieve the intended outcomes?
- Is the program plausible?
- Which aspects of this program are amenable to a subsequent monitoring or impact assessment?

### Major Approaches

Approaches which are consistent with this form include:

- *logic development* or *evaluability assessment*. This involves the

---

[2] The terms *program theory* and *program logic* tend to be used interchangeably in the literature. We will use the term program logic throughout this text to describe the nature of social and educational programming. This will help to distinguish more clearly between program logic and evaluation theory. Evaluation theory can be thought of as a body of knowledge that conceptualises, aids in understanding, and predicts action in the area of evaluative enquiry.

development of program logic using a range of analytical methods including documentation, and interviews with program staff and other stakeholders with a view to constructing a map of what the program is intended to do. We tend to use the term *program logic development* for these processes. The use of these techniques is relatively recent. Rutman (1980) and Smith (1989) have provided definitions and examples of practice using the term *evaluability assessment*—a term used in the United States but not so well known elsewhere. Evaluability assessments were originally seen as an essential step before impact evaluations could be conducted. Now it is commonly agreed that the clarificative evaluation can be thought of as an approach to evaluation in its own right.

- *accreditation*. This involves a determination of the worth of program guidelines, generally in the context of certifying that an agency or organisation can deliver the program for a given period—for example, three or five years. Accreditation, like program logic development, concentrates on the design of a program rather than its implementation. It is a common practice in publicly funded agencies, with a view to providing the public with confidence that the programs delivered by the agency are up to scratch.

Of these Approaches, program logic development and accreditation represent a social science perspective while feasibility studies have a strong management flavour. Clarification evaluation is the focus of discussion in Chapter 10.

## Interactive evaluation (Form C)

### *Purpose or orientation*

Interactive evaluation provides information about delivery or implementation of a program or about selected component elements or activities. Interactive evaluation can be concerned with the documentation or incremental improvement of an innovation, or establishing what is happening to help staff to understand more fully how and why a program operates in a given way. The evaluator provides findings and facilitates learning and decision-making. This Form of evaluation supports programs which are constantly evolving and changing. Thus, evaluators working within this Form provide information orientated towards improving the program; there is therefore a strong formative flavour. In some instances, in particular where the evaluator is an insider, the evaluator may also be involved in facilitating change.

While Impact and Monitoring Forms are more likely to be

addressed to senior managers and funding agencies, findings provided by Approaches within the Interactive Form are more logically directed at middle-level managers and program implementers—those responsible for delivering a program at the local or site level.

### Typical issues

Issues about which an evaluator might be engaged include the following:

- What is this program trying to achieve?
- How is this service going?
- Is the delivery working?
- Is it consistent with the program plan?
- How could the delivery be changed to make it more effective?
- How could this organisation be changed to make it more effective?

### Major Approaches

Approaches which are consistent with this Form include:

- *responsive evaluation*. This involves the documentation or illumination of the delivery of a program, see (Parlett & Hamilton, 1976). In addition to being focused on process, responsive evaluation takes account of the perspectives and values of different stakeholders, and is orientated towards the information requirements of audiences, often the providers of the program.
- *action research*. This involves determining whether or not innovatory approaches to delivery are making a difference.
- *quality review*. Sometimes known as *institutional self-study*, this involves providing system level guidelines within which providers have a large amount of control over the evaluation agenda.
- *developmental evaluation*. This involves working closely with program providers on a continuous improvement process, often on programs that are innovatory and unique.
- *empowerment evaluation*. This involves assisting program providers and participants to develop and evaluate their own programs, as part of a broader goal of giving citizens more control over their own lives and their destiny.

It might be noted that, while Interactive evaluation represents a social science perspective, action research had its genesis in the workplace, and continues to have relevance to improved performance on the shop floor.

## Monitoring evaluation (Form D)

### *Purpose or orientation*

Typically, monitoring is appropriate when a program is well established and ongoing. The program may be on a single site or it may be delivered at several sites, remote from senior management. Staff are aware of specified goals or intentions, have identified program targets and implementation is taking place. There is usually a need for managers to have an indication of the success or otherwise of the program or one or more of its components. This is likely to be linked to the expenditure of program funds.

The evaluation may involve the development of a system of regular monitoring of the progress of the program. Typically, *quantitative performance indicators* have been used as the means of organising data in monitoring evaluations, but more recently there has been a recognition that data management in any evaluation requires the use of a range of techniques, both qualitative and quantitative. There is a growing recognition that indicators do not in themselves provide the last word on program effectiveness. Indicator information needs to be combined with contextual knowledge to provide valid and useful findings.

Evaluations within this Form are likely to be management driven, and key theorists in the area (e.g. Mangano, 1989) have described such evaluation arrangements as having a rapid response capability. Evaluators are likely to be internally located in large-scale organisations.

### *Typical issues*

Issues about which an evaluator might be engaged include the following:

- Is the program reaching the target population?
- Is implementation meeting program benchmarks?
- How is implementation going between sites?
- How is implementation going now compared with a month ago, or a year ago?
- Are our costs rising or falling?
- How can we finetune this program to make it more efficient?
- How can we finetune this program to make it more effective?

46

- Is there a site which needs attention to ensure more effective delivery?

### Major Approaches

Approaches which are consistent with this Form include:

- *component analysis*. This involves the systematic evaluation of a component of a large-scale Program, identified because there are indications that the component needs to be reviewed to bring it into line with organisational goals.
- *devolved performance assessment*. This involves the development by which an organisation or system sets up evaluation procedures by which components can report regularly on their progress.
- *systems analysis*. This involves setting up procedures by which the central management institutes common evaluation procedures to be used uniformly across an organisation.

In all Approaches, the findings of the review are used to provide an indication of performance against some standard, or as a basis for a consequent review (Wholey, 1983). Evaluators are likely to be internally located in large-scale organisations. Alternatively, evaluators might be in the public sector—perhaps part of a government department with responsibility for the delivery of a service provided by local agencies, such as the provision of care to the elderly through nursing homes. In this scenario, the department may be charged with monitoring these homes and this Form provides an evaluative structure with which all agencies must comply. Monitoring evaluation is the focus of discussion in Chapter 12.

## Impact evaluation (Form E)

### Purpose or orientation

Impact evaluation is used to assess the impact of a settled program. It assumes some logical end-point analysis—for example, establishing the outcomes of a completed adult education remedial reading program, or a program designed to teach basic skills in an on-the-job apprenticeship. Typical approaches include the extent and level of attainment of specified objectives, determination of the level of performance on simple outcome indicators, or examining both intended and unintended outcomes.

If the intention of the evaluation is to make a decision about the merit or worth of the program, evaluations of this Form are described as summative evaluations. Summative evaluations assist with decisions about whether to terminate a program or whether to adopt it in another place. It is important, in a summative evaluation, to determine whether the intervention described in the program plan is in place. Thus, while the emphasis in summative evaluation is on outcomes, good summative evaluation may also include a review of the implementation characteristics of the program. These studies are known as *process-outcomes evaluations*.

### Typical issues

Issues about which an evaluator might be engaged include the following:

- Has the program been implemented as planned?
- Have the stated goals of the program been achieved?
- Have the needs of those served by the program been achieved?
- What are the unintended outcomes of the program?
- Does the implementation strategy lead to the intended outcomes?
- How do differences in implementation affect program outcomes?
- Has the program been cost effective?

### Major Approaches

Approaches which are consistent with this Form include:

- *objectives-based evaluation*. This involves judging the worth of a program on the basis of the extent to which the stated objectives of the program have been achieved. It should be noted that objectives-based evaluation represents the foundation of evaluation practice.
- *process-outcomes studies*. This involves not only determining outcomes but also measuring the degree of implementation of the program. The need for attention to implementation arose from the mistaken notion that social and educational programs were always delivered in ways that were consistent with program intentions.
- *needs-based evaluation*. This involves judging the worth of a program on the basis of the extent to which the program meets the needs of the participants. This represents a variation on objectives-based evaluation, and makes the assumption that the objectives of a program do not necessarily represent the needs of the participants.
- *goal-free evaluation*. This involves determining not only the stated goals, but also the unintended outcomes of the program; thus the common name given to this approach is

misleading. Goal-free evaluation has implications for evaluation practice, as getting an indication of unintended outcomes—both positive and negative—implies the use of investigative methods, rather than preordinate designs.

- *performance audit*. A performance audit is an analysis of program efficiency and effectiveness. Performance audits concentrate on program outcomes and generally involve financial and non-financial measures.

Impact evaluations are often used to justify expenditure, which is consistent with the notion of a summative evaluation role. While such evaluations can be handled internally, they are most often undertaken by external evaluators. Impact evaluation is discussed in detail in Chapter 13.

## THE USE OF FORMS IN FOCUSING AN EVALUATION

It is important for all of those involved in any evaluation setting to choose the most appropriate way of proceeding. The Forms just discussed provide a conceptual map by which the evaluator and client can make a decision about how to proceed. The following example illuminates the use of Forms in this way.

### Example 3.1 Evaluation of training for child welfare workers

We were asked to undertake an evaluation of a training program for child welfare workers in a large state agency. In initial negotiations, the stakeholders expressed a strong desire for a traditional outcomes evaluation based on program goals. After further discussions with the program manager and inspection of program documentation, particularly the course plan and materials provided for participants as handouts, it became evident that the program plan was not specific and members of the training team were not clear about fundamental program themes, or about how the various course components linked together.

These deliberations led to a realisation among stakeholders that a Clarificative evaluation was needed. The methodology employed included observation, analysis of all documentation, then some interactive sessions with all members of the training team, including the program manager, to develop a revised plan for the program.

A key feature of the evaluation was that the training team, through the development process, recognised the need for a more systematic plan, and developed a commitment to implementing a program which had greater internal coherence.

In summary, this was a classic Clarificative evaluation.

- The orientation was towards clarification of course description.
- The program was still in a stage of development.
- The focus of the evaluation was on its design.
- It was undertaken during cycles of program delivery.

The revised plan became the basis for ongoing delivery of the training program, offered several times. When it was deemed to be settled, the outcomes evaluation originally suggested by the stakeholders was carried out.

This example emphasises the point that it is essential to decide on the most appropriate evaluation for a given program, taking into account the state of its development (Owen, 1991). It would have been ludicrous to have gone ahead with an outcomes evaluation of an intervention which was incoherent and had little chance, in its original state, of being effective. The evaluative thrust, at least in the first instance, needed to be directed towards program clarification. Later, an outcomes evaluation made sense.

The following scenarios provide an opportunity for you to classify them according to the evaluation Forms just introduced.

**Scenario A:** A suburban hospital offers a set of procedures designed to rehabilitate people who have suffered serious physical trauma, often as a result of motor vehicle accidents. While the procedures are individually well implemented, the staff see a need for someone to develop an overall program plan, to make explicit the links between the range of procedures offered and the overall program objectives.

**Scenario B:** An ambulance training centre adopts a well-documented training program. Management is keen to determine whether the program has made a significant difference to the students and asks an external evaluation group to carry out the evaluation.

**Scenario C:** The Council of a large city is preparing for an expected drought and the chief executive officer has asked one of the staff to examine ways in which the council could develop plans for saving the trees in parks and gardens across the city.

**Scenario D:** There is some concern by senior officials at a museum about the effectiveness and efficiency of the program offered by the astronomical observatory. Information is needed so that decisions can be made about the future of this program. Tenders have been called for the evaluation.

**Scenario E:** The Department of Justice within a state government, responding to a ministerial directive, has set up a set of performance indicators to monitor the effects of its operations.

**Scenario F:** An adult educator is concerned with the ways in which she uses her time in evening classes which involve a large amount of individual student work. She asks a colleague to assist in collecting information about her activities.

**Scenario G:** Over a 20-year period, a national government has spent $123 million on facilities for science in the nation's schools. In the final year of the program, a national research agency is asked to carry out an evaluation of the impact of the project.

Each of these scenarios fits neatly within one of the evaluation Forms—for example, Scenario C can be classified within the Proactive Form and Scenario F belongs to the Interactive Form. The import of this exercise is that we are providing some order for what could be a bewildering array of possibilities for attacking the realities of evaluation practice. There is more guidance at hand to help classify evaluation scenarios and this is provided in the following section.

## FORMS OF EVALUATION: ADDITIONAL DIMENSIONS

Table 3.1 provides a useful framework for deciding what Form is most useful for a given evaluation. However, there are additional dimensions for our conceptual framework. They provide additional guidance, and are described below and outlined in Table 3.2.

- *State* of the existing program. State means the degree to which the program under review has been implemented at the time of the proposed evaluation. State is a variable: at one extreme the program will not be in existence—it needs to be developed; at the other extreme, the program will have been operating for a period of time without modification. If a program can be described in this way, we refer to it as being *fully implemented* or 'settled'.
- *Focus* of the evaluation. Focus refers to the program component(s) on which the evaluation is likely to concentrate. For a given program, four possible focii are:
  - the social, political and economic context in which a program is to be developed;
  - the coherence and adequacy of program design;
  - elements of program delivery or implementation; and
  - program outcomes.
- *Timing* refers to the temporal links between the evaluation and program delivery. For example, a needs assessment takes place *before* a program is developed while action research occurs *during* the delivery of a program.
- *Assembly of evidence*. This refers to the method(s) used to answer the evaluation questions, sometimes called *data management*. Data management involves things such as setting standards, sampling, choice and application of data collection techniques, and data analysis. The end point is to arrive at findings to each evaluation, which may include judgments about program worth.

In summary, each Form can be represented by seven dimensions, represented in Tables 3.1 and 3.2. The inclusion of the state of program, focus and timing variables implies that different evaluation is related to different stages of program development. That is, a Proactive evaluation would logically precede the development of a given program, an Interactive evaluation could take place as the program is being implemented, and an Impact evaluation can be thought of as an evaluation that happens at the conclusion of a program.

## USING THE FORMS IN PRACTICAL SETTINGS

So far we have introduced the Forms as conceptual or heuristic, in order to provide a conceptual overview. It is now time to apply these ideas to practical situations. How can we make these ideas operational to guide evaluators, clients, audiences and other interested parties through the conduct of a given evaluative study? Let

**Table 3.1  Evaluation Forms: orientation, typical issues and key Approaches**

| | Proactive [Form A] | Clarificative [Form B] | Interactive [Form C] | Monitoring [Form D] | Impact [Form E] |
|---|---|---|---|---|---|
| **Orientation** | Synthesis | Clarification | Improvement | Justification/finetuning | Justification/accountability |
| **Typical issues** | •Is there a need for the program? <br>•What do we know about this problem that the program will address? <br>•What is recognised as best practice in this area? <br>•Have there been other attempts to find solutions to this problem? <br>•What does the relevant research or conventional wisdom tell us about this problem? <br>•What do we know about the problem that the program will address? <br>•What could we find out from external sources to rejuvenate an existing policy or program? | •What are the intended outcomes and how is the program designed to achieve them? <br>•What is the underlying rationale for this program? <br>•What program elements need to be modified in order to maximise the intended outcomes? <br>•Is the progam plausible? <br>•Which aspects of this program are amenable to a subsequent monitoring or impact assessment? | •What is this program trying to achieve? <br>•How is this service going? <br>•Is the delivery working? <br>•Is delivery consistent with the program plan? <br>•How could delivery be changed to make it more effective? <br>•How could this organisation be changed so as to make it more effective? | •Is the program reaching the target population? <br>•Is implementation meeting program benchmarks? <br>•How is implementation going between sites? <br>•How is implementation now compared with a month ago? <br>•Are our costs rising or falling? <br>•How can we finetune the program to make it more efficient? <br>•How can we finetune the program to make it more effective? <br>•Is there a program site which needs attention to ensure more effective delivery? | •Has the program been implemented as planned? <br>•Have the stated goals of the program been achieved? <br>•Have the needs of those served by the program been achieved? <br>•What are the unintended outcomes? <br>•Does the implementation strategy lead to intended outcomes? <br>•How do differences in implementation affect program outcomes? <br>•Has the program been cost-effective? |
| **Key Approaches** | •Needs assessment <br>•Research review <br>•Review of best practice [Benchmarking] | •Evaluability assessment <br>•Logic/theory development <br>•Accreditation | •Responsive <br>•Action research <br>•Quality review <br>•Developmental <br>•Empowerment | •Component analysis <br>•Devolved performance assessment <br>•Systems analysis | •Objectives based <br>•Process-outcome studies <br>•Needs based <br>•Goal free <br>•Performance audit |

**Table 3.2  Evaluation Forms: all dimensions**

| | Proactive [Form A] | Clarificative [Form B] | Interactive [Form C] | Monitoring [Form D] | Impact [Form E] |
|---|---|---|---|---|---|
| **Orientation** | Synthesis | Clarification | Improvement | Justification/finetuning | Justification/accountability |
| **Typical issues** | [see Table 3.1] | [see Table 3.1] | [see Table 3.1] | [see Table 3.1] | [see Table 3.1] |
| **State of Program** | None | Development | Development | Settled | Settled |
| **Major focus** | Program context | All elements | Delivery | Delivery/outcomes | Delivery/outcomes |
| **Timing [vis-à-vis Program delivery]** | Before | During | During | During | After |
| **Key Approaches** | •Needs assessment<br>•Research review<br>•Review of best practice [Benchmarking] | •Evaluability assessment<br>•Logic/theory development<br>•Accreditation | •Responsive<br>•Action research<br>•Quality review<br>•Developmental<br>•Empowerment | •Component analysis<br>•Devolved performance assessment<br>•Systems analysis | •Objectives base<br>•Process-outcome studies<br>•Needs based<br>•Goal free<br>•Performance audit |
| **Assembly of evidence** | Review of documents and data bases, site visits and other interactive methods. Focus groups, nominal groups and delphi technique useful for needs assessments. | Generally relies on combination of document analysis, interview and observation. Findings include program plan and implications for organisation. Can lead to improved morale. | Relies on intensive onsite studies, including observation. Degree of data structure depends on approach. May involve providers and program participants. | Systems approach requires availability of Management Information Systems [MIS], the use of indicators and the meaningful use of performance information. | Traditionally required use of preordinate research designs, where possible the use of treatment and control groups, and the use of tests and other quantitative data. Studies of implementation generally require observational data. Determining all the outcomes requires use of more exploratory methods and the use of qualitative evidence. |

us examine a few alternatives, drawn from the thinking and experience of some who have used the Forms in their work.

## Evaluation Forms and the Program Evaluation Continuum (PEC)

Tony Simonelli has incorporated the evaluation Forms into what he calls a Project (or Program) Evaluation Continuum (PEC) (Simonelli, 1996). A basic point of the PEC is that evaluation should and can contribute to decision-making at every key point linked to:

- pre-program;
- during implementation; and
- post-completion.

The PEC is being used to provide a frame for his consultancy work in countries with developing economies. Typically, these projects are funded by an external agency such as the World Bank or World Vision and implemented by local agencies with support from a consultant with expertise in program design and evaluation.

In the pre-program stage, Proactive (Form A) and Clarificative (Form B) evaluations are used for what Simonelli calls *program identification*, and for program design and appraisal. Program identification seeks to identify worthwhile 'investments' which typically address needs or tap developmental opportunities. This approach normally involves some form of situational or trend analysis, problem identification and comparison with a desired state. Evidence is constructed from various information sources such as existing file data, studies undertaken by others and original data. Design and appraisal involve using the information from the previous stage to develop a design, then subjecting it to rigorous examination, assessing its feasibility from every relevant perspective—for example, social, financial, economic, environmental and technical. The end point involves making an assessment of the worth of the project, its cost and how it compares with alternative uses of the available investment resources. This may lead to the refinement of program design on the basis of the actual funds available.

While program identification is generally undertaken by a community or provider group with the assistance of technical support, design and appraisal are undertaken by the funding agency. The major decision at this point is whether to proceed with implementing the program based on the evidence assembled to date. It is evident that the feasibility study involves a benefit for cost analysis as well as an appraisal of the plausibility of the program design. An independent 'expert' may be consulted to aid decision-making.

In the implementation stage, Monitoring evaluation is used to check, first, that the program is on target in terms of its stated objectives. This evaluation seeks to provide up-to-date information on actual implementation progress as compared with targets, so that the emphasis is on deviations from expected performance and suggestive corrective action. Also at this stage, Simonelli incorporates the possibility of invoking an Impact (Form E) evaluation. This could be thought of as a major review of progress, to assess the likelihood that the stated objectives can, in fact, be attained, with a view to identifying changes of a major nature to the program, if warranted.

In the post-completion stage, Simonelli envisages two evaluation strategies. He calls them *terminal* and *impact evaluations*, the difference being that terminal evaluations focus on immediate outcomes and impact evaluations follow after a sufficient time to allow the full effects of the program to be noted. Terminal evaluation is seen as an end-of-project status statement and could be assembled by project management. It focuses on resource use and the actual outcomes to this point in time. The evidence would vary from case to case, but usually seeks to provide an end-of-implementation summary to interested parties, including the funding agency. In Simonelli's terms, impact evaluation provides information about the 'final' outcomes of the program, both expected and unexpected, and thus is most similar to our Impact evaluation. In the context of projects undertaken within developing countries, the Impact evaluation is likely to be done by an outside evaluation consultant who reports to the funding agency.

Simonelli states (1996: 17) that:

I find the PEC useful both conceptually and practically. Others may likewise find it helpful as a conceptual, training or practical evaluation tool. Used conceptually it may make some small contribution to encouraging and application of the associated notions that:

- the principles and techniques of evaluation can be usefully applied to assist decision-making at every phase of the project cycle; and
- preparation of a framework for project evaluation can assist in and should be an integral part of project development and design (not something tacked on after the key decisions have already been taken). As a training tool, it may have particular application for project planners and managers because it relates evaluation concepts to something they would have a firm understanding of, that is, the project cycle.

## Evaluation forms and change management

Example 3.1 on page 49 shows how evaluation Forms were used by someone working on community projects funded by outside agencies. The consultant was working in a local environment to develop a program that would be beneficial to those in that environment. The use of Forms provided information of use to both local providers and funders. Local providers use relevant information to develop their program. Funding agencies need information from which to mount future programs of the similar type, in addition to using the information to account for the funds allocated to the program.

In the next example, Faye Lambert (1996) has linked evaluation Forms to more conventional business and management principles. Note that, in this case the evaluand could be the organisation or an organisational unit within a company or a business—that is, we have moved from an emphasis on an intervention in the form of a program to a work unit. We remind you that, as outlined in Chapter 2, an evaluand can be a program, a policy or an organisation.

This work is grounded in the change management literature and the work of Kotter (1995) in particular. Based on observations from about a hundred organisations, Kotter suggests that eight critical steps need to be taken to successfully manage a major organisational change initiative. The steps are:

1  *Building a case for change.* Key stakeholders, such as staff and shareholders, need to understand why change is necessary, the evidence for the change must be collected and articulated to those affected by the change. Change is about risk, so the risk of not changing needs to be perceived as greater than the risk of going ahead with the change.
2  *Forming a powerful guiding coalition.* This involves moulding a group of individuals into an effective team and providing them with enough power to lead the change effort.
3  *Creating a vision.* What is initially required is a sense of direction, not myriad plans. There is a need for those involved in the change effort to share the vision which could come from a charismatic leader or be developed by the coalition.
4  *Communicating the vision.* The nature of the vision needs to be communicated synergistically to stakeholders.
5  *Empowering others to act on the vision.* This requires administrators to set up structures to support the change and to remove potential obstacles which would stand in the way of its introduction.

6   *Planning for and creating short-term wins.* This is about ensuring that there are tangible signs of improvement early on in the initiative to provide momentum for furtherance of the change. In association, there should be opportunities to recognise and celebrate success.

7   *Consolidating improvements.* This involves incorporating the change into the very fabric of the organisation. This almost always involves both person-centred and resource support from the administration.

8   *Institutionalising new approaches.* This involves making sure that those within the organisation make the connections between the change and outcomes which follow from the change. This is with a view to ensuring that the coalition understands and supports the change.

These steps are set out in Figure 3.1. While the diagram implies a linear sequence, the truth is that implementing change is far more messy, with plenty of recursive loops involving the steps set out above.Where does evaluation fit into this change scheme? Critical diagnostic evaluation should be an integral part of the decision-

**Figure 3.1   Eight critical steps in leading and managing change**

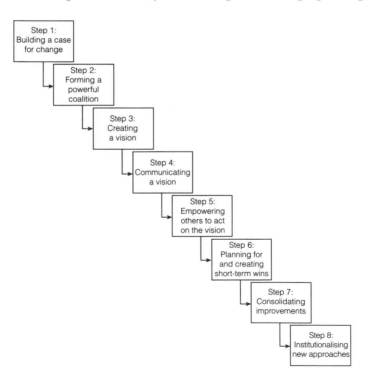

**Figure 3.2    The change process and the use of evaluative enquiry**

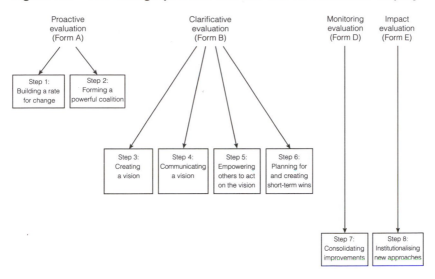

making related to the change process. Lambert's research suggests that the average manager spends about 80 per cent of the available time on implementation, with only around 2 per cent spent on diagnosis, whereas she suggests that 20 per cent of management time should be on the diagnostic effort, and just 40 per cent on implementation. We suggest that a major reason for this discrepancy is that, up to now, the typical manager has had limited understanding of how diagnostic evaluation can aid the change effort.

We show how these links can be forged in Figure 3.2. Proactive evaluation (Form A) would be employed in steps one and two. Clarificative evaluation (Form B) would be employed in steps three to six and so on.

Imagine that a small, forward-looking university has made an in-principle decision to introduce information technology across all departments. The administration decides to use evaluation to help in introducing an information technology policy. A Proactive evaluation could be based around the following questions:

- What are the skills and abilities that will enable students to effectively participate in and shape their world of the future?
- What do we know already about the potential of information technology to help meet their needs?
- How might technology be used to develop those abilities in this college context?

To get people onside, a case for the change must be made, particularly among those with clout—those who Kotter (1995) describes as the 'powerful coalition'. Proactive evaluation would engage staff in discussions about how they could use technology, not simply to familiarise students with technology, but to reshape the college curriculum. Actively involving the coalition in leading staff through a needs analysis would be one way of building support for the change effort.

A Clarificative evaluation (Form B) would be undertaken in conjunction with steps 3 to 6: the design and development of the information technology policy. Typical questions would be:

- What are the intended outcomes from the implementation of the policy?
- What are the underlying assumptions?
- What would it mean to the work of each college department if the policy was implemented?
- What aspects of the program should be chosen for monitoring or for impact evaluation?

The evaluative effort to this stage has resulted in:

- development of a clear understanding of the intended outcomes of the policy and the strategies used to achieve them;
- a basis for monitoring the evaluation process for the program in action;
- a basis for future modifications because the original policy has been based on explicit identification of policy need.

Similar questions could be developed for interactive and monitoring evaluation phases (see Figure 3.2).

Experience suggests that if staff are involved, there is increased understanding that most worthwhile innovations take time to implement. The use of evaluation not only provides useful knowledge, but also helps clarify expectations for the different stages of policy development. Clarifying expectations goes hand in hand with clarifying policy. This alleviates much of the anxiety of the change initiative and can assist with ongoing policy implementation.

Perhaps the most important message from these examples is that 'real evaluations' can span one or more of the evaluation Forms. The following case is an example of this.

### Example 3.2 Evaluating the progress of an innovation

Maher (1996) employed several evaluation Forms in relation to an innovative teaching program titled 'Preparing for the

Victorian Certificate of Education (VCE)'. The program was designed to assist students 'at risk' when it came to passing the VCE which is awarded to students graduating from secondary school. The program was of one week's duration, and was held before the beginning of the conventional school year. Program content focused on research skills, task and time management, and report writing. The study reflected the use of several Forms Approaches which were consciously used in conjunction with the program over a fifteen-month period. They included:

- needs analysis prior to and in the early stages of planning;
- monitoring during the program;
- needs-based outcomes evaluation, designed to answer the question: 'Was it worth doing?', to account for the use of resources, to identify the effects on students, and to document what was done.

## CONCLUSION

Evaluation Forms provide a framework for answering the 'why' question in evaluation. This is reflected in the broad orientation of each Form. The fact that Forms can be moulded into all stages of the organisational or program cycle signifies that the concerns of evaluation change as a program is designed and developed.

However, it is more usual for evaluators and clients to select one Form as the basis for an evaluation. Usually the choice of this Form and one or more Approach within that Form is consistent with a need for a particular kind of evaluation. This, in turn, is determined by the concerns of clients and other key stakeholders.

To encourage the intelligent use of each of the Forms, we go into more detail about each one in Chapters 9 to 13. This involves working down the columns of Tables 3.1 and 3.2. We will devote the discussion to the links between orientation, typical issues, key Approaches and methodologies appropriate to each Form, and provide case studies of evaluations which illustrate each of these Forms of evaluation.

## REFERENCES

Day, S. (1991). 'Casework Evaluation'. Unpublished Paper for the Graduate Diploma in Evaluation, Centre for Program Evaluation, The University of Melbourne.

Kotter, J.P. (1995). 'Leading Change. Why Transformation Effects Fail'. *Harvard Business Review*, March–April 1995, 59–67.

Lambert, F.C. (1996). 'The Introduction of Technology into Classrooms: Change Management and the Role of Evaluation'. In *Expanding Horizons Conference*, Geelong College, Geelong, p. 18.

Maher, M. (1996). 'Educational Evaluation'. Major Project for the Doctorate of Education, Faculty of Education, The University of Melbourne.

Mangano, M.F. (1989). *Rapid Response Evaluation for Decision Makers: The Story of the HHS Inspector General.* Washington, DC: US Department of Health and Human Services.

Owen, J.M. (1991). 'An Evaluation Approach to Training Using the Notion of Form: An Australian Example'. *Evaluation Practice*, 12 (2), 131–9.

Parlett, M. & Hamilton, D. (1976). 'Evaluation as Illumination: A New Approach to the Study of Innovatory Programs'. In G.V. Glass (ed.), *Evaluation Studies: Review Annual.* Beverly Hills, CA: Sage.

Patton, M.F. (1996). 'A World Larger than Formative and Summative Evaluation'. *Evaluation Practice*, 17 (2), 131–44.

Rutman, L. (1980). *Planning Useful Evaluations.* Beverly Hills, CA Sage.

Shadish, W., Cook, T.D. & Leviton, L.C. (1991). *Foundations of Program Evaluation*, Newbury Park: Sage.

Simonelli, A. (1996). 'The Project Evaluation Continuum'. *Evaluation News and Comment*, 5 (2), 13–18.

Smith, M.F. (1989). *Evaluability Assessment: A Practical Approach.* Norwell: MA Kluwer.

Wholey, J. (1983). *Evaluation and Effective Public Management.* Boston: Little, Brown.

# 4

# Negotiating an Evaluation Plan: The Importance of Negotiation and Planning

In Chapter 1 we adopted a description of evaluation as the processes of:

- negotiating an evaluation plan;
- collecting and analysing evidence to produce findings;
- disseminating to identified audiences.

All three stages are essential to the practice of evaluation. Their execution requires those engaged in evaluation to possess a range of complementary skills. In the first stage, the emphasis is on *negotiation* and *planning*. In addition to the ability to synthesise information, interpersonal skills are required in dealing with those who have a legitimate interest in the program. In the second stage, the emphasis is on assembling evidence by data collection and analysis. This is sometimes referred to as the *obtaining* stage. Methodological skills are required. In the third stage, the emphasis is on *information dissemination strategies* and *reporting*. Communication skills are required.

As Barrington (1990) has noted, university and college training programs in evaluation have tended to focus on methodology while neglecting skills needed to undertake the first and third stages. This has left many neophyte evaluators ill-equipped to cope with the pressures encountered in the real world of organisational decision-making and policy research.

During the negotiation and planning stages, an understanding of the evaluation Forms is critical. An evaluator armed with a detailed knowledge of the Forms can help steer an evaluation in a direction from which the findings can have maximum leverage on the issues raised by the stakeholders.

It should be noted that while, for conceptual purposes, we imply that the stages follow each other as outlined, in practice they might overlap. For example, in an evaluation where one phase of data collection is dependent on the findings of a prior phase, the evaluation could be conducted as a set of rolling stages of planning, obtaining and disseminating. It should also be noted that the stages are interdependent. How each stage is approached will have a direct effect on the others. For instance, negotiation and planning will establish the scope of the evaluation and thus set the parameters for the obtaining stage.

The need to develop negotiation and communication skills in addition to data management skills cannot be over-emphasised. Good evaluation is more than good data collection and analysis. This applies whether the evaluator is an outsider, working for an agency that undertakes evaluation work on contract, or an insider, working for the organisation that has commissioned the evaluation.

The inclusion of the planning and communicating stages helps us to distinguish evaluation from some other kinds of research. While both evaluation and research draw on the same range of data collection and analysis techniques, in both the qualitative and quantitative domains, the ways in which research and evaluation are conducted have different epistemological characteristics:

1   Compared with research, evaluators must devote considerable energy and resources to ensuring that an adequate and acceptable plan is developed, and that the evaluation findings are comprehended by clients. In an evaluation of college or university level programs for training teachers, it was estimated that 30 per cent of the resources available for the study were devoted to the planning and dissemination stages of the study (Owen et al., 1985). This left 70 per cent for the obtaining stage. It is important for evaluators to budget for planning and communicating in addition to obtaining when allocating available resources for an evaluation.

2   Research is concerned with general explanations designed to advance the frontiers in a discipline or field of study. A major motivation for research is the search for generalisations and the creation of new knowledge. By contrast, evaluation concentrates on specific policy or programmatic interventions and is motivated by the need to inform decisions about those interventions (Smith & Glass, 1987).

3   Those undertaking research are answerable to the scientific

community at large, while evaluations are generally commissioned enquiries. Evaluators are beholden to some or all of the stakeholders who have a legitimate interest in a given program.

4  Where possible, most scholars undertaking research attempt to adopt a disinterested value position, while the influence of an evaluation may be dependent on the position taken by the evaluator in relation to those held by the various stakeholders.

5  There is a difference relating to the practicalities of data collection and analysis. While there is often a high commitment to elaborate designs in the conduct of research, evaluators often must select from a limited range of evidence from which to present findings and reach conclusions. This applies in particular to *post hoc* evaluations, that is, occurring after the program has commenced or been completed.

Now that we have a firmer view about the meaning of evaluation in practice, we turn to a description of each of the major stages of evaluation. In the remainder of this chapter, we examine the *delineating* or *negotiating* stage. The obtaining or assembly of evidence stage is examined in Chapter 5 and the dissemination stage is discussed in Chapter 6.

## NEGOTIATING AN EVALUATION: KEY DIMENSIONS

Negotiation requires a set of social skills on the part of the evaluator. Fundamental to the ideal of negotiation is the concept that evaluators perform a service to clients who require answers to specific questions about a given program or policy. Evaluators must be prepared to acknowledge the interest framework of the clients, so that the knowledge they produce has salience to ensuing decisions about the evaluand under review.

Thus evaluation is not something the evaluator does without reference to stakeholders, and in particular the clients—those who can be regarded as the primary audience for the study. Attention must be given to client involvement in the planning stage of an evaluation, before any data collection or analysis takes place. There must be reasonable agreement between evaluator and client about the broad parameters of the evaluation so that the parties are clear as to how it will proceed, and aware of what the evaluation might realistically be expected to achieve.

Negotiation is fundamental because it sets the direction for what follows. It determines what questions are important, and to whom they are important. Negotiation may also help to gain access to data needed to answer the evaluation questions. In addition, the negotiation phase should attend to how information about the evaluation and the findings of the evaluation will be disseminated. Up-front planning and negotiation build in support for the evaluation effort. While there may be differences in emphasis in the degree of planning according to the Form selected, effective use of evaluation findings is heavily dependent, in all arrangements and settings, on the degree to which evaluator and clients agree on a plan for the evaluation. This is the 'up-front' agreement which determines the directions the evaluation will take.

At this point, it must be acknowledged that there is often a diversity of views among program stakeholders about the purpose of an evaluation. Different interest groups associated with a given program often have different agendas, and it is essential for the evaluator to be aware of these groups and know about their agendas in the negotiation stage. It is difficult, however, to undertake an evaluation that reflects the needs of *all* stakeholder groups, and at an early stage in negotiations with those commissioning the evaluation, the evaluator must determine *which* stakeholder group(s) will be primarily served by the investigation.

Experience suggests that a given evaluation can address directly the agendas of one or two stakeholder groups. They are the groups with which the evaluator negotiates about the evaluation design, elements such as the key issues to be addressed, the timeline and budget. This does not mean that the findings or products of the evaluation are necessarily restricted to these audiences. Other stakeholders may also receive these findings or products. However, the evaluation design may not answer questions that these stakeholders would like to ask about the given program, nor will the styles of reporting be specifically tailored to their wishes or needs.

It is thus essential to settle on an evaluation plan in advance of any other actions. The plan could be regarded as an agreement between the evaluators and the client(s) about the direction the evaluation will take. This does not mean that everything that follows is set in stone, to be followed in an unyielding fashion. For example, there might be agreement that the direction of the evaluation is determined by what has been found in a previous round of enquiry and reporting back to the primary audience. However, it does mean that the general direction of the evaluation has been decided, and that this direction will be followed unless circumstances are such that follow-through is impossible—for example, if the expected data sources are unavailable. In this case, the evaluation plan should be renegotiated.

An interesting development in evaluation practice is the increasing sophistication of those commissioning evaluations.

While it was once the norm for commissioners to have just a hazy idea of what they required from an evaluation, now it is far more likely that those wanting an evaluation to be done on their behalf will develop a clear brief for the evaluator. Having a well-prepared brief is a great advantage because it provides a clear starting point for negotiation and speeds up the completion of the evaluation plan.

## A FRAMEWORK FOR NEGOTIATING AN EVALUATION

While evaluation plans can have a variety of formats, we have found that the following headings provide a logical and helpful way of presenting the plan. For each of the headings, we have also made some general explanatory comments that come from experience in using this format.

### Specifying the evaluand

What is the object of the evaluation? What is known about the evaluand? How was it developed? How long has it been in existence? What is the nature of the evaluand: policy/program/organisation/product? Who are the key players in its development (actual or projected) and implementation?

### Purpose

What is the fundamental reason for commissioning the evaluation? As we have seen in the previous section, the fundamental purpose of a given evaluation might be to prove that a given intervention is effective, or to improve the delivery of an intervention, or to help develop an intervention. We have discussed the primacy of evaluation Form in determining the orientation of different kinds of evaluation. This implies that a plan for a Proactive evaluation would look very different from a plan for Monitoring evaluation. Consistent with evaluation Form, a key issue is whether the evaluation is primarily concerned with:

- synthesis of information to aid program development;
- clarification of a program;
- improvement of the implementation of a program;
- monitoring program outcomes; or
- determining program worth.

### Clients/audiences

To whom will the findings of the evaluation be directed? As indicated above, it is important to distinguish between the clients, the primary audience for an evaluation and other interested parties. The primary audience is an individual or group that is most likely to use the knowledge, in the form of findings, conclusions or recommendations, produced by the evaluation. Note that the primary audience is not necessarily identical to the commissioners of an evaluation, defined as the group that initiates and provides the resources for the evaluation. The identification of the primary audience(s) implies that it is difficult for a given evaluation to provide the information needs of a wide range of stakeholders. Patton (1997) has discovered that the identification of a key individual who has influence in an organisation during the course of an evaluation can significantly affect the utilisation of evaluation findings. We agree. However, on the basis of working cooperatively with clients in organisations, we have also found that there is often a key small group within an organisation for which the evaluation has particular meaning. Thus an individual or a small group of individuals may have influence over decisions relating to the program under review, and their involvement is vital during the negotiation stage of the evaluation.

### Resources

What human and material resources are available to undertake the evaluation? Someone must be given time to plan, to set up appropriate data management systems and to generally be responsible for all aspects of the evaluation. External evaluators develop structures for coping with the realities of running what is often a complex operation. However, more and more, government departments and businesses have developed internal arrangements so that evaluations can be undertaken in-house—for example departments which have separate budgets and other resources, and trained staff to make evaluation work feasible across the organisation (Love, 1994).

We believe that resources must be identified and made available, even in the case of small-scale studies in which there may be no clear distinction between evaluation and development/ implementation tasks—for example, in the action research Approach. If program deliverers are also expected to engage in evaluation, they should be given time and resources to undertake the research within the range of their day-to-day tasks. The inclusion of this element reminds us that evaluations are always done under resource and time constraints; in fact, the resources available determine the extent of the data management and the range of evaluation findings that can be provided to the primary audiences.

*Focus*

What is the nature of the object or evaluand under review—for example, is it a policy or program or organisational unit? Which elements or components of the evaluand are to be reviewed—for example, the program plan or its implementation? What is the state of development of the evaluand?

The identification of the focus ensures that the evaluators are clear about the object to be investigated, so that the highest quality information can be produced, given the resources available.

### Evaluation issues and key questions

This involves the selection of the most important aspects of a program to be examined. In practice, this is the way in which an evaluation can be made more manageable because it forces clients to think about the fundamental directions the evaluation will take.

It is quite common for clients such as a steering committee, a school council or a middle-level manager to put forward a long list of issues which they would like addressed. The evaluator may need to work with the client to reduce this list. This involves educating the client about the realities of working within a budget, challenging them as to the relative importance of each issue, and identifying those questions which are not amenable to answers through the evaluation.

For the purposes of planning, issues should be turned into a set of evaluation questions. These questions serve to focus the evaluation even more and provide a direction for the collection and analysis of data. Posing a small set of key questions is fundamental for the evaluation to go forward. We discuss the nature of key questions in more detail in Chapter 5.

### Assembly of evidence/data management

For each question, a data collection and analysis strategy should be developed. It is important that the data collection and analysis techniques chosen should be those that best answer the questions. The implication is that the evaluator should have recourse to a range of data-collection strategies, and an understanding that, in the end, there is a need for the evaluator to make sense of the evidence and draw defensible conclusions. The range of possible data collection techniques available is wide and it is in this area that a trained evaluator or someone with research skills is often needed. Also, when making decisions about analyses, the evaluator should bear in mind the sophistication of the audiences and, if possible, ensure that findings from the analysis can be presented in ways that make sense to the primary audience.

### Dissemination of findings

How will information about the evaluation be disseminated? How will the findings and conclusions arising from the evaluation be disseminated? Is there a need for recommendations? If so, who will create them?

It is a truism that many evaluations have failed to have an impact on decision-making because the evaluator has not used effective techniques for disseminating the findings. In particular, the long and/or esoteric report has been shown to be ineffective in transferring information. More creative techniques are called for, including those that allow clients and evaluators to interact. It is fundamental that clients comprehend the findings of the evaluation and understand their implications. The issue of whether recommendations will be developed by the evaluators or by others should be considered during the planning phase of the evaluation. We discuss dissemination in more detail in Chapter 6.

### Codes of behaviour

What are the ethical conditions that underlie the evaluation effort? Standards of conduct underlie the work of professionals such as doctors and psychologists. Evaluators should also ensure that high ethical standards are applied to the conduct of an evaluation. These are discussed in detail in Chapter 8.

### Budget and timeline

Some indication of the amount of resources needed for the evaluation should be included in the evaluation plan. If an evaluation is to be carried out externally, it is necessary for the evaluators to cost their services and associated resources, and to set this out clearly. Working out a week-by-week work schedule helps ensure that the evaluation will be well managed and that the findings will be delivered on time. A schedule must take into account the resources that are available for the investigation. It is important that resources and time are allocated to the negotiation and dissemination phases of the evaluation.

While the evaluation plan has been set out under a set of discrete headings, we wish to emphasise that the overall plan should be coherent—that is, the entries under one heading should be consistent with those under *all* other headings. There is no use in planning an elaborate data collection effort related to many evaluation questions if the budget is $500! In practice, the final evaluation plan generally involves a series of steps. The first one is to respond to the information provided in an evaluation brief, or to the broad concerns of the clients if a formal brief is not available. Generally, the initial brief provides the basis for a second step—discussions between client and evaluator—that leads to the third step—a final evaluation plan.

Without this refinement of evaluation negotiation there is a high likelihood that the remainder of the evaluation effort is likely to be unsatisfactory to all parties. These processes may take up to 15 per cent of the total evaluation budget.

An issue is whether an external evaluator should withdraw if they find that there is some aspect of the proposed evaluation, or the program, with which they have some moral or ethical concern. It should be made clear that the negotiation can include these concerns, and that the final evaluation plan should take into account suggestions from the evaluator in addition to addressing the perceived needs of the evaluation commissioners.

In the course of an ongoing evaluation, it may be necessary to develop a series of evaluation plans as the needs of the clients change over time. It is not necessary for an entire plan to be finalised prior to the first round of data collection. It is possible for an evaluation to have a series of phases, each dependent on one that has gone before. For example, in a study we conducted some years ago, the evaluation team worked to provide feedback on the trials of an innnovatory curriculum designed to increase the participation of girls in school maths/science courses. Over a period of a year, the evaluation team negotiated a series of mini-plans which directed data collection on selected trials. Each of these phases lasted about six weeks. A mini-plan for a subsequent period was to some extent dependent on what had been found in the previous six weeks. This was an example of a situation where the evaluators provided a highly responsive service to program developers. It should be emphasised, however, that for all phases a mini-plan was negotiated to the satisfaction of the evaluators and the program team.

An evaluation planner suitable for use in negotiating evaluation is included as Figure 4.1.

## Figure 4.1  Negotiating evaluations: dimensions of an evaluation plan

**1  Specifying the evaluand**
What is the focus of the evaluation?

**2  Orientation or purpose(s) of the evaluation**
Why is the evaluation being done?

**3  Clients/primary audiences**
Who will receive and use the information?

**4  Evaluation resources**
What human and material resources are available?

**5  Evaluation focus(es)**
Which element(s) of the program will need to be investigated?—program context, program design, program implementation, program outcomes or a combination?

**6  Key evaluation issues/questions**
- *Assembly of evidence/data management*
  What are the key questions and how can we collect and analyse data to answer them?
  For each question, outline the data management techniques to be used.
- *Key questions*
  To what extent does . . .?
  Is there . . .?
  In what way does . . .?

- *Data management*
  What are the most appropriate methods of data collection and data reduction?
  *Collection (some considerations)*
  — Is sampling important?
  — Is anything known about this from other sources?
  — How will the data be collected?
  *Analysis and interpretation*
  — How will the data be analysed to address the key evaluation question?

**7  Dissemination**
- What strategies for reporting will be used?
- When will reporting take place?
- What kinds of information will be included (findings, conclusions, judgments, recommendations)?

**8   Codes of behaviour**
What ethical issues need to be addressed?

**9   Budget and timeline**
Given the resources, what will be achieved at key time points during the evaluation?

**10   Other considerations which emerge in the course of the negotiation**


## THE IMPORTANCE OF EVALUATION PLANNING

If a plan is not negotiated, an unsatisfactory evaluation in practice is likely to be the outcome, as the following example shows.

### Example 4.1 Evaluation of a national school improvement program

This example concerns a national evaluation of school improvement, the Participation and Equity Program (PEP). The first stage of the evaluation was specifically devoted to the development of an evaluation plan. The plan proposed that the evaluation consist of several phases with differing methodologies. For example, one phase involved an analysis of the reaction of different systems (state education departments and private school systems) to PEP. A second phase involved a set of case studies in school and community colleges.

While the plan paid extensive detail to methods, it lacked specificity on other elements of an evaluation plan. For example, there was insufficient attention given to the purposes of each phase, the major audience for the phase, and the likely uses of the findings. There was a general agreement among the evaluators that the commissioning agency, the Department of Education, needed to know about PEP, but beyond this, there was a lack of clarity about the reasons for the evaluation.

One result was that each phase was carried out as if it was a research study with minimal interaction between clients and evaluators. There was also little interaction between staff working on each phase. As each phase was completed, reports were forwarded to the commissioning agency.

A question which arose among those responsible for the case studies was: why are these being undertaken and for whom? The best guess was that they were primarily aimed at enlightening bureaucrats about the impact of their policies at the grassroots level. This was an acceptable use of the case study evaluation findings, but this use was never made specific at any stage during the design or implementation of the evaluation. If it had been negotiated, the case study evaluation team may have decided on more effective forms of reporting other than those used: a series of case reports. For example, an alternative with more likelihood of enlightening key bureaucrats could have been a seminar at which the site developers described their programs and the evaluators followed with a critical review of these programs.

As it was, a decision was made to publish and distribute the case studies to school and school systems twelve months after they had been forwarded to the commissioning agency. Presumably they were seen as being of primary value to practitioners, not to bureaucrats.

If the evaluators and commissioners had decided that practitioners were to be the primary audience, this almost certainly would have had an impact on how the case studies were planned and how the findings were disseminated.

In summary, the evaluators should have devoted more attention during the planning stage to the social interactive elements and less time to the data management. They needed to arrange things so that the evaluation messages were more timely—to set up arrangements through which the bureaucrats could telephone for information when it was needed. Also, it would have been useful for those concerned if there had been some face-to-face meeting between clients and evaluators through the year. These aspects should have been part of the evaluation design, but were not brought up during the initial planning stage of the project.

## AN EVALUATION PLAN: AN EXAMPLE

Recently, a large city (Bigtown) commissioned an evaluation plan with an external evaluator, with a view to moving on to the data management stage of the study. The focus of the study was the SafeT Program, an attempt by Bigtown City Council to improve the quality of life across the metropolis. A meeting was held between the commissioner of the study, the Director of Social Programs at Bigtown, and the evaluator. At this meeting the evaluator also had recourse to key documents about the

SafeT Program. Subsequently the following evaluation plan was prepared.

## Example 4.2 Evaluation plan for the SafeT Program

*Introduction*

This document provides an evaluation plan for the SafeT Program (hereafter, the STP), a major program currently being undertaken by the Bigtown City Council and a number of partners.

The Evaluation Plan should be regarded as indicative, a basis from which those working directly on the STP and the Council can make decisions on the final orientation of the evaluative approaches to be used.

This strategy is based on the notion that those most closely associated with the Program, key stakeholders, need to be involved in final decision-making in order to build commitment to the evaluation processes and the utilisation of the evaluation findings.

These procedures are designed to ensure that key stakeholders have a common understanding, up front, of what the evaluation hopes to achieve, and the products it will deliver.

Based on the negotiation, a final design for the study should be agreed so that the study can proceed to the data management phase.

*Structure of the evaluation plan*

For this discussion, the tentative plan is set out under a set of headings which, taken together, represent an integrated evaluation design. The headings are as follows:

- Object of the study
- Orientation of the evaluation
- Audiences for the evaluation
- Key questions
- Data management
- Reporting
- Timeline and resource implications.

Setting out the proposal for the evaluation under these headings is predicated on an assumption that there are links between them. That is, the plan should be coherent across headings rather than each being seen as independent. This form of planning:

- assists in identifying the key issues to be explored;
- identifies the audience(s);
- ensures that the evidence and conclusions address the key issues of the identified audiences; and
- encourages the utilisation of findings.

So while each area must be treated in turn, it is essential that the reader understand that links must be drawn across the areas.

### Object of the study

In discussing an evaluation design, it is also important to identify clearly the object which is the focus of the evaluation. By object of the study we mean the 'thing' being evaluated. An object can be a policy, a program, a product or a combination of these.

Understanding the nature of the object, its intentions, implementation and planned outcomes, makes subsequent discussions of the evaluation purposes clearer. This, in turn, assists in the development and implementation of the data management phase of the study—that is, decisions about what data to collect and how to analyse it.

For the purposes of clarity, we make the following distinctions between 'objects':

- *Policy* expresses intentions about directions in a given organisation that have priority. The policy in a given area gives guiding assumptions and goals for that area.
- *Programs (capital P)* are administrative umbrellas for distributing and regulating funds under a policy. Experience suggests that while there are one-off Programs, many government programs have extended lives and directions that are only changeable at the margins.
- Programs consist of *projects*, the actual delivery of specific interventions. Projects may differ widely in character, while some are permanent, others may have lives which are shorter than those of the Program of which they are a part. In addition, there can be variation in location of projects and in the personnel involved. Sometimes, projects are referred to as *'little p' programs*.

In this case a major object under consideration is the STP that, reflects the BigTown City Council's policy on safety for citizens. The strategy and the STP are based on the following policy directives:

- a broad and cooperative approach to city safety;
- safe streets and neighbourhoods;
- safe transport;
- well-planned business and appropriate controls;
- activities and special events that are safe for all;
- a reduction in criminal and anti-social behaviour.

In keeping with the generic distinctions above, current STP projects include:

- revitalisation of the west precinct of the city;
- establishment of an accord with proprietors of licensed bars and clubs;
- installation of public surveillance systems in selected areas;
- training for Council's staff in community safety principles.

The object about which conclusions and decisions need to be made is the STP Program. In order to make these decisions and conclusions, the objects that will be the focus of attention will be:

- the documentation and implementation of the STP. This includes ways in which the Program responds 'up' to Council policy, and 'down' to the delivery of specific projects;
- the documentation and delivery of specific projects. This includes the degree to which the projects are consistent with the intentions of the STP, and the individual impact of these projects.

### Orientation of the evaluation

Orientation refers to the conduct of the evaluation, including the primary purpose of the study, and the way the evaluator links to audiences and provides information to them.

The orientation suggested here involves the use of an external evaluator who will work closely with the primary audience: key Program staff. This is based on the notion that the STP is an ongoing program, and that key staff need to have access to evaluative information on a continuous basis in order to:

- make modifications, from time to time, to the Program's objectives and administration;
- make decisions about the effectiveness of existing individual projects, including whether they should be extended, modified, or terminated;
- make decisions about the introduction of new projects under the Program;
- keep key decision-making bodies, such as the SafeTown Executive Committee and the BigTown City Council, informed of the progress of the SCP. They, in turn, need to decide, at a given point in the future, about whether the Program should be terminated, or amalgamated with other Council initiatives.

This approach to evaluation is consistent with what we term *Monitoring evaluation*.. A key element is that the evaluator is seen as an essential supporter for program leaders. Evaluators involved must have a range of evaluation skills; they must also possess knowledge of program planning, and must have the ability to respond rapidly and flexibly to the needs of key audiences. A feature of the work of the evaluator is to provide relevant high-level information to staff for decision-making. This role can be contrasted with a more intensive evaluation in which the emphasis is on large-scale 'end-of-program' evaluation designed to 'prove' that the program has been a success.

The approach to evaluation suggested here is one in which the evaluator adopts a stand consistent with an interested but unbiased expert. It should be stressed that the evaluator would *not* be involved in any aspects of program delivery. Thus there is an element of 'distance' maintained between the evaluative and delivery functions.

### Clients/audiences

The reason for identifying key audiences is to ensure from the outset of the data collection and analysis that the issues for investigation and the dissemination strategies are the most appropriate for them.

From what has gone before, the primary audience for the evaluation is the program management of the STP. We would expect the evaluator to report to the primary audience in a variety of ways, some of which may be informal, and will involve direct interaction with key Program staff. An important issue is to provide relevant and timely information about those aspects of the Program which have high priority at a given point in time.

There are, of course, other audiences for the findings of the study. We regard the secondary audience to be members of the BigTown City Council.

The secondary audiences may wish to make decisions, at *specified points* in time, about the worth of the STP—say, eighteen months after the evaluation commences. One way for this to be provided is for the evaluator to provide an aggregation of information collected throughout the life of the program. It should be recalled that these data will be used for *ongoing* decision-making by the STP staff. We see this as a second important reporting strategy to be undertaken by the external evaluator.

The use of aggregated data in this way allows the evaluator to effectively address the key information needs of both primary and secondary audiences. This is a key aspect of this evaluation design.

*Key questions*

The following questions could be asked at any point in time in the delivery of the STP. In keeping with an evaluation for management approach, an issue for the evaluator is to provide evidence on the existing situation, and to encourage management to consider how the Program could be 'fine-tuned' to lead to improvement.

Program level

- To what extent is the STP consistent with international best practice? How could the Program be modified to be more in line with best practice?
- To what extent is the STP affecting the general level of safety in the city? How could the Program be modified to be more effective?
- To what extent are the objectives of the STP reflected in the design and implementation of individual STP projects? How could consistency between Program and projects be increased?
- How effective has the administrative decision-making of

the STP been in terms of making links between policy and practice? How could the Program be modified to be more in line with community needs?

Project level

For an individual project:

- Is the project plan consistent with the STP?
- What is actually happening within this project?
- Is it meeting the objectives of this project?
- Should it be continued?

Note that these questions apply to each individual project. Posing questions of this nature implies *following a given project over time*. This would be consistent with the needs of the Council to undertake a longitudinal study into the effectiveness of the STP. The number of projects to be followed will be limited by the resources available for the evaluation. Selection of the projects to be monitored should be guided by the priorities of the primary and secondary audiences.

*Data management*

Data management is the term used to assemble evidence from which evaluation questions such as those above can be answered. It should be noted that there is no one 'formula' for obtaining relevant information for a given question. This implies that the evaluator selected for the work must have a range of skills, including those of collecting and analysing data for the evaluation questions.

It is our view that:

- the evaluation of the Program at the Program level is essential;
- the selection of projects to be evaluated would be negotiated, depending on priorities and resources available for the evaluation.

Program level

The following is indicative of how the evaluation questions related to the *Program* could be handled. For simplicity, we have concentrated on the 'what is' here (as distinct from the 'how could the situation be improved' element) for each question.

- To what extent is the STP consistent with international best practice?

  *Review of literature on benchmarking; elite discussions with selected respondents to identify best practice sites; telephone interviews with managers of identified sites; development of criteria for best practice; review of STP in terms of these criteria.*

- To what extent is the STP affecting the general level of safety in the city?

  *Development of indicators that reflect the objectives of the program and their operationalisation; selection of procedures by which data on these indicators could be collected systematically at given time intervals. Note that this will require some creative attention to data management, as most available indicators may have limited face validity.*

- To what extent are the objectives of the STP reflected in the design and implementation of individual STP projects? How could consistency between Program and projects be increased?

  *Evaluator review of STP documentation; review of decision-making processes associated with selected projects; review of project documentation and interviews with project leaders.*

- How effective has the decision-making of the STP been in terms of making links between policy and practice?

  *Individual interviews with key stakeholders, such as senior administrators; use of expert panel on policy implementation.*

Project level

One common test that can be applied to projects is to determine whether they are consistent with the objectives of the Program. The evaluators should provide the STP with a method for this checking process.

However, as there will be a wide variety of projects, each one having its own objectives, evaluation of the implementation and outcomes of individual projects will require its own methodological approach.

It is likely that resources will not allow all projects to be evaluated for outcomes. The evaluator should work with the STP to set priorities in this regard.

*Dissemination*

There should be a high degree of interaction between the evaluators and client audiences for the study. This is based on research that shows an increased probability of evaluation findings being used if there is a strong link between the evaluators and stakeholders during all stages of an evaluation project.

As indicated above, there are two distinct major audiences for the findings of this evaluation:

- The primary audience is the management of the STP. It is proposed that the evaluator use a range of reporting approaches to the management. Consistent with the need for timely reporting, it is envisaged that the evaluator will prepare a series of short reports on selected aspects of the STP and its component projects.
- The secondary audience comprises the BigTown City Council members. It is envisaged that the evaluator will assist the STP management to prepare overview reports, summarising the overall impact of the project at predetermined points in time. This could be at the end of each year of a three-year project.

*Timeline and resource implications*

Finally, while a detailed budget for this study has not been developed, there are implications for the amount of funding that would be needed. One is that new Programs need time for implementation, and that implementation is essential for outcomes to be achieved. Most major interventions need at least two years to 'bite', the more complex the Program the longer is the period needed. The second, implied in this plan, is that evaluators should be 'on tap' regularly during implementation to provide quality information as the Program proceeds.

We believe that the study should be undertaken over a period beginning in the next calendar month for a 27-month period. The wishes of the Council to gauge the impact of the study over an extended period are thus consistent with what we know from other studies about the need to evaluate over a period thus allowing the effects of a Program to emerge.

# EVALUATION PLANNING AND THE INFLUENCE OF EVALUATION FORMS

While it is interesting to examine an evaluation plan developed by others, as in the example above, there is no substitute for doing a plan on a Program yourself. If this is not possible, you might like to develop a tentative plan for the following scenario.

**Example 4.3 Developing an evaluation plan**

Chapelton Community Health Centre (CCHC) offers a two-day educational Program designed for 15–16-year-olds currently attending school.

The Program was devised to meet a perceived need for accurate information about issues such as contraception, sexually transmitted diseases and the impact of drugs on the development of foetuses and young children.

It is delivered by a team consisting of two CCHC nurses and a visiting gynaecologist.

The Program was originally offered to students from nearby schools, but as it has become more widely known, most school groups travel to the CCHC by bus. All groups are accompanied by a teacher.

The Centre's Manager has provided support for the Program through the provision of facilities and nurses' time, but the major mission of the CCHC is to support the general health needs of the local inner urban community.

The Program has two parts. The first involves sessions taught by the team in a formal teaching–learning situation. Some use is made of videos, slides and charts.

In the second half of the Program, students visit a hospital where additional sessions are held and visits are made to labs and wards.

*The Program has been running for several years and is settled as far as the delivery staff are concerned. However, they are finding it difficult to cope with the increasing number of school requests. For the first time, CCHC has an interest in documenting the impact of the Program with a view to having it adopted at other sites.

The State Department of Health and Well-being has made a grant of $15 000 to fund the study. It is the beginning of a new year. You are a member of a small external evaluation agency that has been approached to

> evaluate the program. You have been asked to attend a meeting at the agency before meeting the clients. Use the evaluation planner to develop a tentative plan for the study.

Note that in this case you have been asked to 'scope' the evaluation plan before the negotiation actually begins. We would like to reiterate, at this point, that interaction with the client is essential to finalise the plan before proceeding to data collection and analysis.

Now, just imagine that all the parameters in the example were kept constant except the one that is preceded by an asterisk. Let's change this to the following:

> The Program has been running for almost one year. While the deliverers believe that the Program is generally OK, they need access to information designed to refine it.
>
> It is the beginning of the new year. You, as a member of the CCHC with some evaluation experience, are asked to convene a working party to undertake an internal evaluation. In all, there is the equivalent of one person's time for six weeks to carry out the study, and $2000 for expenses. A plan is needed as the basis for undertaking the evaluation.

You might like to repeat the planning exercise and make a comparison of your two plans.

You will have now realised that the evaluation plan and subsequent stages of the evaluation would be very different for the two scenarios presented in Example 4.3. The first scenario calls for an impact study focused on outcomes and thus is consistent with the Impact Form (Form E). The second calls for an improvement-focused study concerned with program delivery, consistent with the Interactive Form (Form C). Contrast these with Example 4.2, where the evaluation plan is built around the Monitoring Form (Form D).

The Forms provide a framework to aid in the planning and negotiation stage of an evaluation. However, the real power of the evaluation planner discussed in this chapter is that it can be used to plan evaluations for scenarios which fit within any one of the Forms.

## REFERENCES

Barrington, G.V. (1990). 'Evaluation Skills Nobody Taught Me or What's a Nice Girl Doing in a Place Like This?' Paper presented at the American Evaluation Association. Washington, DC: November, 1990.

Love, A. (1994). 'Internal Evaluation: Building Organisations from Within'. In *International Conference of the Australasian Evaluation Society*. Canberra: Australasian Evaluation Society.

Owen, J.M., Johnson, N.J. and Welsh, R.J. (1985). *Primary Concerns: A Project on Mathematics and Science in Primary Teacher Education*. Melbourne: Melbourne College of Advanced Education for the Commonwealth Tertiary Education Commission.

Patton, M.Q. (1997). *Utilization Focused Evaluation*. 3rd edn. Thousand Oaks, CA: Sage.

Smith, M.L. and Glass, G.V. (1987). *Research and Evaluation in Education and the Social Sciences*. Englewood Cliffs, NJ: Prentice Hall.

# 5

# From Evaluation Questions to Evaluation Findings

## INTRODUCTION

In this chapter we link the negotiation/planning stage of evaluation to the second stage. This stage involves the collection and analysis of evidence to produce findings, or what we sometimes refer to as *data management*. What do we mean by data management? It may not be a surprise to learn that social scientists, philosophers and others have engaged for some time in discussion and debate about the nature of data management and, more broadly, the underlying bases of enquiry on which research into physical and social phenomena is based. Here we outline some of these issues before turning to their relevance to evaluation practice. You should note that we can only provide a very brief overview, and we encourage you to pursue them through the extensive material that is now available in the literature.

At the basis of these discussions is the notion of an *enquiry paradigm*. This is:

> a set of interlocking philosophical assumptions and stances about knowledge, our social world, our ability to know that world, and our reasons for knowing it, assumptions that collectively warrant certain methods, certain knowledge claims, and certain actions on those claims. A paradigm frames and guides a particular orientation to social enquiry, including what questions to ask, what methods to use, what knowledge claims to strive for, and what defines high quality work. (Greene & Caracelli, 1997)

A philosophical position about enquiry has implications for the selection of sources, and for the gathering and making sense of data. In recent times, two major paradigms have become pre-eminent. These are the post-positivist and constructivist.

## POST-POSITIVIST PARADIGM

This paradigm is based on a view that social phenomena not only exist in the real world, but that systematic and stable relations exist between them. The regularities that link phenomena together can be expressed in terms of lawful or causal relations, or constructs that underlie individual and social life. The aim of enquiry is to prove or discover lawful or causal relations between elements of the phenomena. Studies consistent with this paradigm seek to establish generalisable knowledge. The fact that most of these constructs are not tangible or visible does not make them invalid. Traditionally, sources of data are large-scale data sets and there is an emphasis on the use of quantitative methods, but there are also examples of smaller-scale studies of an inductive nature which have adopted this perspective.

## CONSTRUCTIVIST PARADIGM

The constructivist paradigm is based on a belief that reality, or at least social reality, is socially constructed—that is, there is no objective reality. The aim is not to find the 'right' description of a program, but to develop an increasingly sophisticated description that incorporates the perspectives of all concerned. An evaluation based on this paradigm would focus on gathering constructions, descriptions and analyses from relevant people, including intended clients, staff and others, jointly reflecting on them, and seeking synthesis and consensus. Evidence would be useful to fill out these descriptions but would not 'prove' their validity. Typically, studies within this paradigm are inductive in nature, adopt an investigatory perspective, and provide knowledge which is specific to the context. There is an emphasis on intensive study, often concentrating on a small number of cases or sites, and on the use of quantitative methods.

An issue that has been occupying the minds of evaluation theorists is the degree to which these 'world views' and others based on other paradigms have and should impinge on the practice of evaluation, and in particular the use of different methodologies. Given the vastness and complexity of the topic, we can only make a summary statement. This is that, while we should be aware of the paradigms mentioned above, there is emerging a more adequate paradigm on which to base the practice of evaluation. This has been described as *emergent realism.*

## EMERGENT REALISM

Like the post-positivist perspective, this paradigm assumes the existence of an external reality. It assumes that evaluators, by the use of a combination of systematic methods, can provide a description of this reality. The more adequately we select and apply these methods, the closer we will get to an accurate description or rendering of this reality. However, a key aspect of the emergent realism perspective is that we must always be aware of the tentativeness of our findings. Emergent realism holds that a synthesis of methods is needed to provide a rich and adequate understanding of evaluation issues (Mark et al., 1998).

The emergent realism paradigm is consistent with the adoption of a *pragmatic* framework. According to Datta (1997), such a framework provides essential criteria for making design decisions which are practical, contextually responsive and consequential. This leads to the following questions:

- Can salient questions be adequately answered?
- Can the design be successfully carried out?
- Is there an optimisation of tradeoffs in the use of different methods—for example, between breadth and depth of understanding of an issue related to a given question?
- Are the results usable?

You may have realised that this is consistent with the orientation and issues based framework which underlies the evaluation Forms. The fact that we have indentified five evaluation Forms implies a set of what could be called 'mini-paradigms' of evaluation within an *emergent realism* perspective. That is, one could regard the Forms themselves as providing alternative epistemological views of evaluation practice. For example, Monitoring evaluation (Form D) tends to be associated with a utilitarian view of the world, with issues such as efficiency and effectiveness, and the use of quantitative methods, as indicators. By contrast, Interactive evaluation (Form C) tends to be associated with the concerns and issues of staff involved in a program, the use of investigatory methods, and qualitative methods.

This is a key point in the development of arguments in this book. We take the view that salient issues are the drivers of the data management phase of evaluation practice. *The choice of the methodology follows from the questions asked, not vice versa.* This is a challenge for practitioners who wish to work across all

Forms, particularly those who come to evaluation practice with a well-honed but selective set of methodological tools which they prefer to use. Employing an investigator with a limited methodological range of skills can lead to the evaluation being methodology dominated, rather than directed by the negotiated concerns of clients and audiences.

So writing evaluation questions and understanding the data management implications is a key factor in successful evaluation. Not only is the writing of evaluation questions fundamental to evaluation planning, in our experience, but even graduate students with experience in evaluation find it difficult to develop them. The remainder of this chapter is thus devoted to:

- question development; and
- data management: ways in which these questions can be answered through empirical enquiry.

## THE NATURE OF EVALUATION QUESTIONS

The primacy of evaluation questions has been recognised by evaluation theorists. For example, one writer says that 'clarification of and discrimination between the various types of questions which evaluations undertake to answer is absolutely fundamental to getting a useful answer at all' (Scriven, 1980). One way of classifying evaluation questions is to locate them in the five evaluation Forms.

To see how different styles of questions can be linked to different Forms, we make use of a case study. Recently, we were involved in a project designed to encourage evaluation practice in the area of adult literacy and basic education [ALBE]. The project was comprehensive in scope and funded by a national education agency. Initially, practitioners working the ALBE area were surveyed to determine:

- ways in which the goals of programs they presented were developed and implemented;
- use of procedures that demonstrated the success or otherwise of programs;
- evaluation instruments used in evaluation; and
- the general level of expertise in evaluation in the adult literacy and basic education community.

Consequently, it was decided that the ALBE field would be enhanced if guidelines were prepared that would make evaluation more meaningful at all levels of ALBE provision. It was also decided that evaluation should not be undertaken in isolation from the larger frame of reference that took into account program design and delivery.

A framework designed to provide basic information about evaluation was prepared by a team led by our colleague, Faye Lambert (Lambert et al., 1995). Subsequently an extensive professional development program was implemented, based on the framework. A key element of the framework was to assist those engaged in evaluation to set evaluation questions. Tables 5.1 to 5.5 represent tables derived from those developed for the ALBE framework.

Table 5.1 contains typical generic questions that could structure studies consistent with the Proactive Form of evaluation. An important feature is the vertical dimension of the grid, the level of provision. The three levels are consistent with:

- Policy development;
- big P program provision and
- little p program provision

which we outlined in Chapter 2 when discussing different evaluands.

Tables 5.1 to 5.5 are in the same format, providing a smorgasbord of *generic* questions that could be asked by stakeholders and audiences relating to a given initiative. It is important to note that, in a given evaluation, those negotiating the evaluation would need to decide on *specific* questions relating to a given policy or program.

## REFLECTING ON THE NATURE OF EVALUATION QUESTIONS

It is clear that there are different styles of questions among the many that have been asked across Tables 5.1 to 5.5.

Difference *is* associated with the Form of evaluation. Different Forms imply different evaluation purposes, so one would expect that questions asked within one Form would differ in substance from those posed within a different Form. A factor which contributes to between-Form differences is the *timing* of an evaluation. Let us confine ourselves here to questions asked at the policy level across Tables 5.1 to 5.5. In Table 5.1, Proactive evaluation questions relate to what *ought* to be, to help decision-makers establish a desirable state of affairs. Proactive evaluation is concerned with policy development. Ideally, we would like Proactive evaluation to establish that a given intervention is of sufficient quality in terms of solving or ameliorating a given social or educational problem. Compare this with questions asked in the Monitoring Form, Table 5.4. Time has passed, and the policy has been implemented. The policy-maker is now concerned with

90

**Table 5.1  Proactive evaluation: typical questions**

Evaluation undertaken to make decisions about a given impending policy or (P) program.

| | Typical questions | Focus | Clients |
|---|---|---|---|
| Policy level (taken at the national level) | What are the current national agendas, priorities, contexts and goals? What part can ALBE play in achieving national goals? Why do we need a program and what should its goals be? What are the current literacy skills of the population? Are there specific areas of need? Which should receive priority? How should resources be allocated to service the total range of needs identified? | Current situation and contexts, policy and goals. Existing infrastructure, skill levels, present and future needs. | Government Ministers Portfolio/departments. |
| Big P Program level (taken at the regional level) | What are the particular needs of this region? What are the region's policies, objectives and priorities? Do they address these needs and are they consistent with national policies, objectives and priorities? What is already happening to meet the region's needs? What else would make the difference? Where should we see new provision and/or innovative provision? | Current situation, contexts, policies and goals. Existing program provision, infrastructure, present and future needs. | Funding agencies, regional planning groups. |
| Little p program level (taken at the provider level, e.g., community college/group within community college) | Are our program policies, objectives and priorities consistent with regional, state and national policies, objectives and priorities? Do they provide a framework for the program? What is the present and future need for the program? Do we know who and where our potential program users/students are? How does our program relate to other programs in the area? What are the local conditions that impact on our program now and in the future? | Current situation, context, program policy and objectives. Existing program design, present and future needs. | Funding agencies, policy makers, program planners and deliverers. |

**Table 5.2  Clarificative evaluation: typical questions**

Evaluation undertaken to make explicit the essential features of a given policy or (P) program.

| | Typical questions | Focus | Clients |
|---|---|---|---|
| Policy level (taken at the national level) | What are the objectives of our policies? Do our policies have internal coherence? Do our policies provide support for program implementation at regional level? Are our policies plausible in terms of guidance for practice? | Policy statements. | Government Ministers Portfolio/ departments/ federal policy makers. |
| | How does the national infrastructure support program implementation in line with policies? Do resource allocation practices reflect our stated objectives and priorities? Does our manpower planning adequately support program development? | Program information and support. | |
| Big P Program level (taken at the regional level) | What are the objectives of our Programs? Do our Programs have internal coherence? Are our Programs plausible in terms of guidance for practice? Is the rationale for offering each Program clear to all involved? | Program statements. | Regional staff/advisory groups, providers. |
| | Is it clear as to how we will disseminate Programs? Do providers know what is expected of them in terms of reporting back? Is Program resource allocation transparent from the provider perspective? Are the principles and objectives of staff development programs designed to support implementation well developed? | Program information and support. | |
| Little p program level (taken at the provider level, e.g., community college/group within community college) | Are our programs consistent with regional objectives? Are they realistic and how are our programs structured to achieve these objectives? | Program design. | Program planners, program staff and college administration. |
| | Are our program plans internally consistent? Has the program logic of our programs been validated? Which of the present programs should be targeted for an impact evaluation? | Program design. | |

**Table 5.3  Interactive evaluation: typical questions**

Evaluation undertaken to make decisions about improvement of a current and/or continuing policy or (P) program.

| | Typical questions | Focus | Clients |
|---|---|---|---|
| Policy level (taken at the national level) | Are the national strategies designed to address literacy needs working? Are these areas in need of improvement? How effectively is the present infrastructure supporting the needs of the states? Are the personnel management policies appropriate or should there be changes? What are the strengths and weaknesses of the professional development delivery strategies? Are there further areas of professional development which are required to improve state, regional and provider operations? How are policies on resource allocation/distribution and curriculum affecting the states/territories, regions and providers? | Processes. | Government Ministers Portfolio/ departments. |
| Big P Program level (taken at the regional level) | How are present Programs affecting providers? Are changes required in priorities for individual programs? What difference is the funding making to the quality of program delivery in the region? How can we improve the delivery of the Program? How can we improve the support for the Program? | Processes. | Regional authorities/ funding bodies. |
| Little p program level (taken at the provider level, e.g., community college/group within community college) | What actually happens in this program? What are practitioners doing that is working well? What is not working so well? How are students affected by the program in action? Is the delivery tailored to meet individual needs and goals of students? Are professional development strategies as identified by staff effective? How has professional development affected program implementation? How could we generally improve the program for the future? | Processes. | Program managers/ program staff and clients. |

**Table 5.4  Monitoring evaluation: typical questions**

Evaluation undertaken to provide checks on the state of a current continuing policy or (P) program.

| | Typical questions | Focus | Clients |
|---|---|---|---|
| Policy level (taken at the national level) | How many people are participating in the programs? Are literacy skills increasing? What is the effect of Commonwealth expenditure for this policy area; can this policy be administered more efficiently? Is the money allocated to strategic areas being expended efficiently? What is the cost of identified outcomes? What difference is increased funding making to the type of student outcomes? How much are we spending on each student? Are our policy guidelines clear and well understood? Are they influencing program provision? Do we need to improve our information dissemination? | Existing policy and related program. | Government Ministers, Finance and Treasury, Portfolio/ departments. |
| Big P Program level (taken at the regional level) | How well are our Programs going? Are they understood by providers? Are they being translated into practice? How many students are graduating from each Program? How does this compare with the situation last year? Has there been an impact on achievement of student learning outcomes and, if so, how does it compare with last year? Are there differences in achievement at different program sites: if so, why? How are our regional support mechanisms working; are they as good as last year? Are there differences in the quality of support across the region? What effect is this having on the quality of programs offered in the region? | Existing Program and related programs. | State and Regional authorities, funding agencies. |
| Little p program level (taken at the provider level, e.g., community college/ group within community college) | How many students are achieving success in our program: how does this compare with last year? What is the attrition rate from our program, compared with other program sites? Are our clients getting jobs or improving job options: is this increasing or decreasing? What proportion of our students are going on to further studies, compared with other similar programs? Does our program exemplify national/regional good practice? Is professional development support acceptable? How much does it cost to run this program? | Existing programs. | Managers and program staff, program co-ordinators and staff. |

**Table 5.5　Impact evaluation: typical questions**
Evaluation undertaken to assess the effects of a given policy or (P) program.

| | Typical questions | Focus | Clients |
|---|---|---|---|
| Policy level (taken at the national level) | How was policy implemented? Were national goals and targets achieved? Was the expenditure justified in terms of gains in literacy and national productivity? Was this the result of the policy initiatives or were other factors involved? Were some regions more successful in implementing their program than others? To what extent was our policy dissemination effective? How well managed was the policy/program interface? Is the policy still appropriate? What should be the direction of future policy in this area? | Existing policy and programs. | Government Ministers and Portfolios. |
| Big P Program level (taken at the regional level) | To what extent have regional goals been achieved? Were the real goals reflected in Program statements? Have some programs performed better than others in achieving desired outcomes? Should some programs be encouraged over and above others? Have there been any unanticipated outcomes, desirable or undesirable, as a result of programs? To what extent were the regional support mechanisms effective in supporting Program provision? | Existing Program. | Policy makers and planners, funding bodies. |
| Little p program level (taken at the provider level, e.g., community college/group within community college) | To what extent was our program implemented? Did implementation lead to the stated outcomes? Were there any unanticipated outcomes? What were the short-term and long-term outcomes for our students? To what extent did the program meet the needs of the students? To what extent did regional support affect the implementation and outcomes of the program? | Existing program. | Regional staff, program managers and staff. |

reviewing what is happening across regions and maybe individual sites. There is a concern now with management decisions, those which can assist the policy-maker to 'report up' to funders and senior bureaucrats, and in some cases to finetune policy direction. So, at different times, there are different evaluation questions which should be asked.

Within each Form, a factor that influences question style is the *level* of Program provision. Policy-level questions are generally different from Program-level questions. In reality, evaluation-based concerns of staff are different depending on their needs for information about the evaluand under consideration. Consider the implementation of a given policy. While the policy developer may need to know how much the implementation of the policy actually costs at the site level, the program manager's concern could be whether the essential elements for implementation have been assembled successfully. A key question might be whether or not the teacher works well with the students, or whether the teaching/learning facilities are adequate, or the extent to which the students have been briefed as to program expectations.

The *focus* for an evaluation actually changes from level to level. In this example, there is a policy at the national level, at the regional level there is a Program and at the local or provider level there are one or more programs. While there will be differences in these details for other situations, the important distinctions between levels of evaluand are likely to remain.

While the style of question asked is linked to Form and level, there are question styles that seem to crop up again and again across all elements in the tables. Perhaps the most pervasive appears as follows: *'What is the situation regarding . . .'* or *'To what extent has . . .?'* or *'What are the . . .?'* An example of this style in Table 5.1 is 'What are the particular needs of this region? This is a Program-level Proactive Form question. In Table 5.3 we find the following: 'What actually works in this program? This is a program-level Interactive evaluation Form question. These questions can be described as *non-causal*—they do not search for cause and effect links. The general question style is as follows: 'What is the state of P?' (where P can be a policy, a Program or a program).

Such a question assumes that we want to know what is happening about P—that is, the assumption is that the evidence in the form of findings and conclusions will be largely in the form of a description of P. If, in fact, P is being delivered at more than one site location, the question implies a cross-site analysis of P to provide comparisons of what is happening within P between sites.

**Example 5.1 Evaluation of the Curriculum and Standards Framework (CSF)**

In 1995, an evaluation of the CSF was undertaken for the Victorian Board of Studies. The CSF was a curriculum policy developed for use across all schools in the state. In addition to general policy, the Board provided the schools with curriculum outlines (which could be regarded as big P Programs). The Board commissioned an external evaluation during the first year of provision.

Among the questions about which senior executives wanted evidence were the following:

- How well is the CSF being disseminated?
- In what ways are schools using the CSF?
- Do the schools value the CSF?

The evaluators collected data by observation, interview and document analysis in a sample of schools over a period of about fifteen months. Data were presented in the form of charts and tables which summarised patterns across the schools. The primary audience was provided with trend data on dissemination and use at intervals over the fifteen-month period. (Owen et al., 1996)

Another kind of common question that might be asked is a causal one, along the lines of: what is it in P that causes O? As we write this chapter, there has been a major landslide at a ski resort, resulting in heavy loss of life. Currently investigation teams are combing the mountain with the object of determining what caused the slide. An underground stream passing under a lodge has been discovered. It is likely that a flood in this stream was a major cause of the landslide.

In the context of posing evaluation questions, let us assume again that P is the evaluand under consideration here and O is a possible outcome of the evaluand. Such a question implies identifying those key elements of P, sometimes called *independent variables*, and their relative contribution to the outcome, sometimes called the *dependent variable*. A study of this nature requires the evaluator to look for evidence within a site or sites which will support the causal links.

The implication of such a question is that the evaluator will also be involved in investigatory approaches to data management, leading to the discovery of the causal link or links. This is consistent with an inductive approach to knowledge creation, and is often linked to the use of intensive qualitative data collection and analysis methods—see, for example, Miles & Huberman (1994).

> **Example 5.2 Evaluation of the Curriculum and Standards Framework (CSF)**
>
> In addition to the questions outlined in Example 5.1, other questions posed during the CSF evaluation were as follows:
>
> - What is the uptake of the CSF in schools?
> - What internal school factors affect the uptake of the CSF?
>
> The second question involved an in-depth analysis of the use of the CSF at whole-school level in nine schools, and a review of what factors seemed to influence use. A 'thick description' of each school was prepared. Arising from the case report, a construct labelled as 'school culture' was identified as a major determining variable—that is, in schools where the uptake was high, school culture was high, whereas in schools where school culture was absent or less evident, uptake was low. (Meyer, 1997)

It is also necessary to ask whether more of some key variable or variables act to cause more of O. This implies identifying key elements of the Program—let us call them X1 and X2—and their relevant impact on the outcome. To test this, we must have cases where there is variation in the amount of X1 and X2 in the Program.

An evaluation question which would encourage this style of enquiry would be as follows: Do different support strategies used by different organisations have differential effects on staff morale? The implications for setting up such a study are that different treatments would have to be implemented, and information collected on the implementation of these treatments and on changes in staff morale. This is a form of investigation that lends itself to an 'experiment', or the use of what is called *multivariate analysis*, that enables the relative effects of X1, X2, etc., to be estimated.

The implication of such a question is that the evaluator will be involved with structured approaches to data management, leading to an estimation of the extent of the causal link or links. This is consistent with a deductive approach to knowledge creation, and is often linked to the use of quantitative data collection and analysis methods. Such an approach is rooted in the canons of the so-called scientific method and has been used widely in some areas of the social sciences. In practice, such approaches have been adopted in evaluation studies, in particular within the Impact evaluation (Form E).

## ANSWERING EVALUATION QUESTIONS

Evaluation questions help us to determine the data management techniques that we use. A distinguishing feature of evaluation practice is a need to have access to a repertoire of methods, to select and use data management methods that are the most suitable for answering the questions which focus the evaluation. This is integral to the provision of plausible and accurate findings.

Figure 5.1 provides an overview of the link between asking for and providing answers to evaluation questions. Essential aspects of data management in evaluation include:

- the assembly of evidence—the collection of data relevant to each evaluation question; and
- analysis of evidence—making sense of these data through systematic data analysis techniques.

**Figure 5.1    Data management in evaluation**

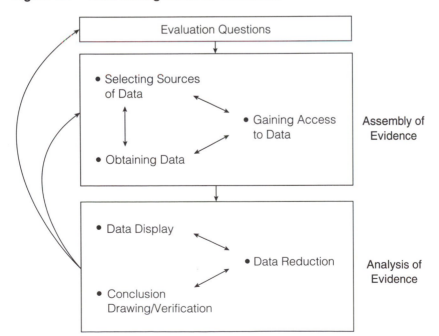

A large range of methodologies are available to evaluators. However, all of these methodologies require the evaluator to be concerned with the elements of data collection and analysis that are outlined in Figure 5.1.

*Assembly of evidence* involves the following interlinked elements:

- *sources of data*, the actual location of the data, such as an existing file, documents, or individuals who possess the information required. This also involves the selection, where necessary, of data sources in instances where all relevant sources will not be consulted. Thus, sampling is a consideration in this element of data collection;
- *gaining access to data*, the means by which the data can be extracted. This involves making contact with data sources and involves aspects such as gaining permission to consult with individuals, determining where and when data can be collected, and ensuring that ethical considerations are being observed; and
- *collecting data*, involving the development of instruments, and the use of these instruments to assemble information from the field. Instruments used in the collection of data include questionnaires, interviews and schemes for document review, as well as the methods used within them. For example, a given questionnaire might incorporate a range of methods—for example, an attitude scale, a semantic differential scale and an item which requires an extended written response.

Ways of collecting data can be summarised as follows:

- directly from individuals identified as a source of information: *self-reports*;
  - diaries or anecdotal records;
  - checklists or inventories;
  - rating scales and semantic differentials;
  - written responses;
  *as personal products*;
  - tests;
  - samples of work;
- compiled by an independent observer: *written accounts*; *observation forms*;
  - observation schedules;
  - rating scales;
  - checklists and inventories;
  *oral responses, either singly or from a group*;

- compiled by use of mechanical devices:
  *audiotape*;
  *videotape*;
  *time lapse and still photography*;
  *other devices*;
  – computer collation of responses;
- through use of unobtrusive techniques (see Webb, 1966);
- from existing records;
  *public documents*;
  *files*;
  *existing data bases*;

*Analysis of evidence* involves a consideration of the following interlinked elements:

- *data display*, the development of an organised assembly of information which leads to the drawing of conclusions about the key questions of the evaluation study;
- *data reduction*, the process of simplifying and transforming the raw information according to some logical set of procedures or rules;
- *conclusion drawing*, making meaning about the data in the broader context of the evaluation question being examined.

It is possible that some studies will need more than 'one round' of data collection and analysis to reach a conclusion. This explains the recursive arrow linking the conclusion drawing and verification element of data analysis back to the data collection stage in Figure 5.1.

As we noted earlier, conclusion drawing is the end point of all evaluative enquiries. However, in others, the evaluator may also be concerned to use the conclusions to:

- *make judgments about the program*. This means placing values on the conclusions by making statements that the program is 'good', or 'bad', or that the results are 'positive', 'in the direction desired', or 'below expectations'.
- *develop recommendations*. These are suggested courses of action, advice to policy-makers, program managers or providers about what to do in the light of the evidence and conclusions.

A detailed knowledge of specific data management techniques is beyond the scope of this book. Readers are encouraged to consult appropriate texts on individual techniques or to seek the assistance of an expert on technical matters of data analysis. Experience suggests that some 'experts' tend to choose methods with which they are comfortable, rather than those which are most appropriate.

Numerous techniques for the analysis of quantitative data have been developed over time and have been made accessible to evaluators through sophisticated computer packages such as Statistical Packages for the Social Sciences (SPSSx). While these techniques vary in specifics, the above principles apply to them all. While it is true that canons or rules of data analysis for quantitative data are better specified and have stood the test of time, rules for the analysis of qualitative data have been developed more recently which also fit within the principles described above (see, for example, Miles & Huberman, 1994).

It should also be noted that, in all evaluations, a combination of common sense and an ability to be analytical can get the evaluator a long way towards conclusions on key evaluation issues or questions. If these attributes are used, it is possible to get by with some assistance from a methodological specialist at the 'right' time. For some years we have continually been amazed at the quality of work done by graduate students if the above combination of factors has been present. This implies that the abilities of the evaluator are important in the collection and analysis of data.

The effective analyst needs mental powers *as well as* the relevant methodological tools. These mental powers required include:

- the ability to *accumulate knowledge*—this involves the acquisition and synthesis of relevant information about the evaluand under review;
- *observational abilities*, in terms of what to look for to recognise the meanings of the data and to be able to perceive and interpret available information;
- *reasoning powers*—the ability to build a line of argument or mulitple lines of argument. This is consistent with the need to come to conclusions which can stand up to scrutiny;
- *intuitive powers*—the power of insight, the ability to make a conceptual leap in the face of lack of direct access to the phenomena of interest (Smith, 1992).

As we indicated earlier, data management is an integral part of evaluation planning and should be scrutinised before any field work is undertaken. All data management plans should be subjected to the following criteria:

- Will the evidence collected give a comprehensive picture of what is being evaluated?

102

- Does the data management strategy make effective use of existing data?
- Will the cost of data collection be justified, given the amount and kind of information it will provide?
- Will the information be reliable?
- Can the data collection be carried out without unduly disrupting the program and taking too much of the time of the program providers?
- Are the data collection procedures legal and ethical?
- Can the data be collected and analysed within the time constraints of the study?

This review may give an impression that data management proceeds in a linear and well-organised sequence of events. In practice, this is not the case. Data management involves a set of micro-level decisions, each contingent on what has been decided before. Together, these determine the direction of the analysis, and lead to the findings of the study. Consistent with the Emergent Reality paradigm is the desire of the conscientious evaluator to arrive as close to the truth as possible while retaining a sense of humility about the certainty of the conclusions reached.

## CONCLUSION

The fact that evaluation can no longer be regarded as a unitary concept is reflected in the different Forms of evaluation, each with identifiable purposes and issues which define them. Once the evaluator has determined which Form is needed for a given investigation, the next step is to develop appropriate evaluation questions.

We agree with Smith (1987) that the evaluation is fundamentally a process of answering questions. Thus the importance of developing good evaluation questions cannot be overestimated. The development of evaluation questions can be conceived of as the beginning of the vital data management aspect of evaluation practice. Clarifying our evaluation questions assists clients and evaluators to see clearly what is needed, as well as helping us to reject questions that are unanswerable and put aside questions that are not important.

As we have emphasised in the second half of this chapter, getting the questions clear should assist the evaluator in the selection of appropriate data management techniques. An effective evaluation is tightly focused, and the key to this focus is for the evaluator to be able to select and use the methods of data collection and analysis which will provide plausible answers.

Chapters 9 to 13 are devoted to a discussion of evaluation for each of the evaluation Forms. These chapters contain case examples which provide a cross-section of the range of data management techniques available. So, while this chapter has provided an overview of methodology, the material in later chapters should also contribute to your understanding of the use of methodologies and their focused use in answering evaluation questions.

## REFERENCES

Datta, L. (1997). 'A Pragmatic Basis for Mixed Method Designs'. *New Directions in Program Evaluation*, 74 (Summer), 33–46.

Greene, J.C. & Caracelli, V.J. (1997). 'Defining and Decribing the Paradigm Issue in Mixed-method Evaluation'. *New Directions in Program Evaluation*, 74 (Summer), 5–17.

Mark, M.M., Henry, G.T. & Julnes, G. (1998). 'A Realist Theory of Evaluation Practice'. *New Directions in Program Evaluation*, 78, (Summer), 3–32.

Lambert, F.C., Owen, J.M., Coates, S. & McQueen, J. (1995). 'A Guide to Program Evaluation'. In *Professional Development for Program Evaluation*. Canberra: National Staff Development Committee for Vocational Education and Training.

Meyer, H. (1997). 'The Impact of the CSF in Schools'. Unpublished Doctor of Education thesis, The University of Melbourne.

Miles, M.B. & Huberman, A.M. (1994). *Qualitative Data Analysis*. Thousand Oaks, CA: Sage.

Owen, J.M., Meyer, H. & Livingston, J. (1996). *School Responses to the Curriculum and Standards Framework*. Carlton, Vic: Victorian Board of Studies.

Scriven, M. (1980). *The Logic of Evaluation*. Port Reyes, CA: Edge Press.

Smith, N.L. (1987). 'Towards the Justification of Claims in Evaluation Research'. *Evaluation and Program Planning*, 10, 309–14.

——(1992). 'Aspects of Investigative Inquiry in Evaluation'. *New Directions in Program Evaluation*, 56 (Winter), 3–13.

Webb, E.J., Campbell, D.T., Schwartz, R.D. & Sechrest, L.B. (1996). *Unobtrusive Measures: Non-reactive Research in the Social Sciences*. Chicago, Ill.: Rand McNally.

# 6

## From Evaluation Findings to Utilisation

### INTRODUCTION

Notions related to use of the products of evaluation have been included in previous chapters. It is now appropriate to provide a more conceptual overview. This chapter is devoted to an examination of ways in which findings and other products of evaluation affect clients and other audiences. Thus we are concerned with:

- the dissemination of information generated through evaluation;
- the utilisation of findings which are produced by the evaluation; and
- factors which affect client utilisation.

As we have indicated throughout, dissemination is an integral component of evaluation. Dissemination requires evaluators and audiences to be in communication. Thus communication skills are an essential part of the repertoire of a skilled evaluator—a fact that is sometimes overlooked in training programs for potential program evaluators.

Dissemination and utilisation of social science knowledge have been written about extensively over the past two decades. The evaluation utilisation literature forms a subset of this knowledge base. Well-known evaluators—for example, Marvin Alkin, Michael Patton and Carol Weiss—have made significant contributions to the theory of evaluation utilisation which we draw on in the following sections.

## EVALUATION TO UTILISATION

From a review of the contributions of these and other theorists, we have developed a framework which summarises key elements in the dissemination and utilisation processes which are presented in Figure 6.1. In this 'model', there are several major elements:

- *evaluation*, which consists of three key stages. As we have indicated previously, these are:

  - negotiation and planning;
  - obtaining—the assembly of evidence and findings; and
  - dissemination.

  We have discussed the negotiating/planning and assembly of evidence and findings in previous chapters. In Figure 6.1, we focus on the following elements:
- *dissemination*, means the use of deliberative strategies for informing identified audience(s) about aspects of the evaluation including its conduct and findings. While reporting of findings is an important and fundamental aspect, it is not the only aspect of dissemination.

  The term 'dissemination' here is a sign that evaluators need to initiate strategies designed to encourage the spread of information resulting from the evaluation. Dissemination is used in preference to diffusion, as the latter connotes a more general and less interventionist percolation of the findings to interested parties.
- *utilisation*, an examination of Figure 6.1 reveals that there are, in conceptual terms, several stages of evaluation utilisation. These are discussed below.

### Meanings of evaluation utilisation

At this stage it is important to describe what we mean by utilisation, as there has been considerable confusion in the literature about the definition of the term. In fact, our view is that utilisation has a range of meanings, and we need to be clear about which meaning we adopt when we discuss the impact of a given evaluation or evaluation Form, or when we are concerned with encouraging the uptake of evaluation findings while in the negotiation and planning stages.

It is worthwhile spending a paragraph or two tracing the evolution of thinking about utilisation. Early studies of utilisation of evaluation took a narrow definition which was based on direct observable effects, such as a policy change or the adoption of a new program initiative. Taking such a perspective, evidence of utilisation would be in the direct and immediate impact of an

**Figure 6.1   Conceptualising evaluation utilisation**

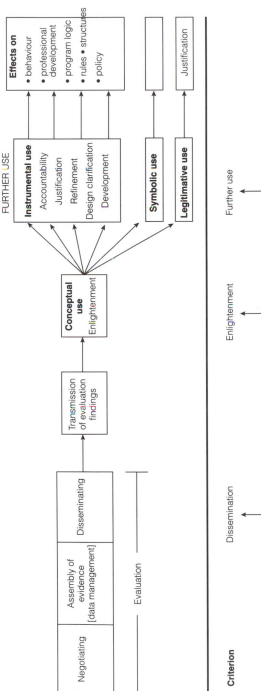

| Negotiating | Assembly of evidence [data management] | Disseminating |

├── Evaluation ──┤

Transmission of evaluation findings

**Conceptual use**
Enlightenment

FURTHER USE

**Instrumental use**
Accountability
Justification
Refinement
Design clarification
Development

**Effects on**
• behaviour
• professional development
• program logic
• rules • structures
• policy

**Symbolic use**

**Legitimative use**
Justification

**Criterion**

Dissemination

Enlightenment

Further use

**Factors affecting criterion**

More dependent on evaluation strategies than audience/organisational characteristics

Dependent on evaluation strategies and audience/organisational characteristics

More dependent on client/organisational characteristics than evaluation strategies evaluation on the program under review. This has been defined in the knowledge utilisation literature as *instrumental use* and refers to examples of an evaluation directly affecting the decision-making, and in some cases actually influencing the program itself—for example, by a change in program implementation. Evidence of this type of utilisation was sought in reported changes to decisions and actions that resulted from the evaluation, including the implementation of recommendations. The implication for studies of evaluation impact was that, if a given evaluation could not be seen to directly lead to instrumental use, that evaluation had not been utilised.

Taking a policy-level perspective, Weiss encouraged an expansion of the notion of utilisation to include *conceptual use*, or enlightenment (Alkin, 1990). Conceptual use refers to cases where an evaluation is used to influence the thinking of the client about a program, but does not lead to decision-making related to the program. Weiss was influenced by her experience with policy-makers who valued findings from good evaluations because they provided evidence about how their policies were being transformed into action in the field, and provided a basis for understanding what they were doing. Weiss also made the point that, over time, a series of evaluations could, cumulatively, affect decision-making about a major policy. Thus, while a series of individual evaluations had a conceptual impact, the sum of individual conceptual impacts could lead to an instrumental impact. This is the way policy changes often occur.

So, whereas evaluation impact was once judged in terms of effects on action, enlightenment was seen as an acceptable end point in the evaluation utilisation chain. Enlightenment can help audiences to:

> understand the background and content of program operation, stimulate reverses of policy, focus attention on neglected issues, provide new understanding of the causes of social problems, clarify their own thinking, reorder priorities, make sense of what they have been doing, offer ideas for future directions, reduce uncertainties, create new uncertainties and provide rethinking of taken for granted assumptions, justify actions, support positions, persuade others, and provide a sense of how the world works. (Weiss & Bucuavalas, 1980)

Those concerned about the impact of evaluations must not devalue enlightenment or learning as a proper use of evaluations (Torres et al., 1996). This has been the case in the past partly because enlightenment had not been accepted as utilisation. Also, enlightenment impact has been difficult to measure and studies of conceptual use have been open to charges that they are 'less objective' than measures which are linked to action.

It should also be noted that the findings of any one evaluation can also add to the knowledge base about a given research issue—that is, evaluation findings can be seen as contributing to our understanding of important educational and social phenomena. There are some evaluators who see a contribution to what could be called 'funded knowledge' as their primary role. However, others would argue that, when the primary purpose of a given investigation is to add to the scientific knowledge base rather than respond to the agenda of stakeholders, such investigations are more aptly labelled 'applied research'.

In the context of policy research, enlightenment has been dissected into three phases as follows:

- *reception*. Utilisation takes place when policy-makers or advisers receive policy-relevant information. When the communication comes to rest in the 'in-basket', so that the data reach the policy-maker rather than remaining on an analyst's desk or in the in-files of a distant consultant firm, reception has occurred.
- *cognition*. The policy-maker must read, digest and understand the study for cognition to occur.
- *reference*. If frame of reference is the criterion, then utilisation somehow must change the way the policy-maker sees the world. If information changes his or her preferences or understandings, utilisation is a reality. Altering frames of reference is important because, in the long run, the policy-maker's new vision will emerge in different policy priorities. (Knott & Wildavsky, 1980)

This suggests that evaluators play an educative role—that is, audiences learn about their program via an evaluation. The evaluator facilitates increased understanding of the design and/or implementation of a program or how an organisation is working, which is consistent with an internal evaluator working inside an organisation committed to learning about itself. In a recent study of trends in evaluation use among members of the American Evaluation Association, it was shown that there had been a large increase in evaluations which had such an emphasis (Preskill & Caracelli, 1996).

Alternative views of utilisation have spawned vigorous debate about the impact of evaluations, and about what can be expected of evaluators in terms of their work making an impact. The kind of utilisation that could be expected depends on a range of factors, not least of which is the nature of the evaluand and the Form of evaluation selected. If an evaluator is working closely with provider staff 'on the ground' in the Interactive evaluation Form, one might normally expect that a well-conducted evaluation would influence the program instrumentally. This is the position Michael Patton (1997) takes in his well known utilisation-focused evaluation approach. Alternatively, at the 'big P' or policy level, for a given Impact evaluation (Form E), the most that can normally be expected is that the audience has become enlightened or educated about the effects of that policy on those for whom it is intended and the organisations charged with its implementation.

We have taken these meanings of utilisation into account and added a couple of additional ones to prepare a 'model' of utilisation in Figure 6.1. In this model, the first stage in utilisation is that the audience(s) become(s) enlightened. Enlightenment means:

- knowledge of the plan and conduct of the evaluation; and
- comprehension of the findings.

As indicated enlightenment can be the end point of the utilisation chain. A decision as to whether the enlightenment or educative aspect is to be the end point should be decided in the planning/negotiation phase of a given study.

In other evaluations, enlightenment is the first stage leading to 'further use'. Further use occurs when findings are applied to the program under review in some way. Evaluations themselves cannot make such applications, so it is necessary for someone to link the information from an evaluation to the existing condition of the program under review. Nevertheless, to engage in rational action, it is necessary for the audience to become enlightened about what has been found during the evaluation. We therefore contend that in *all* evaluations, whether the end point is to be enlightenment or some form of further use, it is incumbent on the evaluator to engage in communication strategies which will inform the audience to the utmost about the findings of the evaluation. This leads back to the need for evaluators to be good communicators and to plan suitable dissemination strategies to ensure that audiences have a high conceptual grasp of the salient outcomes of a given evaluation study.

Three broad possibilities for further use are suggested in Figure 6.1. One possibility is that findings from a given evaluation may be used for legitimative purposes—that is, to justify decision(s) already made about the program. Thus, the evaluation follows decision-making, and provides a way of retrospectively justifying decisions made on other grounds. This form of evaluation is a form of verification. It responds to a concern of the policy-maker for support. Muscatello (1988) defends the legitimative use of evaluation as part of the work of an evaluation unit in an organisation. The circumstance is that:

> the decision has already been made and the evaluation unit is asked to develop data or undertake work which can verify or legitimize the decision (which usually would not be common organisational knowledge until the evaluation effort was complete). When the decision becomes public, an implementation plan is drawn up. This can be a particularly sensitive area for an evaluation manager, who may be required to (a) bring to the attention of the decision maker any data which conflict with the proposed decision, and (b) resolve the conflicts. If resolution is not possible, the final report may have to be structured in such a way that the decision is palatable to the rest of the organisation.
>
> Purists in the evaluation field may take exception to this, considering a verification evaluation not to be an evaluation at all. Pragmatists, however, may be justified in observing that such an effort is nevertheless a valid function of an evaluation unit.

A second possibility is symbolic use. This is consistent with an evaluation being commissioned by an individual or a group with no interest in applying the results. The commissioner has ulterior motives—for example using involvement in an evaluation process to curry favour with a superior, as part of a career advancement, or to include involvement in the evaluation on a *curriculum vitae*. In symbolic use, no modifications to the existing program follow from the dissemination of evaluation findings.

While some would no doubt baulk at these possibilities being counted as utilisation at all, Pelz (1978) believes that two types once represented the dominant usage in complex organisations:

> in the domain of policy making, one suspects that symbolic or legitimative use may be more prevalent than conceptual use with instrumental use appearing rarely.

A third further use possibility is that evaluation findings provide a basis for action. This is instrumental use, introduced earlier in this chapter. In practice, instrumental use can take on a range of meanings which will vary from evaluation to evaluation. Instrumental use may mean making decisions about:

- developing a program;
- clarifying an existing program design;
- refining a program in action;
- justifying the approaches used; and/or

- accounting for the resources spent on developing and implementing the intervention.

These are consistent with different Forms of evaluation.

Associated with the instrumental type of further use are alternative actions. As indicated in Figure 6.1, actions could include changes in one or more of the following:

- program logic;
- program delivery—that is, behavioural changes in people;
- rules of the organisation responsible for the program;
- structures of this organisation;
- the philosophy or mission of the organisation.

In the lower half of Figure 6.1, key criterion variables in the utilisation chain are linked to the influences of key players in the evaluation paradigm. Experience and a brief review of the literature suggest that, along the chain, there is a shift in responsibility for the success of each stage. This is summarised in the following generalisations:

- *Dissemination* is highly dependent on evaluator efforts to be responsive to audience needs in planning and during the conduct of the evaluation. Dissemination is less dependent on 'openness to change' characteristics of the audience(s)/organisation for which the evaluation is intended.
- *Enlightenment* is highly dependent on evaluator efforts to be responsive to audience needs in planning and during the conduct of the evaluation, and on the communication strategies used in the study. 'Openness to change' characteristics of the audience(s)/organisation will also affect the extent of enlightenment.
- *Further use*, particularly instrumental use, is highly dependent on 'openness to change' characteristics of the audience(s)/organisation for whom the evaluation findings are intended. It is less dependent on the evaluator efforts to be responsive to audience needs in planning and during the conduct of the evaluation.

While this section has emphasised that the findings of an evaluation are fundamental to utilisation, Smith (1988) suggests that the *act* of evaluation can in itself stimulate thinking and change in an organisation responsible for a program. This can happen when the evaluator is an insider or where the evaluator works closely and cooperatively in conjunction with organisational groups who actually participate in the evaluation process. In this case, the dissemination of information about the evaluation happens continuously during the evaluation and leads to significant learning. This has been defined as process use, which:

> refers to the cognitive and behavioural changes resulting from users' engagement in the evaluation process. Process use occurs when those involved in the evaluation learn from the evaluation process—as, for example, when those involved in the evaluation later say, 'The impact on our program came not so much from the findings as from going through the thinking process that the evaluation required'. (Torres et al., 1997)

---

**Example 6.1 Evaluation as a stimulus for review**

As an example of this, an outside evaluator assisted a federal agency to develop an evaluation booklet which was used by each of its seventeen regional offices to undertake a self-review of its recent projects. While the findings were of importance for each region, it was found that the processes of developing plans for the evaluation acted as a strategy for sensitising regional committees to a range of current educational issues. Taking part in the evaluation was the means by which regional committees came to grips with recent policy developments at state level. It also forced them to become more in touch with their constituents—in this case, families and community groups within each region.

---

## FACTORS AFFECTING UTILISATION

To this point, we have provided a conceptual map of utilisation. We now turn to considering factors affecting utilisation (see Figure 6.2). This section is based again on the utilisation literature, including a major empirical review (Cousins & Leithwood, 1986), and more recent additional research on the relative importance of these factors (Hudson-Mabbs, 1993).

**Figure 6.2   Simple utilisation paradigm**

By and large, these studies classify factors affecting utilisation into two clusters, relating to the

- characteristics of the evaluation—that is, the way that the evaluation is conducted; and
- characteristics of the setting in which the findings are to be utilised—that is, factors nested in the organisation which has commissioned the evaluation.

### Characteristics of the evaluation

Cousins and Leithwood (1986) discuss six factors shown to affect utilisation. With reference to Figure 6.2, four relate mainly to the conduct of the evaluation. These are:

- relevance;
- credibility;
- quality; and
- findings.

The other two relate mainly to dissemination. These are:

- communication; and
- timeliness of reporting.

*Relevance* of evaluation information includes the needs of the decision-makers, and can be thought of as the degree to which the evaluation was focused on issues relevant to the audience. This implies the identification of primary users and their major concerns during the negotiation phase of the evaluation. There is considerable evidence, particularly at the policy level, that evaluation results will be used to the extent that they are relevant to the issues and interests of the management decision-maker. At this level, Lipton (1992) exhorts one to:

> stay focused on the critical policy relevant questions. Evaluation results have to compete in a political decision-making arena with other weighty desiderata. Focusing on critical issues improves the chances that evaluation results will have an impact. The more undifferentiated 'nice-to-know' material added to the body, the less likely the evaluation report will be utilised and have an impact.

*Credibility* refers to the characteristics of the evaluator and the degree to which the evaluator is credible and believable. While the evidence is variable, there is a trend for utilisation to be linked to an evaluator being an impartial and creditable practitioner. In the context of external evaluators, key attributes include:

- competence and record of successful evaluation work;
- objectivity, credibility and bias;

- specialisation of skills;
- being able to undertake evaluation for minimum cost;
- being flexible and able to use methods which are responsive to the needs of individual evaluations.

In summary the evaluator needs to be credible and there must be user trust in the evaluator. Cummings (1988) suggests that the area of greatest difference between internal and external evaluators is that of evaluator objectivity and credibility. Whereas external evaluators are seen to bring these aspects with them, internal evaluators only gain respect over time through a history of productive evaluations which impress the employer.

*Quality* refers to the conduct of the data management phase—for instance, the choice of methods and the rigour with which the data is analysed to produce findings. One could think of this as being the research component of evaluation. Research quality was reported as being important across nearly half of the studies examined by Cousins and Leithwood.

*Findings* includes the nature of results, the implications for decision-making, and their relationship to the concerns of the audiences. Evaluations must be able to produce relevant and timely information for a given situation. Users must believe what evaluators have to say—that is, the findings must make sense. Weiss and Bucuavalas (1980) showed that decision-makers faced with findings on an issue applied two criteria, a truth test and a utility test, when assessing the potential usefulness of the research to their circumstances. Note that this is one of the few studies where conceptual use is the criterion variable. The study is important because of its conceptual clarity and its use of multivariate analysis.

Dimensions of truth were:

- research quality—the scientific merit of the research; and
- conformity to user expectations—the consistency between the findings of the research and what the reader knows about the subject.

Dimensions of utility were:

- action orientation—the practicability of the information contained in the research; and
- challenge to the status quo—the extent to which the research provides information in conflict with the current policies and operations of the organisation or system.

All four variables explained variations in usefulness of research findings, with research quality having the greatest effect.

The analysis also found that the greater the negative interaction which existed between the two truth dimensions, and the less the findings conformed to the previous ideas of the decision-maker, the more it was necessary for them to have resulted from sound research (and vice versa). There was also a negative correlation between the utility scales—that is, if a study challenged the status quo, it was not so important for it to be action orientated.

This study used research findings as a focus. Given the applied nature of evaluation, there is reason to believe that the results of this study also apply to findings which result from evaluation studies. Relating to dissemination:

*Communication* refers to the quality and quantity of communication during the evaluation study, the clarification of information dissemination and the advocacy of the results. Research has shown a clear and strong relationship between the quality of communication between decision-makers and evaluators and the use of evaluation findings, including during the evaluation process. We discuss communication more inclusively in the section on dissemination below.

*Timeliness* refers to the provision of findings and other products from an evaluation in time to meet the decision needs of the audience. Reviews suggest that timeliness is positively related to utilisation; it is difficult to envisage how it could be negatively related, as studies that do not deliver on time are less likely to be considered. Poor timing can limit or preclude use of evaluation findings; evaluation findings presented at opportune times are more likely to influence decision-makers.

## Characteristics of the setting which affect utilisation

As we have indicated, the organisational setting in which the audience for the evaluation is situated can have a major impact on the extent to which the evaluation findings are used in both conceptual or instrumental ways. Cousins and Leithwood (1986) and Hudson Mabbs (1993) identify seven audience related or organisational factors which affect utilisation. These are:

- commitment;
- information needs/competing information;
- personal characteristics;
- decision-making;
- political climate; and
- financial climate.

*Commitment* relates to features such as audience participation and their attitude towards the role of evaluation in program and

116

policy change. Many studies have shown a link between commitment and knowledge use. There is an assumption that, through involvement in negotiation and planning, audience commitment can be developed or enhanced. For example, Greene (1988) found that audience participation in evaluation increased the likelihood that the findings of the evaluation would be used.

Commitment needs to be built through the negotiation of an appropriate plan that is acceptable to clients and evaluation commissioners (Owen et al., 1994). Generally, this means a plan that has been sanctioned by them. Giving the primary audience a say in the plan increases the chances of the evaluators asking salient questions. Negotiation checks that the evaluation is worthwhile, and that it addresses issues which merit investigation. If the scope of an evaluation is too narrow, utilisation could be minimal because the findings do not address substantive issues. Negotiation also helps set realistic time limits and encourages the use of reporting methods which can be comprehended by the audience(s).

Negotiation contributes more towards utilisation than merely agreeing on an evaluation plan. Interaction between evaluator and client within the negotiation process can build up personal and professional rapport between them. Personal rapport means that evaluator and client enjoy each other's company and are able to extend that compatibility to their discussion of evaluation matters. Professional rapport is more task-oriented and is manifested in a shared interest in the nature of the program and the means used to evaluate it. These forms of rapport are often found together and, when they are, the likelihood of utilisation of evaluation information is enhanced. Put simply, the involvement of potential users in the planning stage is designed to build the commitment of the users.

In some evaluations, the line between program and evaluation components can be blurred. There may be instances when the term 'evaluation' may never be mentioned. For example, in some Approaches in the Interactive evaluation Form—such as action research—the integration of evaluation with program delivery makes sense for several reasons. The first is that it increases the chance of obtaining good data if the participants perceive that the evaluative component can also make a contribution to their learning. For example, in evaluating a training program, the evaluators may ask participants to reflect on the knowledge base they bring to the training. They may also be asked to explain why they came to the training and what they expect to learn. These data can serve as a 'pre-test' for determining the impact of the training as a baseline for collecting post-course data. Second, program/evaluation interaction can reduce the cost of evaluation if it can be incorporated into proceedings. For example, it may be possible for the data collection to be administered by program staff. Third, this approach may increase the chances that the findings will be useful to the program staff and for administration purposes.

---

**Example 6.2 Evaluation of supervision training**

In an evaluation of a supervision training program conducted by a state Community Services Department, we worked closely with program deliverers to develop a plan in which the evaluation data collection was part of the program. In the first session of the program, participants were asked to complete a short form which listed their present levels of knowledge on key supervision issues, and their reasons for attending the program. This was immediately used by deliverers and participants as a means of refining the goals and procedures of the program. This information was also used as a basis for collecting information on the immediate impact of the program and on changes to participant performance in the workplace. (Owen & McLeod, 1991)

---

In the context of increasing the use of evaluations conducted by internal evaluators, Muscatello (1988) believes that the determination of evaluation priorities is a first step to increasing commitment to the use of findings. He developed a difficulty rating procedure and a prioritising grid for determining which of competing evaluation proposals should proceed to implementation. In the same context of internal evaluation, Mowbray (1988) suggests that there are six steps for maximising utilisation findings. These are:

- marketing evaluation as a worthwhile service;
- developing and focusing policy questions;
- planning and designing the evaluation;
- conducting the evaluation;
- translating the findings;
- making people pay attention to the evaluation results.

It is worth noting that the first and last steps are outside the functions usually associated with the roles of evaluators. This may be because most of the debate about utilisation assumes that the evaluator is externally based. Mowbray implies that when an evaluator is internal to the organisation, there is a need to remind

others continually of the benefits of evaluation findings in decision-making. Mowbray and others suggest that internal evaluators
are well placed to increase impact, at least to the enlightenment
stage of use.

> **Example 6.3 Making a difference in decision-making**
>
> In an evaluation of competing programs or streams within a
> postgraduate course in teacher education, an internally based
> evaluation group played a strong role in decisions about the
> future of the competing programs. This was possible because
> the evaluation team was known to the stakeholders, the
> steering committee sponsoring the evaluation, and had built
> up the practice of interacting with them throughout the study.
> There was attention to dissemination throughout the study
> as well as transmission of the findings. In terms of further
> use, the evaluators were influential in turning over a decision
> in principle to axe one program which was difficult to
> administer and more costly to implement. The evaluation
> findings showed clearly that this program was educationally
> superior. Data which supported this claim were personally
> presented at steering committee meetings. The evaluators
> were on site and 'on tap' to interact with key decision-makers
> during a crucial period of negotiation about the future of the
> programs. (Owen, 1984)

There may also be instances where an internal evaluator takes
up the responsibility for instrumental use of the evaluation, by
having at least a partial say in the decision-making which follows
an evaluation.

*Information needs* relate to the perceived need for information
and the types of information that audiences turn to for decision-
making and problem-solving. It has been found that the more an
organisation looks outwards for new knowledge, the more likely
it is that the organisation will turn to evaluation and use evaluation findings. Associated with this is *competing information*,
which refers to alternative sources of information. Numerous
writers have found that the existence of additional information
about a program, in the form of other studies, is an important
factor influencing the use of findings from a given evaluation.
This is particularly so in the case of policy evaluation. Evaluation
findings are often used in conjunction with other credible sources,
such as information provided by advisers—something that has

proven more useful than that from evaluations (Alkin & Dalliak, 1985).

*Personal characteristics* refer to the attitudes of individuals to evaluation and their influence and experience in organisations. Patton (1997) has documented in detail the role of a significant individual in influencing the application of findings to program change and improvement. Characteristics of such an individual include leadership, interest, enthusiasm, determination, aggressiveness and access to power. In government, this has been noted for some time; in a review of evaluation use in government it was noted that:

> over and over again, the most important factor in assuring the use of evaluation findings was not the quality of the evaluation but the existence of a decision maker who wants and needs an evaluation and has committed himself [sic] to implementing its findings. (Chelimsky, 1977)

The implication of this for the planning stage is that evaluators need to identify a significant individual or group with the inclination and power to use the findings—should they be judged adequate—in program decision-making. Alkin et al., (1979) suggest the following categories:

- people who can use the information;
- people for whom the information makes a difference;
- people who have questions they want answered; and
- people who care and are willing to share responsibility for the evaluation and its utilisation.

In some cases, an organisation has an entity, a single person or small group of people, which is the key to further use. While this entity is sometimes the commissioner of the evaluation, in other instances this will not be the case. For example, in a nationally funded evaluation of university/college-based pre-service teacher education programs, the steering committee decided that staff of the appropriate departments of the colleges were to be the primary audience for the study. This was in recognition that these staff would have the major responsibility for implementing recommendations from the evaluation (Owen et al., 1985).

*Decision-making* refers to the context in which decisions about the program are made, and the type of decision to be made regarding the evaluand. Cousins and Leithwood (1986) found that this was a constant factor affecting utilisation across studies. As we have seen, a range of decisions can be linked to the instrumental use of evaluation findings. Clearly there is a difference between what might be called *retrospective* decisions for justification and accountability reasons, and *prospective* decisions—for example, to develop or modify a program. The type of decision that is likely to be made should be identified in the planning stage; research suggests that such a strategy will increase the chance of utilisation.

*Political climate* includes the existing political orientation of the organisation. There is a greater likelihood that evaluation findings will be used if they are consistent with the existing political realities that impinge on the organisation. Empirical studies reviewed by Cousins and Leithwood (1986) found that evaluation utilisation was politically influenced at both the organisational and extra-organisational levels.

*Financial climate* relates to the current level of support for the program under review and for changes suggested by the evaluation. There is some evidence that, where findings suggest changes that involve only moderate costs—as distinct from high costs—findings are more likely to be adopted. The presence of this factor reminds us that it is incumbent on evaluators to give consideration to the financial implications of their findings.

In considering this section, we must emphasise that these findings have been drawn from diverse studies, most of which have used instrumental use as their criterion. That is, very few studies have attempted to measure conceptual use. We should also draw attention to the interactive nature of the variables that lead to use, and the fact that almost no studies have been able to look at multiple causes of use. Finally, we believe that use is contextual: what influences use in one setting will not be important in another. The major purpose of this review should be to alert those who are planning evaluations to the possible factors that will affect use in their own setting. These should be considered carefully in the planning and negotiation phase of the evaluation and reviewed throughout the study.

Finally, we include some generalisations from our own experience in evaluation practice which suggest the following:

- The more the evaluator consults with audiences during the planning phase, the more the findings will be used.
- The more the evaluator pursues questions of importance to the audience(s), the more the findings will be used.
- The more interactive the form of communication, the more the findings will be used.
- The less complex the mix of audiences, the more the findings will be used.

- The more proximate the evaluator is to the audiences through-out the evaluation, the more likely the findings will be used.
- The more assistance the evaluator provides with implementation of the findings, the more the findings will be used.
- Any evaluator who thinks his or her study will have an exclusive impact on change in the program or organisation under review is suffering from a delusion.

## DISSEMINATION AND REPORTING

Dissemination involves strategies designed to inform audience(s) about relevant aspects of an evaluation. In a well-executed evaluation, therefore, the client is kept informed about all aspects of the study. For this to occur, channels of communication must be kept open throughout the study. Dissemination relies on dialogue between stakeholders and their audiences. For example, towards the end of a study, there may be merit in promoting opportunities for an open-ended two-way communication through which findings of the evaluation and associated implications for action are explored, rather than being provided as recommendations by the evaluators.

### Findings

Findings include the following:

- *evidence*—the data and other information which has been collected during the evaluation;
- *conclusions*—the synthesis of data and information. These are the meanings made by those involved in the evaluation through the synthesis of data. This involves evaluators in the processes of data display, data reduction and verification;
- *judgments* in which values are placed on the conclusions. Criteria are applied to the conclusions stating that the program is 'good' or 'bad', or that the results are 'positive', 'in the direction desired' or 'below expectations';
- *recommendations*—suggested courses of action, advice to policy-makers, program managers or providers about what to do in the light of the evidence and conclusions.

All evaluation involves the collection and analysis of evidence and the reaching of conclusions. However, there will be variations from study to study regarding the degree to which findings incorporate the making of judgments or recommendations. In some Forms—for example, those within the Proactive evaluation Form—there will be little concern with making judgments in a

122

traditional sense. In this case, the evaluator's role could stop at the conclusion-drawing stage.

Some studies will include recommendations, others will not. Whether or not recommendations are included is something that should be negotiated during the planning stage of the evaluation. It should be noted that recommendations are qualitatively different from other types of findings. Recommendations relate to what needs to be done in the future, while most other findings relate to what is or what has been done. To make useful recommendations, there would appear to be more needed than what has been found through the evidence collected unless such evidence is deliberately orientated towards future action. One example of evidence of this nature is a search conference. Based on a contribution by Hendricks & Papagiannis (1990) the list below provides guidance for making effective recommendations.

- Use the planning/negotiation stage to determine whether recommendations are part of the findings.
- If recommendations are to be made, decide who is to make them—evaluators or clients or evaluators/clients working together.
- Consider all issues to be 'fair game' for recommendations.
- Don't wait until the end of the evaluation to begin thinking about recommendations.
- Link recommendations to the evidence where possible.
- Work closely with clients throughout the evaluation.
- Consider the context(s) in which the recommendations will be implemented.
- Offer only realistic recommendations.
- Decide how specific the recommendations are to be.
- Think twice about recommending fundamental changes.
- Outline the future implications of your recommendations.
- Make the recommendations easy to understand.
- If possible, stay involved after the recommendations have been accepted.
- If a recommendation is not accepted, look for other opportunities to recommend it again.

We have found that interspersing recommendations, or in some cases 'issues for consideration', within the text of an evaluation report provides the link some readers need to establish the credibility of the findings. The following example is a paragraph from an evaluation study conducted for a national educational research organisation. It was written when reviewing the evidence on the internal distribution of newsletters and other materials which come into schools from the organisation.

## Example 6.4 'Issues for consideration' within an evaluation report

Across the more active disseminators, there seems to be two sequential steps. The first involves the Principal distributing the newsletter to other senior staff—for example, the curriculum coordinator, deputy principal, etc. Another ploy is for the Principal to send it to a specific staff member who has interests in the material covered by the newsletter. Another strategy is to send it to the librarian, to a teacher resource or professional development section. A small proportion of schools routinely discuss newsletter issues at staff meetings. The second step involves deposition of the newsletter in a consolidated location, presumably for future reference. This could be the teacher reference section in the library, a rack or similar in the staff room. In other schools there is a filing system kept by a senior member of staff.

*Issue for consideration*

Some intensive studies of exemplary school internal information dissemination which focused on other resources besides the newsletter, including materials for the classroom, would be useful for the research organisation to establish more effective ways of presenting information for dissemination. (Owen et al., 1996)

All 'issues for consideration' were also included in an executive summary at the beginning of the report.

### Styles of reporting

While it was once the norm for evaluators to rely on a major end-of-study written report as the major style of reporting, concerns about the lack of impact of this strategy have led to an examination of alternative forms of communication.

In reporting findings, issues which need to be decided include:

- strategies for reporting;
- types of reports; and
- effective ways of presenting material within these reports.

### Strategies

As we have seen, timely dissemination is critical, as decision-makers must have the information when it is required. There is little point in executing an elegant evaluation design if the findings are too late to influence decisions about the program.

It is not always possible to anticipate the timing of information needs of audiences. In some cases evaluators must release information in response to audience requests before the final analyses are complete. There is then a need to compromise between completeness and utility. Our view is that requests for information should be responded to with the clear caveat that the information is the 'best available' at the time the request was made. In addition, for most of the evaluations we have undertaken over the past decade, it has been the norm to build into the evaluation design strategies that will allow dissemination in instalments rather than as a single end-of-evaluation tome. This implies that an evaluation can be divided into defined stages, each with its own products and findings.

There are advantages, in terms of audience comprehension, in reporting information in a series of smaller chunks rather than a monolithic tome at the conclusion of the project. An audience is more likely to read smaller reports in this situation, and to absorb the essential messages, than they would if they were presented within a large report. In the case of reports to management, there is evidence that, due to work pressures, bureaucrats find it difficult to absorb large amounts of complex information. In addition, serial reporting allows for the release of specific information that may be required at different times. There is also an advantage in that smaller reports spread the workload of evaluator document preparation. On the other hand, a disadvantage is that findings of the study may appear more fragmented if reported over time, and it is sometimes necessary to adopt some form of overview document to minimise this. It is also possible that many—if not most—of the salient findings will not be known until near the end of the evaluation.

### Types of reports

When planning dissemination strategies, evaluators should take into account the following dimensions. Options here include:

- written versus oral;
- progress versus final;
- substantive (main report) versus secondary (such as technical details of data management);
- summary versus main report;
- formal versus informal;
- descriptive versus recommendatory.

*Formats*

Possible formats of written reports include acceptable professional writing and less formal styles, perhaps without referencing and composed in a more vernacular style. There is some evidence that interactive reporting and the use of strategies other than formal reports increases the chances of audience utilisation of evaluation findings. Quotations designed to highlight key findings can also be embedded within the body of the report. Also, there may be merit in using briefer reports. Examples suggested by Macy (1981) include:

- evaluation briefs at the end of main reports;
- an executive summary;
- googles—these are one-liners designed to make members of the audience appear intelligent and well read.

In addition to written reports, other forms of presentation, such as oral reports, displays and photography/videos, may be used. Displays in the form of graphs and charts can summarise and present large amounts of information in an attractive way.

The detail of reporting will vary from evaluation to evaluation and should be negotiated during the planning stage of a study. Generally, a combination of reporting methods is necessary, to take into account the needs of different audiences.

## EFFECTS ON ACTION

The ultimate in the evaluation utilisation chain presented in Figure 6.1 is the effects of evaluation findings on action. In some cases, evaluations have implications for organisations which develop and implement programs. Downs (1967) suggests that action which results from evaluation has implications for four aspects of an organisation and its members:

- *behaviour*—changes in the behaviour of an organisation's members, making it closer to the way they would behave if they were totally in agreement with the organisation's goals. For example, this means that staff trainers in an organisation would be encouraged, through the evaluation, to offer programs which are as consistent as possible with the mission statement of the organisation;
- *rules*—changes in the organisation's formal procedures covering how employees should act in producing the organisation's products or services;
- *structures*—changes involving the hierarchy containing the distributions of power, information and prestige among the members of the organisation;

126

- *purpose or raison d'être*—changes in the fundamental values underlying the goals and actions of an organisation.

Using Down's categories, Johnston (1988) undertook an analysis of recommendations made in evaluations conducted by the US General Accounting Office (GAO). He found that the majority of recommendations were related to changes in behaviour and that these were more likely to have been implemented than those in the other categories. The implication of this finding is that behaviour is more likely to be addressed within an evaluation and that it is easier to change through evaluation than through altering structural aspects within organisations.

The transition from enlightenment to action and change is an area where evaluators have traditionally not involved themselves. However, there is patently a need for assistance with change *per se*, and if change to programs and organisations based on evaluations is to take place, then the evaluator is a candidate to assist with the implementation of the change effort. This has been an increasing feature of our practice and that of evaluators who are being asked to facilitate change in agencies which have adopted a learning organisation focus.

---

**Example 6.5 Implementing change arising from evaluation findings**

This was the focus taken in a recent review of the middle school program of a large inner-city high school. The evaluation recommended that the program should be completely overhauled and linked more closely to what went on before and afterwards up and down the school. Consequent to the dissemination of findings to the school, one of the evaluators worked continuously to implement these findings, a process that took almost two years before all the recommendations were implemented.

Based on this study, we proposed four major principles for evaluation practice which adopted an 'effects focus'. These included:
- negotiation of a plan which is acceptable to stakeholders;
- heightening awareness about the evaluation by making data collection procedures visible to stakeholders;
- using interactive and timely synergistic techniques of reporting; and
- providing guidelines and ongoing personal-level support for the implementation of findings. (Owen et al., 1994)

The inclusion of the fourth of these principles implies that evaluators should possess knowledge about organisational change and implementation theory, and skills in working with practitioners to implement changes which are suggested by the evaluation. Evaluators are in a unique position to assist stakeholders to maximise the instrumental use of findings. If the evaluator has sound human relations skills, he or she is uniquely placed to encourage an informed and balanced use of the findings. Such use by the stakeholders, acting alone, cannot always be guaranteed. Evaluation findings can often be misinterpreted by those to whom they are directed. Our view is that evaluation findings have a much greater chance of impacting on action if the evaluator takes on the role of change consultant. This has particular implications for the creation of positions in learning organisations. One could envisage the creation of a position of a 'Director of Learning', with the holder of such a position being required to undertake the evaluation and change roles outlined in this paragraph.

## BROADER USES OF EVALUATION

While this chapter has focused on the use that is made of the information produced by an evaluation, we need to remember that program evaluation can have broader impacts—both positive and negative—beyond the use of information by its intended audience. There are many processes involved in program implementation apart from just formal decision-making by those in authority.

Program evaluation can also have an impact on these other processes, such as the informal operating routines of front-line staff, the cooperative problem-solving of small work groups, and alliances and conflicts between different organisational units (Rogers & Hough, 1995). By considering these broader impacts when we plan and implement evaluations, we can increase the likelihood of achieving positive impacts and take steps to mimimise negative impacts.

Funders and managers can often be quite deliberate in using the process of an evaluation itself to generate change. An evaluation can signal that certain issues are important, and direct staff to attend to them more carefully. An evaluation can be used to reduce complacency about performance, or to resolve conflict between groups with different views, or to start a longer change process (Floden & Weiner, 1983). Patton (1997) has described how the process of gathering people together to talk about a program can have effects on their motivation and ability to cooperate to solve problems, quite apart from the utility of the information that is subsequently reported.

The effect of program evaluation on emotions and group interactions is particularly important, because these factors directly influence program implementation and also influence people's receptivity to evaluation information. While we have discussed utilisation as if it is a linear process, in reality there needs to be what Huberman & Cox (1990) have called a 'learning and bargaining process'. The intended audience of evaluation findings should not be thought of as a passive vessel into which the information is loaded, but rather as:

> a vessel already filled with other cargo that will need to be partially reloaded, redistributed, relabelled by people who will inevitably have different ideas about which parts of the cargo require unloading, redistribution and relabelling . . . In other words, there is not only a long uneven learning process involved, but an equally unkempt process of institutional negotiation involved in the treatment of evaluative findings. (Huberman & Cox, 1990)

For successful utilisation, an evaluation may need to be designed in such a way that it offers opportunities for cycles of learning. For example, Patton's (1997) utilisation-focused approach to evaluation encourages cycles of evaluation. By answering the questions raised in the first cycle well, an evaluator can help to build a climate for being able to ask, answer and deal with the answers to harder questions—such as questions about more sensitive or threatening topics, or questions which have answers that are complicated or unwelcome, or which are based on better understandings of the programs and the needs they are intended to meet.

## REFERENCES

Alkin, M.C. (1990). *Debates on Evaluation*. Newbury Park, CA: Sage.

Alkin, M.C. & Dalliak, R. (1985). *A Guide for Evaluation Decision Makers*. Beverly Hills, CA: Sage.

Alkin, M.C., Daillak, R. & White, P. (1979). *Using Evaluations: Does Evaluation Make a Difference?* Beverly Hills, CA: Sage.

Chelimsky, E. (ed.). (1977). *A Symposium on the Use of Evaluation by Federal Agencies*. McLean, VA: Mitre Corp.

Cousins, J.B. & Leithwood, K.A. (1986). 'Current Empirical Research on Evaluation Utilisation'. *Review of Educational Research*, 56 (3), 331–64.

Cummings, O.W. (1988). 'Business Perspectives on Internal/External Evaluation'. *New Directions for Program Evaluation*, 39, 59–74.

Downs, A. (1967). *Inside Bureaucracies*. Boston, MA.: Little Brown.

Floden, R.E. & Weiner, S.S. (1983). 'Rationality to Ritual: The Multiple Roles of Evaluation in Government Processes'. In G. Madaus, D.

Stufflebeam & M. Scriven (eds), *Evaluation Models: Viewpoints on Educational and Human Services Evaluation*. Boston, MA: Kluwer-Nijhoff, pp. 177–88.

Greene, J. (1988). 'Stakeholder Participation and Utilisation in Program Evaluation'. *Evaluation Review*, 12, 91–116.

Hendricks, M. & Papagiannis, M. (1990). 'Do's and Dont's for Offering Effective Recommendations'. *Evaluation Practice*, 11 (2), 121–5.

Huberman, M. & Cox, P. (1990). 'Evaluation Utilisation: Building Links Between Action and Reflection'. *Studies in Educational Evaluation*, 16(1), 157–79.

Hudson-Mabbs, S. (1993). 'Influences on the Use of Evaluation Information'. Unpublished Master of Education (Hons) thesis, Murdoch University, Western Australia.

Johnston, W.P. (ed.) (1988). 'Increasing Evaluation Use: Some Observations Based on Results at the US General Accounting Office'. *New Directions in Program Evaluation*, 39, 75–84.

Knott, J. & Wildavsky, A. (1980). 'If Dissemination is the Solution, What is the Problem?' *Knowledge: Creation, Diffusion, Utilization*, 1 (4), (June), 537–75.

Lipton, D.S. (1992). 'How to Maximise Utilisation of Evaluation Research by Policymakers'. *ANNALS of the American Academy of Political and Social Science*, 521 (May), 175–88.

Macy, D.L. (1981). 'Research Briefs'. In N.L. Smith (ed.), *Communication Strategies in Evaluation*. Beverly Hills, CA: Sage.

Mowbray, C.T. (1988). 'Getting the System to Respond to Evaluation Findings'. In J. McLaughlin, L.J. Weber, R.W. Covert & R. Ingle (eds), *New Directions in Program Evaluation* 39 (Fall) (pp. 21–33).

Muscatello, D.B. (ed.) (1988). 'Developing an Agenda that Works: The Right Choice at the Right Time'. *New Directions in Program Evaluation*, 39, 21–33.

Owen, J.M. (1984). 'Evaluating Teacher Education in Australia: The Use of National Guidelines in Assessing the Worth of a Program in Action.' Paper presented at the Annual Meeting of the American Educational Research Association. New Orleans, LA: October 1984.

Owen, J.M., Getty, C. & Simonelli, A. (1996). *Responding to the Educational Needs of Schools: Implications for the Australian Council for Educational Research*. Evaluation Report. Melbourne: Centre for Program Evaluation, The University of Melbourne.

Owen, J.M., Johnson, N.J. & Welsh, R.J. (1985). *Primary Concerns: A Project on Mathematics and Science in Primary Teacher Education*. Melbourne, Melbourne College of Advanced Education for the Commonwealth Tertiary Education Commission.

Owen, J.M., Lambert, F.C. & Stringer, W.S. (1994). 'Acquiring Knowledge of Implementation and Change: Essential for Program Evaluators?' *Knowledge: Creation, Diffusion, Utilization*, 15 (3), 273–94.

Owen, J.M. & McLeod, J. (1991). *A Detailed Proposal for Protective Services Training Evaluation. Report to the Manager, Child Protection Services*. Community Services Victoria. Centre for Program Evaluation, The University of Melbourne.

Patton, M.Q. (1997). *Utilisation Focused Evaluation*. 3rd edn. Thousand Oaks, CA: Sage.

Pelz, D. (1978). 'Some Expanded Perspectives on Use of Social Science in Public Policy'. In J.M. Yinger & S.J. Guther (eds.), *Major Social Science Issues: A Multidisciplinary View*. New York: The Free Press, pp. 346–57.

Preskill, H. & Caracelli, V.J. (1996). 'The Past, Present and Future Conceptions of Evaluation Use'. Paper presented at the Annual Meeting of the American Evaluation Association. Atlanta, GA; November, 1996.

Rogers, P.J. & Hough, G. (1995). 'Improving the Effectiveness of Evaluations: Making the Link to Organisational Theory'. *Evaluation and Program Planning*, 18 (4), 321–32.

Smith, M.F. (1988). 'Evaluation Utilization Revisited'. *New Directions in Program Evaluation*, 39, 7–20.

Torres, R.T., Preskill, H.S. & Piontek, M.E. (1996). *Evaluation Strategies for Communicating and Reporting: Enhancing Learning Organisations*. Thousand Oaks, CA: Sage.

——(1997). 'Communicating and Reporting: Practice and Concern of Internal and External Evaluators'. *Evaluation Practice*, 18, 2, 105–26.

Weiss, C.H. & Bucuavalas, M.J. (1980). 'Truth Tests and Utility Tests: Decision Makers Frames of Reference for Social Science Research'. *American Sociological Review*, 45 (April), 302–13.

# 7

# Key Players and Resources

## INTRODUCTION

Resourcing looms large for all those involved in evaluation. Resources available for evaluation are finite and often stringent and the evaluator must work within set limits. The reputation of an evaluator or evaluation group is likely to rest on the ability to do the best possible evaluation work given the resources available.

In a time of economic rationalism and accountability, it is essential that the true total costing of an evaluation be undertaken as part of the planning and negotiation stage of a study. Commissioners of evaluation must be realistic about their expectations. Clearly what can be accomplished with a $250 000 budget should be greater than if a $5000 budget were available for an investigation.

In general terms, resources needed for an evaluation can be divided between human resources, the costs of evaluation personnel, and material resources. To come to grips with the ways in which evaluation can and is supported, we should first look at the human resource element of evaluation work. For, while it is important that there be funds in evaluation to support the development of data collection instruments, travel and accommodation and the printing of evaluation reports, the most valuable resource for every evaluation is the evaluator or the evaluation team. This is implicit in the skills the evaluator brings, and is explicit in the costing out of the time the evaluator spends on a study.

There are variations in the ways that evaluation can be resourced by organisations. In this chapter, we turn our attention to:

- ways in which evaluators can work for and within organisations;
- roles and influences of internal evaluators;

- roles and influences of external evaluators as consultants;
- costing of evaluation work.

## RESOURCE PROVISION AND USAGE: KEY PLAYERS IN EVALUATION

To pursue these issues further, we need to consider how the evaluator relates to others who control the resources and benefit from their expenditure. In general terms, key players for a given evaluation include:

- the provider of the resources for the evaluation, those who commission the evaluation;
- the beneficiaries of resource expenditure—those for whom the evaluation findings are intended (i.e. the client or evaluation audience(s)); and
- the consumer of the resources—the evaluator or the evaluation team.

Collectively, commissioners and clients can be regarded as the major stakeholders for the evaluation.

The identification of key players, the working relationships between them, their contributions within the evaluation and their information needs must be clarified during the negotiation stage of an evaluation. If they are not, then the resources provided for the evaluation could be wasted. The following example emphasises this.

**Example 7.1 Key players in a national evaluation**

Owen et al., (1985) undertook a national evaluation of university (college) teacher education programs in science and mathematics, commissioned and funded by a national agency.

A steering committee was set up to oversee the program. It comprised representatives of the agency and teacher educators from the colleges which offered the programs under review.

The first meeting of the steering committee proved to be crucial. At this meeting, the committee decided that, while the agency had a legitimate right to the findings of the study, the most important issues to be investigated were those of direct concern to the teacher educators who taught the programs in the colleges. Further, the committee wished to see some evaluation resources devoted to informing staff in these colleges about the findings on these issues. College staff became the clients for the study.

The identification of key issues and audiences was crucial. Regarding issues, whereas the agency was keen for the evaluation to undertake an analysis of student entry characteristics in these programs (for example, how much science they had studied in secondary school), teacher educators wanted information about effective curriculum and teaching, and saw a need for the development of networks and information about innovatory programs in mathematics and science teacher education.

On the need for informing college staff about the findings, the evaluators devoted a substantial proportion of the resources available to hosting a conference of the clients to disseminate and discuss the findings. It was estimated that about 20 per cent of the total resources for the evaluation were devoted to the dissemination phase. This cut the amount of resources available for data collection and analysis.

The first steering committee meeting not only set the agenda for the evaluation. It also determined who would benefit directly from the expenditure of the evaluation resources. In this case, the commissioners provided the resources for the direct benefit of others.

In the above case, the commissioners, the clients and the evaluators were different entities. At the other extreme, it is possible for the commissioner, the audience and the evaluator to be one and the same.

### Example 7.2 Self-evaluation

Consider the case of an educational trainer interested in determining whether or not a program in which she is involved makes a difference. She decides to videotape some of her classes to provide feedback about the quality of her delivery. In addition, she administers a simple skills test to course participants. The findings help her make changes to the way the training program is delivered. In this case, there are no external resources required for the evaluation, which is done in the trainer's 'own time', or as part of her professional work as an educator.

This is what House (1980) calls a private evaluation, as distinct from one which is open to a wider audience for discussion and debate. Private evaluations are part of the practice of the dedicated professional, and the processes outlined above are consistent with the ongoing use of evaluative activities as part of self-improvement (Schon, 1983). If a formal group, such as a department within an organisation, decided to undertake self-evaluation of its programs and their implementation entirely for the benefit of those within the department, this would be another example of a private evaluation. In this case, as in the situation described in Example 7.2, the commissioner, the client and the evaluator would be one and the same.

While the configurations illustrated in the above examples do occur, the most likely arrangement is one in which those funding an evaluation see themselves as a primary audience or client for information which results from the study. Further, the commissioning agent is the primary audience, and the evaluators are a distinct entity. For the sake of examining the resource implications for the remainder of this chapter, let us concentrate on links and the resource exchanges between the client and the evaluator.

## INSIDERS AND OUTSIDERS

Conceptually, we can distinguish between insiders and outsiders when it comes to the resource arrangements involving evaluators and audiences for an evaluation:

> An insider is an entity (individual or group) directly associated with the conduct and/or impact of a program.
>
> An outsider is an entity external to the program, who, for one reason or another, has a vested interest in the conduct and/or impact of the program. (Hogben, 1977)

In Example 7.2, the evaluator was an insider, a member of the organisation responsible for the program, while in Example 7.1, the evaluator was outside the program under review. Evaluators and clients can be identified as insiders or outsiders according to the above definitions. Figure 7.1 suggests four configurations of insiders and outsiders taking into account the status of the evaluator and client.

Each configuration carries certain assumptions about how evaluators and audiences are linked, and how such studies are resourced. These should be thought of as normative positions derived from an informal review of current practice.

**Figure 7.1   Insiders and outsiders**

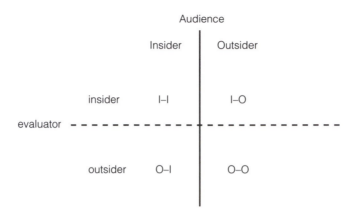

## Configuration I–I (insiders for insiders)

Configuration I–I represents situations where the evaluator and deliverer are within the program, or at least inside the organisation responsible for the program. Remember that the program may be an intervention such as a training course, or a departmental division responsible for statewide delivery of a service to the community. Evaluation is 'in-house', findings of the study may not be made available to the general public, and evaluation information may be informally presented to key decision-makers. Sometimes internal evaluations adopting this configuration are referred to as *institutional self-study* in the evaluation literature.

The focus in this arrangement is generally on organisational learning and program improvement. This approach to evaluation relies for its validity on the availability of internal expertise. This implies that institutions see benefits in providing human and material resources for evaluation support for programs.

The insiders for insiders model manifests itself in various ways. Generally it requires an organisation to adopt a commitment to the accumulation of knowledge about itself—that is, it adopts a continuous learning focus (Morris, 1995). This includes the generation and documentation of new knowledge on the services it provides to clients, experiences about individual programs that might be extrapolated to other like situations, and on the internal work climate of the organisation itself (Torres et al., 1996). It might also be interested in reviewing the ways in which it generates new knowledge: one could think of this as a sort of meta-evaluation of evaluation (Byth, 1997). The primary audience could be delivery staff or management, including those in leadership positions.

Generally, insider for insider configurations must be supported by organisational leaders, both in terms of policy and resources. This has occurred in some national and local school systems in some countries—for example, the United States and Australia (Alkin, 1990). However, this has led to a requirement that teachers take on evaluation as an addition to day-to-day administrative and classroom tasks. In practice, teachers have sometimes been asked to undertake evaluation work without the benefit of any evaluation training. This, in addition to the fact that evaluation is often treated as an 'extra' on top of a normal teaching load, leads to frustration and cynicism about the benefits that evaluation can provide. Insider for insider evaluation can exhaust participants but, when well resourced, it can have a powerful impact on the staff and programs of a school (Brennan & Hoadley, 1984).

Experience suggests that evaluation can be extremely useful for within organisation decision-making if adequate person-centred resources are made available. The American National Education Association's Mastery in School project was a case where a small number of schools were supported by an external evaluation and development consultant who, to all intents and purposes, became an additional staff member of the school (Holly, 1990).

Generally, insider for insider evaluations tend to use Approaches belonging to the Clarificative and Interactive evaluation Forms, although there has been more emphasis recently on organisations documenting the outcomes of their programs (Hatry & van Houten, 1996). It is important to note that an evaluator can act as an insider without necessarily being employed by the organisation commissioning the evaluation. The key is that the evaluator acts as a 'psychological' insider—that is, he or she is in tune with the organisation and is willing to provide evaluative advice designed to improve its functions. This does not mean that the evaluator provides only findings that the primary audience wants to hear. It is consistent with a view that clients genuinely want information, both positive and negative, which will be used to make their programs more effective. Our experience working in this mould is that many organisations committed to learning about themselves are keen to employ 'critical friends' who are fearless in giving advice and, when the occasion is right, will extend a helping hand to assist with implementing changes which flow from the evaluation (Telford, 1991).

While it is rare for educational institutions to have trained evaluators on the staff, other organisations employ evaluators; in some cases, there are identifiable evaluation groups within an organisation. Muscatello (1988) provided an example of this situation in a large public authority, in which the evaluator provided guidelines for prioritising evaluation issues and under-taking those which were of most importance to the authority.

Cummings (1988) and others see the following advantages of internal over external evaluators:

- They reduce evaluation costs.
- They are in a position to alter evaluation designs quickly if it becomes apparent that an evaluation activity is not produc-tive.
- They know the nuances of the organisation and are thus able to see ways in which an evaluation can make a difference.
- They can build a strong credibility over time and can foster stakeholder commitment and promote the use of evaluation findings.

On the other hand:

- Their objectivity may be affected or compromised by the policies of the organisation and its underlying value system.
- They could become a public relations tool of the organisation to the detriment of other more legitimate roles such as encour-aging program improvement.

### Internal evaluation and change management

Organisational decision-makers are increasingly looking for assis-tance with process re-engineering and people-related facets of change management. The distinction between organisational devel-opment consultants and evaluators is becoming blurred. Often the organisational development consultant will be brought in to accomplish a range of tasks including diagnosing organisational culture, working with the staff to identify change initiatives and undertaking a training needs analysis. These tasks fall within the domain and skill set traditionally associated with the practice of evaluation and could be handled by a skilled internal evaluator.

Mathison (1994) suggests that a critical distinction which separates evaluation from organisational development is the sep-aration between evaluative judgments and prescription. She claims that evaluators are ill-equipped to provide recommendations because these require much greater knowledge than can be sub-sumed by the evaluation study itself. However, increasingly, there is an opportunity for evaluators to adopt a more participatory framework for conducting evaluations—one which recognises the importance of involving program stakeholders in the evaluation process. Such collaborative arrangements clear the way for the creation of prescriptions involving evaluator and stakeholders. We have documented the advantages of internal and external evaluators working in such a mode elsewhere.

> we believe that an evaluator with these additional skills and knowledge is in a unique position to assist stakeholders to maximise the instrumental use of the findings. It is the evaluator who has worked with the organization over a period of time through the various states of negotiation, data collection, and reporting back. Given sound human relations skills, the evaluator has the opportunity to build a strong sense of trust and a high level of rapport with those within the organisation, and to develop a shared understanding of the meaning and the implications of the assembled information. With a high personal stake in the quality of the study, the evaluator is then in a position to encourage an informed and balanced use of the findings. (Owen et al., 1994)

There is a clear role for evaluators to work directly with those in leadership positions. This could be seen as the organisational equivalent of Michael Patton's (1997) advice to identify a significant individual to target evaluation findings. It is not necessarily always the case that those in formal positions of responsibility will be the leaders in the organisational change or program improvement effort.

Some of the more radical aspects that an internal evaluator could focus on include surfacing and challenging assumptions, analysing organisational culture, assisting with strategic thinking and planning, and promoting learning within the organisation. These issues have been identified from the organisational learning literature as key to the success of a learning organisation (Owen & Lambert, 1998).

While some evaluators may be uneasy about adopting a strongly developmental role, the reality is that some organisational development consultants are already working in these ways without the benefit of extensive training in evaluation design or data analytical methods, or a well-developed underlying epistemological basis. With more and more evaluative work being nested in organisations (Love, 1994), there should be increasing opportunities for those with strong analytical and communication skills to play an influential role in influencing key decision-making. As with all hard-nosed business decisions, a judgment about the advantages of employing an internal evaluator will depend on whether those who control the purse strings see a pay-off for the evaluative services provided.

## Configuration I–O (insiders for outsiders)

Configuration I–O represents self-evaluations but in these situations the findings are addressed to an audience or audiences outside the program. A typical scenario for this kind of evaluation is one in which an organisation has obtained external funding for an internally designed program. A condition is that insiders are expected to report to the funders, setting out the benefits which have accrued as a result of program implementation. As this is an accountability exercise, there is usually an emphasis on program outcomes, consistent with the tenets of the Impact evaluation Form.

One issue related to this configuration of evaluation is the validity of evaluation findings. Continued funding of programs may be dependent on the conclusions of the evaluation report and in such circumstances it would be a brave organisation which gave a heavy emphasis to negative aspects of program impact. A negative report may also have implications for program directors and reduce the chance that funding will be granted for other projects. It is up to the primary audience in this case to be aware that program development and implementation involve risk-taking and that a balance in reporting involving positive and negative outcomes is to be expected. In fact, an enlightened funding agency should become suspicious of an evaluation report which is entirely positive.

### Example 7.3 Accreditation

The accreditation in some hospital systems is an evaluation consistent with the I–O configuration. For example, as part of a mandated accreditation process, a large inner-city hospital was asked to undertake a total review of its programs. The collection, analysis and compilation of evidence were handled by a small team headed by a senior member of the hospital administration. The team undertook a complete analysis of all existing program documentation and, in addition, staff profiles were developed and a list of facilities tabulated. The information was made available to a visiting panel from the accrediting agency before the panel visited the site. During the one-day visit, the panel made an inspection of the hospital, interviewed selected nursing staff and held an extensive meeting with the hospital evaluation team. The hospital was subsequently accredited for the next five years.

In addition to hospitals, I–O configurations are well known in the areas of nursing and aged care, and college (university) accreditation, especially in the United States. One end-product of an accreditation is a refined program design (Clarificative evaluation). The report to outsiders is in the form of a justification for the evaluation procedures undertaken and the decisions made about the revised program.

In this case, the problem of validation of the information collected by insiders is solved by reference to externally developed procedures and the use of visiting panels of 'experts'. Sometimes, system-wide standards are used in conjunction with the internal evaluation. This is designed to prove that the programs within a hospital or a university have credibility in the eyes of the general public, and in particular to prospective clients (patients, students) of the program.

### Configuration O–I (outsiders for insiders)

Configuration O–I represents situations where an external evaluator is asked to review a program for an internal audience. The selection of this configuration is predicated on the need for special expertise and a requirement for an 'objective' view of the program under review.

---

**Example 7.4 Evaluation of a human development program**

Hurworth et al. (1988) undertook an evaluation of a program designed to educate 15–16-year-olds about issues relating to contraception, sexually transmitted diseases and the dangers of drug abuse.

The major reason for the evaluation was to establish program worth before a decision was made to promote it for adoption by other health centres across the state. The clients saw a need for an external evaluator to add credibility to the findings.

The design of the evaluation was decided upon through consultancy with the clients, the providers of the program (two nurses and a doctor), and included a strong outcomes emphasis. The findings showed that the program promoted learning and was well regarded by students and their school teachers.

The evaluators reported to the clients and to the administration of the health centre through a written report. A seminar which was attended by key health care decision-makers was also part of the reporting process.

---

There is always a problem of threat from the presence of an outsider. Thus outside evaluators working within this configuration should become familiar with the needs of the internal audiences and ensure that the evaluation is responsive to the needs of the organisation. Experience suggests that the more the evaluator can work with the insiders from the outset of the evaluation, the more clients will come to trust the evaluator and use the findings to make changes suggested by the evaluation (Owen, 1990).

In recent times, the O–I arrangement has been used by organisational management to provide a basis for downsizing organisations. In many cases unscrupulous managers have used external reviewers—generally highly paid business management consultants—to help them with 'hatchet jobs' which have led to staff layoffs and/or considerable reductions in inputs to organisational operations. The term 'unscrupulous' can be applied particularly to managers who have already decided that layoffs are to take place, and subsequently influence the organisational review to provide findings that are consistent with decisions that have already been made. This has not only occurred in the private sector, but is also evident in government and higher education sectors. Such reviews could not be regarded as an evaluation, as the consultant's work is unlikely to meet the code of behaviour set by the evaluation profession (see Chapter 9 for details of the standards and principles recently developed in the United States).

## Category O–O (outsiders for outsiders)

Category O–O situations are those in which evaluations have a heavy accountability emphasis and a perceived audience need for expertise and objectivity. There is a sense of an evaluation 'done on' a program or programs of an organisation. Program personnel are not involved in the planning of the evaluation; they are expected to provide information but are unlikely to benefit directly in terms of feedback of information or support to improve their work. Evaluation findings are targeted to a 'higher authority'.

### Example 7.5 Evaluation of the Participation and Equity Program (PEP)

A national Participation and Equity Program (PEP) was the linchpin of a national educational strategy for reform of secondary schools and Technical And Further Education (TAFE) colleges. PEP was a three-year intervention but, despite its scope and importance, no monitoring procedures had been built into the funding for the initiative.

Owen & Hartley (1988) undertook an analysis of the impact of the national PEP program on TAFE colleges. Insiders in this case were TAFE colleges which were recipients of assistance to develop programs for educationally disadvantaged young people.

The analysis involved a state-by-state review of systemic responses to the PEP initiative, and a series of case studies of specific examples of the implementation of programs supported by PEP. Findings were presented in an extensive report and a volume of case studies. The primary audience were officers in the government department which was responsible for the PEP initiative and it was to these officers that the report was presented.

Under these circumstances, it is understandable that college staff responsible for the delivery of the program might find excuses for non-cooperation, especially if the findings may be potentially damaging to them in one way or another. Nevertheless, we have found people from a range of social program areas willing to assist in large-scale outsider for outsider studies. In many cases, the motivation is altruistic. In practice, this facilitates the compilation of information, which assists decision-makers, generally policy-makers, to make decisions about existing social programs.

## Guidelines for evaluation by insiders

An in-principle organisational commitment to internal evaluators and to internal evaluation implies that managers foresee a net benefit in providing resources for internal evaluative work. To keep faith with management, internal evaluators need to understand how to operate within an organisational framework which acknowledges the hierarchy, and the internal structure and culture of the organisation.

A review of practice suggests that internal evaluations are more effective if the administration accepts the following principles:

- Involve the staff, or those staff directly involved in the delivery of the program under review, as much as possible in the planning and implementation of each study. The more staff have a say in evaluation decisions, the more enthusiastic they will be. Meetings at which staff have an opportunity to understand concepts and ideas, and the advantages of self-evaluation, can be very useful.

- There should be an identifiable group responsible for the day-to-day management of the evaluation. This might include staff with limited evaluation expertise in addition to the internal evaluator. During the evaluation planning stage, specify the responsibilities and limitations of the team—for example, collecting and analysing data, but not drawing conclusions.

- Ensure that there is consensus, or almost consensus, on the evaluation plan, even if this appears to take a large amount of time and effort. Make sure that key staff such as the leadership are aware of the details.

- Ensure that the evaluation team has access to resources to collect and analyse the data. This may involve technical advice from the internal evaluator or an outside expert on data collection and analysis at some stage. If the evaluation is concerned with Monitoring (Form D), establish an ongoing record-keeping system. Develop procedures which ensure that the data can be entered into the system at regular intervals.

- Encourage the evaluators to report on their progress even if they are not in a position to report on their findings.

- Use the findings to reflect on the program or organisational aspects (the evaluand) under review. Decide on what changes should be made and to what—for example, whether implementation processes should be modified so that objectives can be achieved.

- Develop a systematic plan by which program changes can be put in place. Changing the program can be the most difficult, but it is probably the most important in terms of improving the evaluand and benefiting those served by the program.

### Guidelines for evaluation by outsiders

As we have noted, consultants are increasingly being employed to assist organisations to solve internal problems. While business consultancy has always been used within the corporate world to solve problems that could not be handled internally, there has been a rapid increase in the use of consultants in the public sector in countries where governments have adopted a policy of devolving the responsibility of the basic provision of goods and services to others.

The move towards tendering out of program provision is likely to be followed by more reliance on external consultants to undertake evaluation. This has already begun in association with:

- providing strategic advice to leaders, as outlined earlier in this chapter;
- change management; and
- insiders who have the responsibility for internal reviews.

For example, outsider consulting is undertaken by:
- international accounting firms such as Price Waterhouse;
- local business management organisations;
- university departments and centres devoted to research and evaluation in a range of disciplines (public policy, health, social work); and
- independent one- or two-person agencies.

Michael Scriven (1995) has some advice aimed particularly at those in the last of these categories, the small-scale or solo consultant. He believes that solo consultants have a hard time making a go of it because of the competition for work from those in the other three categories, in particular from university departments and centres, which are effectively subsidised to do external consulting work by their institutions. Solo consultants need to acknowledge that they must attend to the following tasks:

- managing their companies on a day-to-day basis;
- making and extending contacts;
- undertaking evaluative studies;
- maintaining and extending a repertoire of evaluation skills; and
- making a contribution to the theory of evaluation.

Scriven calculates that the consultant can really only expect to spend half of a 'working year' on undertaking evaluative studies. If we see a working year as 2000 hours (50 weeks by 40 hours per week), this leaves 1000 hours to actually work on evaluation studies. He reckons that a one-person consultant without a secretary and from a home office would need to gross $55 000 to clear $40 000, given overheads, company costs and other expenses, including indemnity insurance. This means charging $55 per hour, or about $500 per day. Scriven also makes the point that the effective solo consultant has to be good at managing and at finding and maintaining contacts, which he refers to as 'hustling' for jobs. This has little to do with the skills normally associated with evaluation work. Individuals who move from paid employment to consulting often do not make it as a solo consultant because they are unable or unwilling to put in the sustained effort to bring in a steady stream of work.

All consultants need to keep an eye out for evaluation projects and be in a position to land those they find attractive.

Commissioning agents use a variety of methods to find outsiders for their studies. In some there is an invitation for a consultant to undertake a study, but it is more common for organisations to invite consultants to tender for a given investigation. In some cases, a selected small number of consultants are asked to apply, while in others commissioners advertise more widely for consultants to undertake evaluations on their behalf. Notification about how to tender usually appears in newspapers with national coverage. More detailed evaluation briefs are then sent to those who respond to the advertisement.

It is important that the brief gives a clear indication of parameters such as the objectives of the evaluation and the amount of resources available, and that it allows sufficient time for submissions to be prepared and submitted. They should contain enough information for the evaluator to provide a submission consistent with the headings we used for the evaluation planner in Chapter 4 (see Figure 4.1). Associated with an increasing organisational knowledge of evaluation, the briefs we see now are far more sophisticated than those available a decade ago. However, it is often necessary for the tenderer to acquire additional information from the contact person given in the brief.

The selection of an external evaluator should proceed by iteration. An outline plan is developed, followed by an interview with the stakeholders which is designed to enable them to select a tender. The successful tenderer should then negotiate the final form of the evaluation plan before any field work is undertaken.

During the data management phase, we have found that ongoing communication with the organisation and the primary audiences is important, even if no findings have become known. Audiences like to know about the progress of the evaluation. Attention must also be given to putting into action the communicating strategies outlined in the plan.

External evaluations rely on good teamwork if more than one evaluator is involved. If junior staff are involved, it is necessary to provide direction and support. It is common for studies to get out of hand if they are not managed carefully. There is a need to stick to timelines and to keep an eye on expenditure. It is best for an external evaluator to adopt an interested but unbiased approach to the conduct of these studies.

### Costs of evaluation studies

The costs of evaluation studies will obviously vary according to the scope of the work done; however, there are obviously some limits on the amount of resources that should be spent on a given study. For example, it would be ludicrous for an evaluation of a program to exceed the cost of the program itself. When pressed to provide a 'ball park' figure by those planning to build in evaluation from the beginning of a program—an admirable strategy—we suggest a figure of 10–15 per cent.

The tender submission should always include a statement of the budget based on the cost of personnel, travel and overheads. The following is a hypothetical example based on an actual evaluation of a major educational policy.

---

**Example 7.6 Budget for the evaluation of a major educational policy**

The evaluation plan requires that evaluators spend extensive periods of time in eighteen case study schools. Non-participant observation will be the approach used. This includes the use of interviews, observation of key events and meetings, and examination of documents at each site. It will be necessary to visit each site regularly during the school year. Staff with a knowledge of schools and an ability to collect and understand the data will be needed.

As indicated in an earlier part of the plan, the study needs to be coordinated so that there are common methodological approaches in both the collection and analyses phases. This will require an evaluation director with these skills.

It will be necessary for one full-time field worker to be employed for the duration of the study, a period of twelve months, supported by the Director of the Consulting Firm.

*Costing*

*Evaluation Staff.* Salary of one field coordinator $42 198 plus 29 per cent on-costs for 52 weeks:
$54 400

*Evaluation Director.* The study will require a director who will be responsible for coordination of the evaluation and the development of the data management approach. The Director will be involved for one day a week for 40 weeks (0.8 year at 0.2 time) during the year at an annual salary of ($66 461 x 0.2 x 0.8) plus 29 per cent overheads:
$10 600

*Administrative/Secretarial.* On the basis of one day per

---

week for 40 weeks (0.8 time). Salary ($29 000 x 0.2 x 0.8) plus 29 per cent overheads:

$4600

*Travel*. On the basis of 30 days' accommodation out of Melbourne @ $150 per day, plus miscellaneous metropolitan travel ($500):

$5000

Printing of report and distribution:

$400

Miscellaneous (computer analyses, telephone, etc.):

$1000

Total:

$76 000

Add organisational oncosts @ 40 per cent:

$30 400

Grand total:

$106 400

It can be seen here that the consulting firm built in a 40 per cent 'overhead' to allow for the 'other tasks' that consultants need to do, as indicated by Scriven earlier in the chapter. Even so the cost of evaluation personnel amounts to just less than two-thirds of the budget.

As an alternative to setting out details of salaries and other costs, some larger consulting firms calculate a daily cost of an employee for consulting. This varies according to several factors, including the base salary of the employee. Daily rates for a highly regarded evaluation consultant can go as high as $3000 per day. While some consultants have fixed rates, others vary their charges according to what the market can bear. Some university-based centres of evaluation adopt a sliding scale of rates according to the client, charging less for work done where the client may have very limited resources.

## CONCLUSION

While the discussion in the last section revolved around external consultants, the truth is that evaluations always need resources, whether external or internal evaluators are employed. All evaluation work should be costed. Costing must be realistic, and detailed where feasible. For those moving into consulting, there are the stark facts to be faced about the fate of small businesses, over half of which fold within three years of setting up. Thus there is a need for good financial planning, yet another skill that the evaluator must acquire in order to be successful.

## REFERENCES

Alkin, M.C. (1990). *Debates on Evaluation*. Newbury Park, CA: Sage.

Brennan, M. & Hoadley, R. (1984). *School Self Evaluation*. Melbourne: Education Department of Victoria.

Byth, V. (1997). 'Evaluating Organisational Knowledge'. Unpublished Paper for the Post-graduate Diploma in Evaluation, Centre for Program Evaluation, The University of Melbourne.

Cummings, O.W. (1988). 'Business Perspectives on Internal/External Evaluation'. *New Directions for Program Evaluation*, 39, 59–74.

Hatry, H.P. & van Houten, T. (1996). *Measuring Program Outcomes*. Washington, DC: United Way of America.

Hogben, D. (1977). 'Curriculum Evaluation: By Whom, For Whom?' Paper presented at the Annual Conference of the American Educational Research Association, Canberra, November, 1977.

Holly, P. (1990). 'Growth from Within: A New Paradigm for Educational Evaluation'. Paper held at the Centre for Program Evaluation, The University of Melbourne.

House, E.R. (1980). *Evaluating with Validity*. Beverly Hills, CA: Sage.

Hurworth, R.E., Owen, J.M. & Griffin, L.D. (1988). *The Impact of the Richmond Community Health Centre Pre Pregnancy Program*. Melbourne Centre for Program Evaluation, The University of Melbourne.

Love, A. (1994). 'Internal Evaluation: Building Organisations from Within'. In *International Conference of the Australasian Evaluation Society*. Canberra: Australasian Evaluation Society.

Mathison, S. (1994). 'Rethinking the Evaluation Role: Partnerships Between Organizations and Evaluators'. *Evaluation and Program Planning*, 17 (3), 299–304.

Morris, L.E. (1995). 'Developing Strategies for the Knowledge Era'. In Chawla, S. & Renesch, J. (eds), *Learning Organisations*. Portland, OR: Productivity Press.

Muscatello, D.B. (1988). 'Developing an Agenda that Works: The Right Choice at the Right Time'. *New Directions in Program Evaluation*, 39, 21–33.

Owen, J.M. (1990). 'Encouraging Small Scale Evaluation: Roles for an External Evaluator'. *Evaluation Journal of Australasia*, 2 (3), 41–50.

Owen, J.M. & Hartley, R. (1988). *Case Studies in Five TAFE Colleges*. Melbourne: Department of Employment, Education and Training.

Owen, J.M., Johnson, N.J. & Welsh, R.J. (1985). *Primary Concerns: A Project on Mathematics and Science in Primary Teacher Education*. Melbourne: Melbourne College of Advanced Education for the Commonwealth Tertiary Education Commission.

Owen, J.M. & Lambert, F.C. (1998). 'Evaluation and the Information Needs of Organisational Leaders'. *American Journal of Evaluation*, in press.

Owen, J.M., Lambert, F.C. & Stringer, W.S. (1994). 'Acquiring Knowledge of Implementation and Change: Essential for Program Evaluators?' *Knowledge: Creation, Diffusion, Utilization*, 15 (3), 273–94.

Schon, D. (1983). *The Reflective Practitioner: How Professionals Think in Action*. London: Temple Smith.

Scriven, M. (1995). 'Evaluation Consulting'. *Evaluation Practice*, 16 (1), 47–57.

Telford (1991). 'Responsive Evaluation for Development in Self Managing Schools'. Unpublished paper for Doctor of Education, The University of Melbourne.

Torres, R.T., Preskill, H.S. & Piontek, M.E. (1996). *Evaluation Strategies for Communicating and Reporting: Enhancing Learning Organisations*. Thousand Oaks, CA: Sage.

# 8

# Codes of Behaviour for Evaluators

## INTRODUCTION

In this chapter, we examine current codes of behaviour which could be applied to evaluative enquiry. These guidelines are predicated on a belief that evaluators, stakeholders and others should have reference points from which to judge whether evaluation practice is acceptable. We have mentioned these codes in passing earlier in the text, in Chapter 4. Here, they are described and discussed in more detail.

## CODES OF BEHAVIOUR FOR APPLIED SOCIAL SCIENCE RESEARCH

Among agencies and professions which support social science research, there has been growing concern that the procedures and methods used by investigators be directed towards acceptable ends. This includes the protection of the rights and welfare of participants. For example, the informed consent of participants is commonly required for all research undertaken by university and government agencies. Informed consent is a procedure by which individuals choose whether or not to participate in a study after being presented with information that impinges on this decision. All research designs put forward by academic staff are rigorously reviewed by ethics committees before proceeding. Issues which these committees consider include:

- the rationale and need for the study;
- the quality of the design;

- whether the research is supervised by a competent and qualified practitioner;
- adequate material support; and
- appropriate selection of participants or groups.

In some instances, there must be evidence that adequate reparations can be made to those who may be disadvantaged by the findings of the study.

When professionals with accredited credentials undertake research, they are expected to abide by the code of behaviour of their professional body. Associations such as the Australian Psychological Association and the American Anthropological Association have developed codes of behaviour for members. They are expected to become acquainted with them as part of their induction to these associations. Also, agencies such as the United States Accounting Office have codes of practice for staff working on audits conducted by the office. Codes of behaviour generally consist of a set of standards of practice. Each standard can be regarded as a principle mutually agreed to by people engaged in a given profession—a principle that, if met, enhances the fairness and quality of that practice.

The existence of professional standards presents moral dilemmas for the researcher working within or for an organisation. This is almost always the case for evaluators. In such contexts, the investigator often performs multiple roles, which give rise to ambiguous and conflicting expectations. For example, the investigator might not agree with the goals of a given programmatic intervention, or be at odds with the ways in which management has implemented the program. In an analysis of ethical relationships, it was concluded that the very nature of an organisational system necessitates that researchers need to approach participants and ethical issues differently from those in non-applied settings— for example, in laboratory experiments (Mirvis & Seashore, 1982). In such contexts, participants in research cannot be approached as individuals. This is because of the hierarchical and interdependent nature of roles and relationships.

Within an organisational situation, researchers do not have the power to resolve all ethical dilemmas—for example, to ensure the wellbeing of participants, or to make assurances that the research will be carried out as planned. This conclusion led Mirvis and Seashore (1982) to suggest that researchers need to modify their approach to ethical standards in such settings by moving from applying prescriptive guidelines and standards to using these standards more flexibly, according to the situation at hand. Having reached what might be regarded as a realistic position, it is up to the researcher to communicate these expectations to stakeholders and clients. In summary, it is the researcher's responsibility as ethical decision-maker 'to create roles that are mutually clarified and compatible, and, in creating them, to affirm general ethical norms governing human research' (Mirvis & Seashore, 1982).

The researcher and the organisation need to reach agreement on the ethical principles that underlie an investigation. The implication is that, if such agreement cannot be reached early in the study, the researcher should withdraw.

## CODES OF BEHAVIOUR FOR EVALUATIVE ENQUIRY

Evaluative enquiry is one branch of applied social science research. The discussion in the previous section can be applied to most evaluations. Many of these issues will be familiar to those who have undertaken evaluation, even if they have not been aware of evaluation codes of behaviour. For example, the evaluator needs to honour promises of anonymity and confidentiality. Evaluation plans which involve using control groups need to be carefully examined for potential ethical risks. Reporting ought to include fair attention to the strengths and weaknesses of programs.

Evaluation is always conducted within the context of the needs of individuals or organisations, be they from the helping professions, government agencies or private organisations. The evaluator can be regarded as an outsider or insider relative to the client and the evaluative contribution might include those of consultant, educator or change agent. These in itself provides a series of ethical dilemmas. These might include conflict for the evaluator whose reputation and career depend on providing accurate and fearless information, and program managers whose reputation and career are bound up with the provision of successful programs: 'speaking truth is a risky and painful task, but this is what the evaluator has to do' (Chelimsky, 1995).

Over the past decade, the development of codes of behaviour or practice has become a major issue for the evaluation profession. Guidelines have been developed in Australia and Canada. The Australasian Evaluation Society produced its Guidelines for the Ethical Conduct of Evaluations in early 1998. However, by far the most activity has been in the United States. Because of the comprehensiveness of the results of this activity, the remainder of this chapter is devoted to recent developments in that country. These are:

- the Program Evaluation Standards; and
- the Guiding Principles for Evaluators.

Each of these is now discussed in turn.

## The Program Evaluation Standards

The Program Evaluation Standards are the result of the work of the Joint Committee on Standards for Educational Evaluation. This committee was created in 1975 with a brief to develop standards for educational evaluation after earlier work had been done on the needs for standards in test construction and administration. The major products have been the Standards for Evaluation of Educational Programs, Projects and Materials (1981), Personnel Evaluation Standards (1988), and the Program Evaluation Standards (Sanders, 1994). The Joint Committee is sponsored by fifteen organisations including the American Evaluation Association. In 1989, its operating procedures were accredited by the American National Standards Institute (ANSI), which subsequently approved the Program Evaluation Standards in 1994 (Sanders, 1995).

There are 30 standards grouped within four areas:

- utility;
- feasibility;
- propriety; and
- accuracy.

They are formalised in an extensive document which provides an overview of each standard, case studies showing how they can be used, and how they can be violated. The characteristics of the standards are outlined below.

*Utility standards* are intended to help plan evaluations that are informative, timely and influential. Utility standards are concerned with whether an evaluation provides practical information needs for a given audience. The utility standards are listed below.

*U1 Audience Identification*
Audiences involved in or affected by the evaluation should be identified so that their needs can be addressed.

*U2 Evaluator Credibility*
The persons conducting the evaluation should be both trustworthy and competent to perform the evaluation, so that their findings achieve maximum credibility and acceptance

*U3 Information Scope and Selection*
Information collected should be of such scope and selected in such ways as to address pertinent questions about the object of the evaluation and be responsive to the needs and interests of specified audiences.

*U4 Valuation Interpretation*

The perspectives, procedures and rational used to interpret the findings should be carefully described, so that the bases for value judgments are clear.

*U5 Report Clarity*

The evaluation report should describe the object being evaluated and its context and the purposes, procedures, and findings of the evaluation, so that the audience will readily understand what was done, why it was done, what information was obtained, what conclusions were drawn, and what recommendations were made.

*U6 Report Dissemination*

Evaluation findings should be disseminated to clients and other right to know audiences, so that they can assess and use the findings.

*U7 Report Timelines*

Release of reports should be timely, so that audiences can best use the reported information.

*U8 Evaluation Impact*

Evaluations should be planned and conducted in ways that encourage follow-through by members of the audiences.

*Feasibility standards* recognise that evaluations are generally conducted in natural settings. Feasibility deals with issues such as value for cost, practical issues such as availability of data, and political issues such as impact of findings. Feasibility standards call for evaluations to be realistic, diplomatic and financially well-managed. The feasibility standards are listed below.

*F1 Practical Procedures*

The evaluation procedures should be practical, so that disruption is kept to a minimum, and that needed information can be obtained.

*F2 Political Viability*

The evaluation should be planned and conducted with anticipation of the different positions of various interest groups, so that their cooperation can be obtained, and so that possible attempts by any of these groups to curtail evaluation operations or to bias or misapply the results can be averted or counteracted.

*F3 Cost Effectiveness*

The evaluation should produce information of sufficient value to justify the resources expended.

*Propriety standards* relate strongly to ethics. They are aimed at ensuring that the rights of people influenced by the program and its evaluation will be protected. Propriety standards require an evaluation to take into account legal and ethical issues, including the welfare of program participants and those affected by evaluation results. Proprietary standards are listed below.

### P1 Formal Obligation

Obligations of the formal parties to an evaluation (what is to be done, how, by whom, when) should be agreed to in writing, so that these parties are obligated to adhere to all the conditions of the agreement or formally to renegotiate it.

### P2 Conflict of Interest

Conflict of interest, frequently unavoidable, should be dealt with openly and honestly, so that it does not compromise the evaluation processes and results.

### P3 Full and Frank Disclosure

Oral and written evaluation reports should be open, direct, and honest in their disclosure of pertinent findings, including the limitations of the evaluation.

### P4 Public's Right to Know

The formal parties to an evaluation should respect and assure the public's right to know within the limits of other related principles and statutes, such as those dealing with public safety and the right to privacy.

### P5 Rights of Human Subjects

Evaluations should be designed and conducted, so that the rights and welfare of the human subjects are respected and protected.

### P6 Human Interactions

Evaluators should respect human dignity and worth in their interactions with other persons associated with an evaluation.

### P7 Balanced Reporting

The evaluation should be complete and fair in its presentation of strengths and weaknesses of the object under investigation, so that strengths can be built on and weaknesses addressed.

### P8 Fiscal Reporting

The evaluator's allocation and expenditure of resources should reflect sound accountability procedures and otherwise be prudent and ethically responsible.

*Accuracy standards* determine whether an evaluation has produced truth and require that the data management reflects the key evaluation issues, whether the information is technically adequate, and that the conclusions and recommendations (if any) reflect the analysis of the data. The overall accuracy of an evaluation against these standards indicates whether the evaluation has produced valid and reliable knowledge about the evaluation. Accuracy standards are listed below.

### A1 Object Identification
The object of the evaluation (program, project, material) should be sufficiently examined, so that the form(s) of the object being considered in the evaluation can be clearly identified.

### A2 Context Analysis
The context in which the program, project, or material exists should be examined in detail, so that its likely influence on the object can be identified.

### A3 Described Purposes and Procedures
The purposes and procedures of the evaluation should be monitored and described in enough detail, so that they can be identified and assessed.

### A4 Defensible Information Sources
The sources of information should be described in enough detail, so that the adequacy of the information can be assessed.

### A5 Valid Measurement
The information-gathering instruments and procedures should be chosen or developed and then implemented in ways that will assure that the interpretation arrived at is valid for the given use.

### A6 Reliable Measurement
The information-gathering instruments and procedures should be chosen or developed and then implemented in ways that will assure that the interpretation arrived at is reliable for the intended use.

### A7 Systematic Data Control
The data collected, processed, and reported in an evaluation should be reviewed and corrected, so that the results of the evaluation will not be flawed.

### A8 Analysis of Quantitative Information
Quantitative information in an evaluation should be appropriately and systematically analysed to ensure supportable interpretation.

### A9 Analysis of Qualitative Information
Qualitative information in an evaluation should be appropriately and systematically analysed to ensure supportable interpretation.

### A10 Justified Conclusions
The conclusions reached in an evaluation should be explicitly justified, so that audiences can assess them.

*A11 Objective Reporting*

The evaluation procedures should provide safeguards to protect the evaluation findings against distortions by the personal feelings and biases of any party to the evaluation.

## Guiding principles for evaluators

The Guiding Principles for Evaluators have been recently developed by a task force of the American Evaluation Association, being approved by a vote of the membership in 1994 (Shadish et al., 1995). The five principles and their elaboration are as follows:

### Systematic inquiry

Evaluators conduct systematic, data-based enquiries about whatever is being evaluated.

1  Evaluators should adhere to the highest appropriate technical standards in conjunction with their work, whether that work is quantitative or qualitative in nature, so as to increase the accuracy and credibility of the evaluative information they produce.

2  Evaluators should explore with the client the shortcomings and strengths both of the various evaluation questions it might be productive to ask, and the various approaches that might be used for answering these questions.

3  When presenting their work, evaluators should communicate their methods and approaches accurately and in sufficient detail to allow others to understand, interpret and critique their work. They should make clear the limitations of an evaluation and its results. Evaluators should discuss in a contextually appropriate way, those values, assumptions, theories, methods, results and analyses that *significantly* affect the interpretation of the evaluative findings. These statements apply to all aspects of the evaluation, from its initial conceptualisation to the eventual use of the findings.

### Competence

Evaluators provide competent performance to stakeholders.

1  Evaluators should possess (or, here and elsewhere as appropriate, ensure that the evaluation team possesses) the education, abilities, skills and experience appropriate to undertake the tasks proposed in the evaluation.

2  Evaluators should practice within the limits of their professional training and competence, and should decline to conduct evalu-

ations that fall substantially outside those limits. When declining the commission or request that is not feasible or appropriate, evaluators should make clear any significant limitations on the evaluation that might result. Evaluators should make every effort to gain the competence directly or through the assistance of others who possess the required expertise.

3    Evaluators should continually seek to maintain and improve their competencies, in order to provide the highest level of performance in their evaluations. This continuing professional development might include formal course work and workshops, self-study, evaluations of one's own practise, and working with other evaluations to learn from their skills and expertise.

### Integrity/honesty

Evaluators ensure the honesty and integrity of the entire evaluation process.

1    Evaluators should negotiate honestly with clients and relevant stakeholders concerning the costs, tasks to be undertaken, limitations of methodology, scope of results likely to be obtained, and uses of data resulting from a specific evaluation. It is primarily the evaluator's responsibility to initiate discussion and clarification of these matters, not the clients'.

2    Evaluators should record all changes made in the originally negotiated project plans, and the reasons why the changes were made. If those changes significantly affect the scope and likely results of the evaluation, the evaluator should inform the client and other important stakeholders in a timely fashion (barring good reason to the contrary, before proceeding with further work) of the changes and their likely impact.

3    Evaluators should seek to determine, and where appropriate be explicit about, their own, their clients', and other stakeholders' interests concerning the conduct and outcomes of an evaluation (including financial, political and career interests).

4    Evaluators should disclose any roles or relationships they have concerning whatever is being evaluated that might pose a significant conflict of interest with their role as an evaluator. Any such conflict should be mentioned in reports of the evaluation results.

5    Evaluators should not misrepresent their procedures, data or findings. Within reasonable limits, they should attempt to prevent or correct any substantial misuses of their work by others.

159

6   If evaluators determine that certain procedures or activities seem likely to produce misleading evaluative information or conclusions, they have the responsibility to communicate their concerns, and the reasons for them, to the client (the one who funds or requests the evaluation). If discussions with the client do not resolve these concerns, so that a misleading evaluation is then implemented, the evaluator may legitimately decline to conduct the evaluation if that is feasible, and appropriate. If not, the evaluator should consult colleagues or relevant stakeholders about other proper ways to proceed (options might include, but are not limited to, discussion at a higher level, a dissenting cover letter or appendix, or refusal to sign the final document).

7   Barring compelling reasons to the contrary, evaluators should disclose all sources of financial support for an evaluation, and the source of the request for the evaluation.

### Respect for people

Evaluators respect the security, dignity and self-worth of the respondents, program participants, clients and other stakeholders with whom they interact.

1   Where applicable, evaluators must abide by current professional ethics and standards regarding risks, harms, and burdens that might be engendered to those participating in the evaluation: regarding informed consent for participation in the evaluation; and regarding informing participants about the scope and limits of confidentiality. Examples of such standards include federal regulations about protection of human subjects, or the ethical principles of such associations as the American Anthropological Association, the American Educational Research Association, or the American Psychological Association. Although this principle is not intended to extend the applicability of such ethics and standards beyond their current scope, evaluators should abide by them where it is feasible and desirable to do so.

2   Because justified negative or critical conclusions from an evaluation must be explicitly stated, evaluations sometimes produce results that harm client or stakeholder interests. Under this circumstance, evaluators should seek to maximise the benefits and reduce any unnecessary harms that might occur, provided this will not compromise the integrity of the evaluation findings. Evaluators should carefully judge when the benefits from doing the evaluation or in performing certain evaluation procedures should be foregone because of the risks or harms. Where pos-

sible, these issues should be anticipated during the negotiation of the evaluation.

3    Knowing that evaluations often will negatively affect the interests of some stakeholders, evaluators should conduct the evaluation and communicate its results in a way that clearly respects the stakeholders' dignity and self-worth.

4    Where feasible, evaluators should attempt to foster the social equity of the evaluation, so that those who give to the evaluation can receive some benefits in return. For example, evaluators should seek to ensure that those who bear the burdens of contributing data and incurring any risks are doing so willingly, and that they have full knowledge of, and maximum feasible opportunity to obtain, any benefits that may be produced from the evaluation. When it would not endanger the integrity of the evaluation, respondents or program participants should be informed if and how they can receive services to which they are otherwise entitled without participating in the evaluation.

5    Evaluators have the responsibility to identify and respect differences among participants, such as differences in their culture, religion, gender, disability, age, sexual orientation and ethnicity, and to be mindful of potential implications of these differences when planning, conducting, analysing, and reporting their evaluations.

### Responsibilities for general and public welfare

Evaluators articulate and take into account the diversity of interests and values that may be related to the general and public welfare.

1    When planning and reporting evaluations, evaluators should consider including important perspectives and interests of the full range of stakeholders in the object being evaluated. Evaluators should carefully consider the justification when omitting important value perspectives or the views of important groups.

2    Evaluators should consider not only the immediate operations and outcomes of whatever is being evaluated, but also the broad assumptions, implications and potential side effects of it.

3    Freedom of information is essential in a democracy. Hence, barring compelling reason to the contrary, evaluators should allow all relevant stakeholders to have access to evaluative information, and should actively disseminate that information to stakeholders if resources allow. If different evaluation results

are communicated in forms that are tailored to the interests of different stakeholders, those communications should ensure that each stakeholder group is aware of the other communication. Communications that are tailored to a given stakeholder should always include all important results that may bear on interests of that stakeholder. In all cases, evaluators should strive to present results as clearly and simply as accuracy allows so that clients and other stakeholders can easily understand the evaluation process and results.

4    Evaluators should maintain a balance between client needs and other needs, Evaluators necessarily have a special relationship with the client who funds or requests the evaluation. By virtue of that relationship, evaluators must strive to meet legitimate client needs whenever it is feasible and appropriate to do so. However, that relationship can also place evaluators in difficult dilemmas when client interests conflict with other interests, or when client interests conflict with the obligation of evaluators for systematic enquiry, competence, integrity, and respect for people. In these cases, evaluators should explicitly identify and discuss the conflicts with the client and relevant stakeholders, resolve them when possible, determine whether continued work on the evaluation is advisable if the conflicts cannot be resolved, and make clear any significant limitations on the evaluation that might result if the conflict is not resolved.

5    Evaluators have obligations that encompass the public interest and good. These obligations are especially important when evaluators are supported by publicly generated funds; but clear threats to public good should never be ignored in any evaluation. Because the public interest and good are rarely the same as the interests of any particular group (including those of the client or funding agency), evaluators will usually have to go beyond an analysis of particular stakeholders' interests when considering the welfare of society as a whole.

The evaluation journal *New Directions for Program Evaluation* (Shadish, 1995) devoted an edition to the discussion of their evolution, their usage and comparisons with the Program Evaluation Standards. A major contribution to this edition of the journal was an article by Jim Sanders (1995), who compared the Program Evaluation Standards developed under his chairmanship, with the Guiding Principles for Evaluators. He concluded that:

I can safely say that there are no conflicts or inconsistencies between the two. Although there may be minor disagreements about where the AEA statements should be placed within the Joint Committee Standards, the overall advice is very consistent, with both documents strongly emphasising accuracy of results, inclusion of stakeholders in the evaluation process, regard for the welfare of evaluation participants and a concern for service to stakeholders, the community and society.

Now that we have outlined the extensive work that has been done in this area, we would like to discuss the terminology used. You may recall that we have used the word 'standard' to refer to the required level of attainment on the scale of a variable. This was in Chapter 1, when we were judging how much of a given variable had to be present for the evaluand under review to be judged as 'worthy'. So, in the context of this discussion, it seems that the use of the term 'standard' to indicate the important parameters of acceptable practice is a little confusing. Also, it is easier to use a common term to refer to the two different ethical frameworks. We will use the term *codes of behaviour* in a generic fashion to refer collectively to the standards and to the guiding principles, and dimensions of acceptable professional practice more generally.

## APPLYING EVALUATION CODES OF BEHAVIOUR

Of the two major codes of behaviour just described, the Program Evaluation Standards provide evaluators with more practical directions for use. For each standard, there is a scale with the following anchor points:

- The standard was deemed applicable and to the extent feasible was taken into account.
- The standard was deemed applicable but could not be taken into account.
- The standard was not deemed applicable.
- Exception was taken to the standard.

The scale is used in a checklist to help evaluators determine whether the code of behaviour for a given study is acceptable to clients and other stakeholders. The availability of these resources is part of an impressive attempt by the developers of the standards to make them user-friendly. This is in recognition that the standards are not only for the professional evaluator undertaking well-funded studies, they are also accessible to small-scale insiders for insider studies.

As we indicated earlier in this chapter, the evaluator should be judicious in invoking the standards or principles. It is a mistake

163

to think that they should be applied 'chapter and verse' in a slavish or unthinking way to an evaluation study.

An analysis of the use of the Program Evaluation Standards shows that, very often, the standards of Accuracy and Feasibility can collide. For example, to get a very accurate estimate of the population, we may need a sample size so large that the survey becomes too expensive to undertake.

In this case, we may decide to use a small sample, knowing that the population estimate will vary considerably, or we may use key informants' estimates of the population size, if they are likely to be sufficiently accurate for our purposes, or we decide not to proceed until sufficient resources are available to undertake the large surveys required.

The standards of Utility and Accuracy may also be at odds, particularly in terms of the trade-off between timeliness and comprehensiveness. It is sometimes important to get a set of more tentative findings to the client in time to inform a key decision, rather than to provide a more thorough analysis of the evidence which is only available after the deadline.

Token or superficial evaluation generally does not involve these considered trade-offs. For example, studies which routinely report client feedback data, based on the small and unrepresentative sample of clients who volunteer to return evaluation forms, are using data management techniques which are not good enough.

As a minimum, we believe that all evaluators, whether they be professional evaluation consultants or those working on internal evaluations as part of a broader role in an organisation, should know what the standards or principles contain and what they imply for a code of practice.

## USING PRINCIPLES IN REAL EVALUATIONS

It is a long step from getting people to understand a code of practice to having then accept that code to the extent that it forms a basis for their action. Experience suggests that knowing about the standards or principles is not enough: there is a need for them to be acted on. An obvious move is to encourage practitioners to use them in real evaluation studies. Beginning in the negotiation stage, it is up to the evaluator to take the initiative on their use. This is why we have included the notion of a code of behaviour in the evaluation planner, outlined in Chapter 4 (see Figure 4.1). Negotiating should include determining which of the principles or standards should form part of the evaluation agreement and be included in the final evaluation plan. Where possible, the evaluator should look for any problems encompassed by the principles or standards which might arise in the data management and dissemination stages.

## USING PRINCIPLES IN TRAINING EVALUATORS

One way in which the use of codes of behaviour can be encouraged is during the training of neophyte evaluators. One source of new evaluators is through formal graduate training in colleges and universities (Owen, 1998). However, the general consensus among academics is that most college or university courses in evaluation concentrate on methodology and do less than justice to many of the basic principles of evaluation practice, including an analysis of principles and their usage in real situations. Blaine Worthen (1996), who has had extensive experience in training evaluators in university settings, believes that codes of behaviour for evaluation cannot be taught in isolation from more general concerns about ethical behaviour. He maintains that the inculcation of appropriate standards of practice must sensitise students to more general concerns about how we treat fellow human beings. Worthen believes that the formal training of evaluators should also involve modelling of appropriate behaviour by university staff responsible for training. This implies that university staff must set high standards for the way they conduct themselves professionally and that they should be 'honest and upstanding'. Good training also involves teaching of standards and/or principles in an experiential format. This involves applying them, first of all, to simulated situations, and then to projects in the field. During this stage, students would be asked specifically to adhere to a code of behaviour based on the standards or the guiding principles (Worthen, 1996).

This implies a rigorous and extensive training program. There remains the problem of how those new to evaluation who do not have the benefit of extensive college training can employ a suitable code of behaviour in their work. There has been extensive discussion within evaluation associations, at least in the United States and in Australasia, about ways in which the certification of evaluators might proceed. If there is a move towards certifying evaluations and evaluators, there will be a need to upgrade the quantity and quality of training for evaluators working in these countries.

# META-EVALUATION: USING THE STANDARDS OR PRINCIPLES TO REVIEW PRACTICE

Another way in which the standards or principles can be used is as a framework for reviewing practice. This is known as meta-evaluation, literally the evaluation of evaluations. Meta-evaluations can be undertaken at a strategic time—strategic, that is, in the sense of checking that a suitable code of behaviour has been built in to a study. This is the principle by which universities, colleges and other entities invoke the use of organisational ethics committees. For evaluations, this generally does not involve an external party in an overseeing role. It is more likely that an informal meta-evaluation is undertaken by a steering or advisory committee for the evaluation. However, it is our experience that such undertakings are rare.

An alternative procedure is to undertake a retrospective meta-evaluation at the completion of a study. This should be undertaken by a third party, not the evaluators or the clients. We have had some success in using graduate students to undertake meta-evaluations based on the principles of conduct, especially the Program Evaluation Standards. This has been a service to an organisation interested in determining the quality of an evaluation which has been completed recently; both internal and external evaluations have been reviewed. Generally the review is based around one of the four clusters—for example, Utility. The reviewer typically examines documents and interviews key stakeholders and, in some cases, the evaluator. In addition to the service to the organisation, the exercise provides an opportunity for the graduate student to 'get inside' the codes of behaviour, by using them for a major postgraduate paper.

## IMPACT ON THE FIELD

There is a dearth of empirical studies on the use of codes of behaviour and factors affecting their use in the field. Two important studies stand out in the literature. The first asked a sample of experienced evaluators to rank the frequency of a set of violations to good practice, each one linked to one of the 30 standards in the Program Evaluation Standards. It was found that the respondents found that Utility and Feasibility standards to be more frequently violated than those of Accuracy and Propriety (Newman & Brown, 1992).

A subsequent and more extensive study asked 700 members of the American Evaluation Association to report on their experiences with ethical problems in their work. An open-ended methodology was used to get respondents to describe:

- ethical problems they had faced most frequently in their work; and
- the single most serious ethical problem they had ever encountered (Morris & Cohn, 1993).

The 459 responses were subjected to content analyses, based on another set of principles, the Standards for Program Evaluation (SPE). The SPE consists of 66 principles, clustered under six headings:

- Formulation and Negotiation;
- Structure and Design;
- Data Collection and Preparation;
- Data Analysis and Interpretation;
- Communication and Disclosure;
- Use of Results.

(It is worth noting that these principles, which are now largely superseded by those we have discussed above, correspond closely to the key steps in the evaluation planner (see Figure 4.1) which we introduced in Chapter 4.)

Key findings of this study included the following:

- Almost 65 per cent of respondents encountered ethical problems in their work.
- Ethical problems were more likely in external evaluations— that is, when the evaluator was an outsider.
- Ethical problems were more likely to be associated with process and outcome evaluations rather than enquiry related to needs assessment or cost-benefit analysis.
- Evaluators who had a background in education were less likely to have encountered ethical problems than evaluators with backgrounds in other disciplines.

Most problems were located in the post-data managment phase. These included:

- conflicts over the presentations of findings such as pressure to alter a presentation, or being reluctant to fully outline findings due to them being at odds with the expectations of the client;
- disagreement over disclosure of findings, such as disputes concerning the ownership and dissemination of a final report; and

- misinterpretation or misuse of the final report, such as the findings being suppressed or ignored by the client.

Morris and Cohn (1993) prepared a 'composite portrait' of an evaluator's nightmare based on these findings, as follows:

> The client informs the evaluator at their initial meeting that it is extremely important to demonstrate that the program is having a significant beneficial effect on participants. Later, when the data indicate that the program's effects are not as positive as the client had hoped, the client exerts pressure on the evaluator to exaggerate the 'good' findings and downplay the 'bad' ones. At this point the client also questions the evaluator's right to discuss the findings with individuals outside of the organisation, an issue the evaluator thought had been resolved during the contracting phase. Finally, after the final report has been submitted, the evaluator discovers that the document has been 'deep sixed'. The client has not shared it with other stakeholders within the agency, and does not appear to be using the study's results or recommendations in decision-making concerning the program.

This has a familiar ring, reminding us of a study we undertook in the mid-1980s, in which the client was a federal government department. At the draft report stage, we received telephone calls from senior bureaucrats asking that the findings of an executive study be 'rearranged' by putting the more positive findings at the front, with the more negative ones relegated to the rear and downplayed. At about the same time, one of the evaluation team presented a report at a national education conference about some of the findings, which resulted in a threatening call from a senior bureaucrat to the director of the evaluation. Fortunately, after pressure from other stakeholders, some of the findings were distributed to the wide range of stakeholders; however, a major report with some criticisms of the roles of federal officers in liaising with their counterparts in the states was never released. The result of this and other studies suggest that ethical problems relate to the transmission of findings and their use, rather than to the negotiation and data management stages of an evaluation study.

## CONCLUSION

In an address at the Australian Council for Educational Research in July 1997, Ernest House reviewed a series of evaluations undertaken by well-known evaluation agencies for the Federal Department of Education in Washington. In the course of the discussion, it became clear that in none of these large-scale studies were ethical standards or principles *ever* broached by evaluators or clients. If this situation can be extrapolated to the field, the application of codes of behaviour represents a major challenge for evaluation associations and their members.

We have suggested several ways in which codes of behaviour can be brought to the attention of new evaluators. We also believe that the more emphasis there is placed on codes of behaviour in the negotiation stage of evaluations, the more likely that stakeholders will become aware of them.

A further advantage of incorporating codes of behaviour into the design of evaluations is that there will be fewer problems with ethical issues in the later stages of an evaluation. However, as others have pointed out, there is always the potential for conflict because of the basic difference in orientations of evaluators, concerned with the veracity of their evaluations, and managers, if the findings threaten the programs in which managers have a high stake (Kimmel, 1988).

## REFERENCES

Chelimsky, E. (1995). 'Comments of the Guiding Principles'. *New Directions for Program Planning*, 66 (Summer), 53–5.

Kimmel, A.J. (1988). *Ethics and Values in Applied Social Research*. Newbury Park, CA: Sage.

Mirvis, P.H. & Seashore, S.E. (eds) (1982). *Creating Ethical Relationships in Organisational Research*. New York: Springer Verlag.

Morris, M. & Cohn, R. (1993). 'Program Evaluation and Ethical Challenges: A National Survey'. *Evaluation Review*, 17 (6), 621–42.

Newman, D.L. & Brown, R.D. (1992). 'Violations of Ethical Standards: Frequency and Seriousness of Occurrence'. *Evaluation Review*, 16, 219–34.

Owen, J.M. (1998). 'Towards an Outcomes Hierarchy for Professional University Programs'. *Evaluation and Program Planning*, in press.

Sanders, J. (1994). *The Program Evaluation Standards*. Thousand Oaks, CA: Sage.

Sanders, J.R. (1995). 'Standards and Principles'. *New Directions for Program Evaluation*, 66 (Summer), 47–52.

Shadish, W.R., Newmann, D.L., Scheirer, M.A. & Wye, C. (eds) (1995). 'Guiding Principles for Evaluators'. *New Directions for Program Evaluation*, 66.

Worthen, B. (1996). 'Mechanisms for Making the Program Evaluation Standards Meaningful to Graduate Education'. Paper presented at the Annual Meeting of the American Evaluation Association, November, 1996. Atlanta, GA.

# 9

## Proactive Evaluation

### INTRODUCTION

This chapter outlines the rationale and Approaches to evaluation designed to inform front-end decision-making about the structure and content of policies and programs. There are two major situations to which this Form of evaluation is logically applied. The first is in a 'nothing to something' situation where the aim of the evaluation is to provide findings to aid decision-making about a new program, one being developed from scratch. In the second, a program exists but there is a need for a major review, with the likelihood that this existing program will be altered radically or even replaced by a new and more appropriate one.

Because, in both instances, these evaluations provide information in order to assist decisions about a future or projected program, evaluations of this nature are described as Proactive evaluations (Form A). Note that, in a previous edition of this book, this Form of evaluation was labelled Evaluation for Development.

*Proactive evaluation* is concerned with:

- the extent of the need among a defined population for a program in a given area of provision;
- synthesising what is known in the existing research and related literature about an identified issue or problem;
- critically reviewing ways in which an identified issue or problem has been solved through programs mounted in other locations.

The essential features of Proactive evaluation are summarised in Table 9.1.

**Table 9.1   Summary of Proactive evaluation (Form A)**

| Dimension | Properties |
| --- | --- |
| Orientation | Synthesis |
| Typical issues | • Is there a need for the program?<br>• What do we know about this problem that the program will address?<br>• What is recognised as best practice in this area?<br>• Have there been other attempts to find solutions to this problem?<br>• What does the relevant research or conventional wisdom tell us about this problem?<br>• What could we find out from external sources to rejuvenate an existing policy or program? |
| State of program | None |
| Major focus | Program context |
| Timing (vis-à-vis program delivery) | Before |
| Key Approaches | • Needs assessment<br>• Research review<br>• Review of best practice (establishment of benchmarks) |
| Assembly of evidence | Questionnaire, review of documents and data bases, site visits and other interactive methods. Focus groups, nominal groups and delphi technique useful for needs assessments. |

Table 9.1 shows that the *orientation*, or purpose of evaluation, of a Proactive Form is to provide evidence to aid the synthesis of programs. Given that the *state* of these programs is that either no program exists or that radical changes are needed to an existing one, the timing of the evaluation can be conceived of as occurring 'before development'. The *focus* from which evidence is drawn is the context or milieux within which the program will or may be developed, or like contexts in other locations.

Employing Approaches within this Form assumes that policy and program development should be informed by the best and most appropriate evidence about the problem to be addressed. For example, an analysis of needs, combined with information on available resources, is fundamental to making decisions about the provision of services. Such knowledge enables planners at the policy, Program and program levels to:

- determine priorities in geographic areas, among client groups and across areas of support;
- train and allocate staff appropriately;
- locate services and facilities to achieve maximum effect;
- substantiate the allocation of resources.

The evaluator's task is to harness and provide knowledge for those who will be involved in program planning. The logic for Proactive evaluation seems to be beyond challenge. However, in practice, extensive examples of the application of real-life examples are hard to locate. This suggests that decisions about providing available resources have traditionally been based on the intuition of program planners, long-used practices or personal preferences, or have been unduly influenced by political pressures. The use of evaluation to aid decision-making before programs are developed is a call for a more analytical and rational approach to the allocation of precious resources such as those applied to social and educational interventions.

## KEY APPROACHES TO PROACTIVE EVALUATION

Three major Approaches to Proactive evaluation (see Table 9.1) are:

- needs assessment;
- research review; and
- review of exemplary practice (and the establishment of benchmarks).

Each of these approaches will now be considered in turn.

### Needs assessment

Needs assessment is the most well-known Approach within this Form. Over the past decade, an extensive conceptual literature has emerged. The American Evaluation Association has supported a strong Topical Interest Group on Needs Assessment, an indication that this Approach is acknowledged as an important subset of evaluation practice, a position central to this book.

In a recent and extensive text on the subject, a needs assessment is defined as:

> A systematic set of procedures undertaken for the purpose of setting priorities and making decisions about program or organisational improvements and allocation of resources. The priorities are based on identified needs. (Witkin & Altschuld, 1995)

172

To undertake a needs assessment, one must come to grips with the notion of a *need*. This is not an easy notion to deal with, as there are many views on what we actually mean by a need (Scriven, 1991). Using 'need' as a noun provides a basis for making a needs assessment operational. Need as a noun describes a gap between the present and a desired situation. The need is the difference between the desired and the present situation or condition. Need is thus a discrepancy. This contrasts with the use of the term 'need' in everyday parlance as a verb. Using 'need' as a verb focuses on solutions—for example, a community might say: 'We need a new health centre in the neighbourhood.' We are now talking about the program to fix the need, rather than the investigation which should precede it. According to Witkin and Altschuld (1995), these two meanings are often confounded, and it is essential that the notion of 'need as a noun' remains uppermost in the minds of those commissioning or undertaking needs assessments.

Spelling out the essential features of a need leads us to be concerned with five elements, as follows:

- the desired or ideal condition or state of affairs, or what ought to be;
- the present or actual condition or state of affairs;
- discrepancies between desired and actual conditions;
- reasons for the discrepancies; and
- deciding which needs should be given priority for action through a treatment or program.

According to Roth (1990), need can be generally defined as follows:

$$N = D - A$$

where N is the need or discrepancy, D is the desired state and A is the actual state. Roth points out that need is not a unitary concept. There are different meanings as indicated in Table 9.2.

**Table 9.2  Different meanings of 'need'**

| N | | D | | A |
|---|---|---|---|---|
| Goal discrepancy | = | ideal state | – | actual state |
| Social discrepancy | = | normative state | – | actual state |
| Essential discrepancy | = | minimal state of acceptability | – | actual state |
| Want discrepancy | = | desired state | – | actual state |

For each of these situations, the desired state differs and thus, in a given context, the discrepancy is likely to be different, both in nature and amount. For example, the gap between minimal and actual state would be smaller that between ideal and actual. Note that in the fourth of these definitions, there is a shift from needs to wants. It is important to distinguish a need from a want. An example may clarify this.

---

**Example 9.1 Undertaking a needs assessment in a school of nursing**

The example is organised around the five stages outlined above:

1 the desired or ideal state of affairs;
2 the present or actual state of affairs;
3 discrepancies between 1 and 2;
4 reasons for the needs or discrepancies; and
5 which needs should be given priority for action through a treatment or program.

Imagine that a review is being undertaken of teaching methods in a school of nursing which has a reputation for being conservative. An agenda for the evaluation, sponsored by the managing committee of the school, is to make the school more responsive to recent developments in teaching and learning.

One possibility is to carry out a wants discrepancy.

1 An evaluator is asked to review the actual methods used. This is done through observation of classes and interviews with teachers.
2 At the same time, the evaluator surveys nurse education teachers working in the school about teaching methods they would prefer to use.
3 The evaluator determines differences between the actual and desired state. The analysis shows that there is little difference between methods used and preferences expressed.
4 The evaluator notes the size and the nature of the (wants) discrepancy. Some comments about the reasons or causes for the discrepancy are given on the basis of the knowledge of the context of the evaluation.
5 The evaluator presents his or her conclusions about the size and nature of the discrepancy to the management

---

committee. The committee notes the findings, which imply minor policy and practice changes.

A second possibility is to carry out a social discrepancy.

1   The evaluator also reviews the latest guidelines on effective nursing teaching which appear in educational documents and visits other like schools to determine methods commonly in use.
2   This stage is identical to that undertaken in the wants assessment.
3   On the basis of this information the evaluator prepares a statement of an 'ideal' state for teaching in the school, a direction to work towards through staff development. This is the social discrepancy.
4   The evaluator notes the size and the nature of the (needs) discrepancy. Some comments about the reasons or causes for the discrepancy are given on the basis of the knowledge of the context of the evaluation.
5   The evaluator presents his or her conclusions about the size and nature of the discrepancy to the management committee. The committee notes the findings, which imply major policy and practice changes. Among them is the need for new directions in teaching practice and a program of professional development for teaching staff.

*Comparing the two assessments*

If both assessments were carried out, the evaluator could note that the two discrepancies are very different both in size and nature. Some comments about the reasons or causes for each discrepancy could be given on the basis of the knowledge of the context of the evaluation. Decisions about action by the committee would depend on their collective opinions about which of the two assessments is more valid in terms of the aims or mission of the school.

The existence of these two types of needs can be explained by the context within which the evaluations are conducted. Determination of what ought to be is the basis for each discrepancy. What ought to be depends on the frame of reference for the evaluation. Needs assessments, like other evaluations, are political activities. Needs or wants are conditional. In the social discrepancy example above, the need for staff development is conditional on the assumption that more up-to-date teaching methods are required. In this case, establishment of the need comes down, to the need for students in the nurse education programs to learn more effectively.

Needs assessment in practice has three major stages: planning, data management and utilisation. This is consistent with our description of evaluation introduced in Chapter 1. The planning stage culminates in a management plan, which includes the purposes of the study, an outline of the methods to be adopted, and the potential uses of the findings. Data management includes locating existing sources of information—often an important source of data for needs assessments—and the collection of new evidence. This must include evidence about both the actual and desired conditions. In the utilisation stage, needs are prioritised if competing needs have been found. In some cases, action plans to ameliorate the needs are developed. In these cases, there is a strong link between the evaluative and development aspects of program provision. This is achieved by the evaluators working closely with clients and adopting an insider for insider perspective on the evaluation (see Chapter 8).

It is essential that all three stages are included for a study to be classed as a needs assessment. Reviews of the field have shown that studies often fall short of one or more of these criteria. A review of hundreds of these studies showed that their major shortcomings included:

- confusing solutions with needs;
- not attending to the establishment of the desired state or condition;
- relying on one method of data collection, usually a questionnaire;
- equating the administration of a questionnaire with the needs assessment;
- failing to attend to the establishment of need(s);
- neglecting to assist clients with setting priorities for action (Witkin & Altschuld, 1995).

## Research review

A second Approach to Proactive evaluation is to synthesise research relevant to a particular issue or problem which is the target of future policy or program development. This Approach is predicated on the assumption that 'funded knowledge', the results of relevant pure and applied prior research, should be taken into account when planning programs. There has been a tendency for those working at the coal face of program provision to ignore findings of research. We believe that the findings of rigorous social enquiry can inform practice, and that efforts should be made to harness relevant scientific knowledge and apply it to policy and program provision where such knowledge exists.

For example, we recently attended a seminar on trends in poverty. The reported research was carried out with scientific rigour, involving adequate sampling and careful data collection and analysis, and the results presented stretched over more than seven years. Among the findings was one which suggested that, while 10 per cent of households were chronically poor, another 15 per cent of households were in a low-income situation for only one or two years out of a seven-year period. These findings, taken together with other related information, could be used in framing interventions designed to identify the least well-off and alleviate their social and economic circumstances.

The most obvious method of analysing information within this Approach is to undertake a literature review. There are established procedures that are available in well-equipped libraries for carrying out such a search. This involves the essential step of defining the boundaries of the search, perhaps with the aid of a thesaurus. Computer-based storage facilities, such as CD-Rom, and on-line facilities enable large-scale data bases to be scanned quickly and effectively, and allow evaluators to conduct research reviews without necessarily undertaking the evaluation in the library itself.

The synthesis of research Approach typically includes the following steps:

1   formulating the area of enquiry;
2   collecting data;
3   evaluating the data;
4   analysis, interpretation and integration;
5   presenting the findings.

Several writers have provided advice on carrying out literature reviews for the purpose of undertaking further research and writing research theses see, for example, Cooper (1984) and Neuman (1997). This advice has been adapted for use when undertaking research synthesis as an Approach to Proactive evaluation (Smallwood & Hurworth, 1998). Principles of research synthesis include the following:

- The area of enquiry must be related to the proposed area of intervention or policy development.
- The search should be focused from the outset.

- The reviewer must be flexible about the relevance of individual contributions to the topic.
- Existing meta-reviews and annotated bibliographies can short-cut the review process.
- The reviewer must be systematic in documenting the progress of the search.
- In addition to the literature in journals, other sources may be consulted—for example, census records, parliamentary debates, unpublished reports, etc.
- The use of computer-based search engines is essential.
- There will be wide variation in the quality of the research reported and the reviewer must adopt criteria for evaluating each report.

The result of a literature synthesis is a 'reasoned description or interpretation of a body of literature'. Therefore, the report should first address the specific area of enquiry by providing a contextual background for the work and provide a progressive understanding of developments in the area. For evaluative purposes, the review must address the concerns of the audience and the purpose for which it was developed, taking into account the nature of the primary users.

The format of reporting is critical. The review must engage the client through the inclusion of:

- an introductory paragraph that introduces the evaluation issues;
- an overview of the organisation of the review;
- a descriptive discussion about the existing state of the research knowledge on the issues;
- conclusions about the major findings and their implications for future practice;
- an indication of those areas (if they exist) where the literature has little or nothing to say about the issues.

### Review of best practice (establishment of benchmarks)

There is no doubt that benchmarking has been one of the 'buzzwords' or vogue terms in management in the 1990s (Bendell et al., 1993). Basically, benchmarking is the search for best practices that can be applied with a view to achieving improved performance. Benchmarking is a systematic and continuous process of measuring and comparing an organisation's business processes against those of leaders anywhere in the world, to gain information which will help drive continuous improvement (Sharp, 1994).

Establishment of benchmarks in industry is consistent with the idea of 'a continuous systematic process of evaluating companies recognised as industry leaders, to determine business and work processes that represent best practices and establish rational performance goals' (Cross & Iqbal, 1994) Benchmarking involves systematic processes which involve searching for, introducing and implementing best practice. The search may focus on any of the major types of evaluands: organisations, policies, programs, services or products (Evans, 1994).

Because of the focus of this book, we concentrate on one particular type of benchmarking, that described as a data-driven model. In this model there is a heavy reliance on the use of information, collected directly from organisationally specific comparisons (Sharp, 1994) or from secondary sources, such as data bases (MacNeil et al., 1994). Cases of 'best practice' are located and identified, and the principles documented as an input to developing policies or programs based on the findings. This may involve comparisons with competitors. The documentation is the basis for assisting an organisation to create, implement and monitor programs based on the principles identified in the best practice cases.

A key is to locate practitioners who have shown that their practice has a superior edge in the provision of services or products in a given area. If possible, a range of case examples should be used to assemble evidence. Inductive methods of analysis are used to draw out the underlying assumptions and principles of action across the cases.

This Approach is based on an assumption that best or innovatory practice in the workplace should be disseminated and used more widely (Spendolini, 1992). Procedures must be employed to capture and transfer this knowledge to other users. The evaluator's role can be thought of as synthesising evidence from cases located at the hub of a wheel. Assembling the findings is akin to the evidence travelling inwards on spokes to the hub. Policies and programs are synthesised at the hub and are disseminated to other practitioners via other spokes of the wheel.

Initially popular in business, benchmarking has more recently been applied to the provision of government services. While a range of interpretations exist, benchmarking by an organisation generally includes the following stages:

1  the identification of the area of operation to be benchmarked;
2  identification of 'best practice' in selected organisations or sections of organisations;
3  collection and analysis to determine the common characteristics of this practice;

4 development of best practice indicators and levels to be achieved on these indicators;
5 communication of best practice indicators internally and gaining of acceptance;
6 development and implementation of plans to achieve these levels;
7 progress monitoring;
8 full integration of practice into the functioning of the organisation.

The organisation could move through these stages again at a later time, with a focus on a different area of operation.

For the purposes of this discussion, we divide the benchmarking process into two phases. The first relates to stages 1–4, the second to stages 4–8. We regard stages 1–4 as the establishment of benchmarks, while stages 5–8 represent the application of benchmarks to the operations of the organisation. In this Approach we are concerned only with the *establishment* of benchmarks, as this is consistent with an 'evaluation for development' perspective of Proactive evaluation. The *application* of benchmarks falls within the study of Monitoring evaluation Form (see Chapter 12).

Simply described, the establishment of benchmarks attempts to answer the following questions:

- Who is doing best?
- How do they do it?
- How well are we doing relative to the best?
- How good do we want to be, relative to the best?

In more formal terms, benchmarking establishment involves an organisation in:

- the targeted identification of best practice, and a consideration of whether this practice applies to the organisation;
- a thorough, sustained program of external analysis and investigation;
- the ability to reduce the findings of best practice to indicators which are meaningful as a management tool within the organisation.

## PROACTIVE EVALUATION: TRENDS AND CASE STUDIES

### Use of creative data management

Assembling evidence by the collection and analysis of data is an integral part of all evaluation studies. While the underlying principles of assembling evidence are the same across Forms, there are certain methods which are more likely to be useful for a given Form. Table 9.1 presents a summary of the most useful ways in which evidence can be assembled for studies which fit within the Proactive Form. For most evaluations, more than one type of data collection is required. The following example uses a combination of data collection techniques.

---

**Example 9.2 Workplace communication**

A state-level education department was preparing to develop a workplace basic education project, in which classes in reading, writing and oral communication could be provided during work time for employees. An important objective was to develop a program that would be responsive to the changing needs of industry, while at the same time acknowledging the need for a basic education for working people. It was important to locate workplaces where the need for such a program was greatest, and to use the most effective teaching strategies.

A needs assessment was the means of assembling information by which a responsive program could be developed. To determine the 'desired state', it was decided that a better knowledge of communication requirements in the workplace was necessary. A group of service providers agreed to support an evaluation team to identify and investigate workplace communication. The result was an in-depth review of the communication needs of workers on the job. Later, the 'existing state' of the workers' communication skills was established by administering a series of tests. This allowed an analysis of the gaps in the existing communication skills of the workers. The findings were used to plan a program that was designed to reduce the gap between the actual and desired situations.

---

In a more extensive study in the area of community-oriented needs assessment, Neuber (1980) used the following sources:

- information from public records to create demographic statistical profiles. The profiles included birth and death rates, and statistics on employment, crime and mental health;
- key informants, defined as people having direct contact with individuals having problems with living. Random samples were drawn from several relevant populations, including doctors, school counsellors and social agencies;

- consumers, for in community-orientated needs assessment, consumers must be consulted. Data were collected by individually interviewing a random sample of the adult population in the geographical area served by the projected program or service.

The advantage, from the point of view of drawing conclusions, is the use of triangulation—that is, the collection of data from three different but linked sources for comparison purposes. By focusing on similar issues it is possible to be more certain of conclusions than if the information were obtained from one source only.

Some Approaches within Proactive evaluation require the use of some creative and unique ways of assembling evidence, not used in other Forms. Generally, there is a need for investigatory and inductive methods of data collection and analysis. These methods are designed to gauge opinions of key players, or to gain consensus about the desired state for a prospective program, or the direction for action. These include:

- *Delphi technique.* This term is applied to methodology in which respondents work independently to pool their written ideas about a relevant issue. Each person is then given a copy of the collected ideas, appropriately developed into a set of scaled items, and asked to assess their relative importance. There is often more than one round of assessment, with the view of obtaining consensus (Dixon & Harding, 1990).

> **Example 9.3 Needs of staff employed in the welding industry**
>
> The Edison Welding Institute (EWI) is an umbrella organisation representing the interests of member companies and the welding industry at large in the United States. EWI employed an evaluation team to undertake a Delphi study of immediate and future educational needs of welding staff.
>
> Preliminary discussions were held with stakeholders to determine the major purposes of the study and the methodology to be used, including sampling.
>
> The purposes of the study were to:
>
> - identify critical education and training needs that could be addressed by the company within six to twelve months (immediate needs) and during the next three years (future needs);

- rank order each set of needs according to priorities of EWI member organisations;
- obtain respondents comments about these needs; and
- provide this information for use in planning EWI programs.

Regarding sampling, questionnaires were sent to official representatives of EWI member organisations across the United States. In addition, the project identified companies which might fall under the umbrella of the EWI in the future and sought the information from them.

Regarding methodology, the Delphi technique was reviewed and approved by the stakeholders of the project. It was decided to concentrate on industry-wide, rather than company-specific, problems as the basis for structuring the data collection.

Official representatives of EWI member organisations were initially contacted by telephone, as a means of establishing and maintaining a high degree of cooperation and commitment from the respondents. This strategy was based on research which showed that questionnaires work best when a bond is formed between respondents and evaluators. Approximately 300 telephone calls were made to 108 companies.

Representatives of the Institute across the country participated in the two Delphi rounds. In the first, an open-ended questionnaire encouraged respondents to offer ideas about immediate and future training needs. About 30 immediate problems and 40 future needs were synthesised from this procedure. A feature of the analysis was the use of technical knowledge of EWI staff to make sense of the problems and needs suggested by the respondents.

Based on these responses, a second questionnaire was developed. Respondents were asked to read 30 needs statements related to immediate problems, and to identify the seven most important. Space was also provided for respondents to comment on the items and to suggest additional items. An identical procedure was used for the 40 future needs statements. The analysis consisted of simple tabulations of rankings of these responses.

The study reported the following:

- Twenty-nine immediate problems and 40 future needs were synthesised from the results of Q1.

- High priority immediate and future education and training needs were identified by ranking 62 responses to Q2. Few comments or additional educational and training problems were submitted.

  The study thus provided EWI with base data for establishing both immediate and future education and training needs. In addition, the evaluators indicated that needs of employers were likely to change and that the Institute should consider routinely assessing the needs of its members. (Thomas & Altschuld, 1985)

- *Search conference*. A search conference is an event designed to give direction to a projected program or policy. It involves program staff and administration in a search for appropriated solutions, given their knowledge of the context in which the program is to be developed and delivered. To be effective, it must be carefully planned and custom designed. It is based on an assumption that people want to create their own futures, that they will act creatively and purposefully to achieve this end. In a search conference, participants will be engaged in issues such as: Where have we come from? Where do we want to go? What are the barriers and drivers to achieving desirable programs and activities? Participants are engaged in these questions as they relate to contextual issues and the system or organisation in which they work (Emery, 1990).

- *Nominal group forum*. The nominal group approach was developed to assist people to deal with problems, set priorities and review possibilities. The four essential stages of nominal group method are:

  1 the generation of ideas;
  2 recording of each idea;
  3 discussion of the ideas; and
  4 voting on the ideas.

- *Concept mapping*. Concept mapping is a technique used by groups to develop an understanding of a context in order to guide program planning. The term *structured conceptualisation* is used to define processes which involve a sequence of operationally defined steps leading to a conceptual representation of the context. There are six steps in concept mapping. These are:

184

1    preparation, which includes the selection of participants and the development of a focus to the exercise;
2    the generation of statements about the focus;
3    structuring these statements;
4    using statistical techniques such as multi-dimension scaling and cluster analysis to represent these statements as cluster maps;
5    interpretation of the maps; and
6    utilisation of findings (Trochim, 1989).

- *Focus group*. The focus group is a technique designed to collect information about an issue from a small group of selected people through group discussion. Compared with Delphi, where consensus is the desired outcome, the aim of focus groups is to get a range of views on an issue. The focus group has its origins in the work of Merton et al. (1956). In this seminal work, *The Focused Interview*, Merton found that valid and useful information could be collected from a small group of people through the creation of a relaxed and permissive environment. A key aspect of focus groups is the use of an expert moderator. The approach used in groups is to move from broader to more specific and substantive issues through the discussion. As with all data management techniques, the quality of data collection and analysis is crucial to the process. The technique has assumed wide popularity in market research and in political polling in recent times, and has been the subject of numerous texts (see, for example, Krueger (1988)).

### Proactive evaluation as an agent of change

As indicated earlier, Proactive evaluation can support radical changes in an existing program that is seen to be out of date or not serving the needs of those for whom it was intended. The following is an example of this scenario in which a research review was the evaluation Approach used.

### Example 9.4 Is the music curriculum in dire straits?

Policy-makers in the curriculum branch of a Ministry of Education were concerned about the content and practice in the teaching of music in government schools. While most schools offered music programs, some officials believed that the curriculum was unresponsive to the needs of the large majority of students. An evaluation study was commissioned to investigate the accuracy of these perceptions and to provide guidelines for a revision of music curriculum policy. An important aspect of the evaluation was a major review of recent research on essential elements of school music programs designed to respond to the interests and needs of young people. The review involved a computer-based literature search of worldwide publications in the area, an analysis of recent national documentation, and interviews with music curriculum personnel in the Ministry and in selected schools. An extensive review was written, based on the material collected. (Stringer & Owen, 1986)

The next example is also one where the study was designed to encourage change to the status quo. In this case, the Approach used was a best practice review, rather than a research synthesis. The use of this Approach requires the evaluator to identify examples of best practice from which to collect evidence. This involves the selection of sites and is basically a question of sampling. The evaluator may have to develop criteria for site selection. In some cases, the evaluator may have to rely on the advice of experts when selecting sites. This was the case here.

## Example 9.5 Youth culture and the arts

This study, funded through a national arts project, was designed to document ways in which teachers of the arts incorporated the interests of youth into the curriculum of the senior secondary school. The data base was eight case studies of exemplary practice in schools in four states. A set of criteria was assembled and arts consultants in these states were asked to identify teachers whose practice was consistent with these criteria. The sites were visited throughout the year to discover the essential characteristics of the programs and factors which led to their development. The data were used in a cross-site analysis to discover common features of the innovative programs. This was the subject of a major report that was distributed to policy-makers and schools across the nation.

# IMPETUS OF BENCHMARKING

Supporting best practice by both the private and public sectors has become a major theme in most Western democracies over the past decade. This has been fuelled by global competition and the need for these democracies to be competitive and maintain standards of living for their citizens.

---

**Example 9.6 The Australian Best Practice Program**

Announced by the Federal Government in March 1991, the program's objectives were to:

- stimulate Australian enterprises to adopt international best practice;
- identify effective methods and approaches for the implementation of best practice in Australian enterprises; and
- promote a wider understanding of best practice and benefits of its adoption by Australian enterprises.

The program had two components:

- *funding best practice projects within companies* which were used as role models for industry. Funding included a demonstration element which required companies to share their experiences with others in the business community. This included hosting visits, speaking at seminars, and preparing case studies.
- *dissemination of experiences*, including a comprehensive program of conferences, seminars and site visits across the country.

Benchmarking has also influenced the public sector. There are promising signs of the creative development and use of benchmarks within local government. In a small-scale study, it was found that city councils responded to a National Benchmarking Project by comparing the way they undertook the provision of services with other councils known to be leaders in the area. One council concentrated on services such as parks and gardens maintenance, valuations and drainage. The other concentrated on its election processes, community consultation and community grants.

---

There are indications that the evaluative aspect of benchmarking initiatives has been hampered by a lack of internal evaluative skills in both the private and public sectors. This will have to be ameliorated if the full effect of transferability of quality practice implied in the benchmarking movement is to be transferred into full effect across systems embracing its ideals.

## CONCLUSION

This chapter discusses the Proactive Form of evaluation. These are sometimes known as 'up-front', in that they are undertaken before policies and programs are planned and implemented. The role of the evaluator is to marshal evidence and provide findings which will assist in decision-making about whether a program should be mounted and, if so, the content and strategies to adopt in a given social intervention.

As with all evaluations, it is important that Proactive evaluation be responsive to the concerns of the client, which in this case is the potential developer. Three major Approaches and some methodological techniques have been outlined. The choice of Approach, and the methods within each Approach, must be made with knowledge of an individual situation. This is up to the evaluator in consultation with the client, to decide. Choosing between evaluation options requires the evaluator to have a repertoire of skills. In Proactive evaluation, some novel data management techniques have been employed. There is clearly a need for expertise in 'up-front' evaluation Approaches and opportunities currently exist for evaluators to specialise in this Form of evaluation.

## REFERENCES

Bendell, T., Boulter, L. & Kelly, J. (1993). *Benchmarking for Competitive Advantage*. London: Pitman Publishing.

Cooper, H.M. (1984). *The Integrated Research Review: A Systematic Approach*. Beverly Hills, CA: Sage.

Cross, R. & Iqbal, A. (1994). 'The Rank Xerox Experiment: Benchmarking Ten Years On'. In A. Rolstadas (ed.), *Benchmarking: Theory and Practice*. London: Chapman and Hall, pp. 3–10.

Dixon, J. & Harding, G. (1990). 'DELPHI Forecasting Methodology'. In *Proceedings of the National Conference of the Australasian Evaluation Society*. 1. Sydney, pp. 255–8.

Emery, M. (1990). 'The Search Conference as Evaluation Planning'. In *Proceedings of the National Evaluation Conference of the Australasian Evaluation Society*. 1 Sydney, pp. 259–62.

Evans, A. (1994). *Benchmarking*. Melbourne: Information Australia.

Krueger, R. (1988). *Focus Groups: A Practical Guide for Applied Research*. Newbury Park, CA: Sage.

MacNeil, J., Testi, J., Cupples, J. & Rimmer, M. (1994). *Benchmarking Australia*. Melbourne: Longman.

Merton, R.K., Fiske, M. & Kendall, P.L. (1956). *The Focused Interview*. Glencoe, MA: The Free Press.

Neuber, K.A. (1980). *Needs Assessment: A Model for Community Planning*. Beverly Hills, CA: Sage.

Neuman, L.W. (1997). *Social Science Research Methods: Qualitative and Quantitative Approaches*. 3rd edn. Boston: Allyn & Bacon.

Roth, J. (1990). 'Needs and the Needs Assessment Process'. *Evaluation Practice*, 11 (2), 39–44.

Scriven, M. (1991). *Evaluation Thesaurus*. 4th edn. Newbury Park, CA: Sage.

Sharp, C.A. (1994). 'Industry Best-Practice Benchmarking in the Evaluation Context'. *Evaluation News and Comment*, 3 (1), 27–33.

Smallwood, H. & Hurworth, R.E. (1998). 'Literature Synthesis for Program Planning and Policy Development'. *Evaluation News and Comment*, 7, 1 (June), 37–44.

Spendolini, M.J. (1992). *The Benchmarking Book*. New York: AMACOM.

Stringer, W. & Owen, J.M. (1986). *Is the Music Curriculum in Dire Straits?* Melbourne: Centre for Program Evaluation, Melbourne College of Advanced Education.

Thomas, P.M. & Altschuld, J.W. (1985). 'Evaluators as Needs Assessment Consultants: An Application of the Delphi Technique to the Study of Education and Training Needs'. Paper presented at the joint meeting of the Canadian Evaluation Society, Evaluation Network and Evaluation Research Society. Toronto, ON.

Trochim, W.M.K. (1989). 'An Introduction to Concept Mapping for Planning and Evaluation'. *Evaluation and Program Planning*, 12, 1–16.

Witkin, B.R. & Altschuld, J.W. (1995). *Planning and Conducting Needs Assessments*. Thousand Oaks, CA: Sage.

# 10

# Clarificative Evaluation

## INTRODUCTION

More than ever before, there is widespread concern for the effective and efficient use of resources provided for policy and program provision, especially in the public sector. Once there was a naive belief among politicians and the public at large that, by merely increasing the level of funding to an area of need, the wellbeing of groups targeted for support would improve. This has been problematic. For example, reviews of programs to support indigenous communities in North America and Australasia reveal that, unless wise and responsive program planning was undertaken in conjunction with the provision of these funds, resources have been squandered, leaving target groups little or no better off.

In business, managers who release funds for interventions such as staff development want to be satisfied that the funds they provide for training are likely to contribute to the productivity of the organisation. Yet executives of many organisations report no additional benefits of training despite massive resource inputs, due to the fact that the principles underlying the training are unsound, or the delivery of training is incomplete (Brinkerhoff, 1989).

In the helping professions, planners and providers have been committed to a view that social and educational interventions, taken collectively, will have the desired effects on participants and lead to a society which is better educated, healthier and more just. However, to be more certain that these ends are achieved, sound and responsive program planning is a must. Yet experience suggests that this is an area where systematic methods and expertise

**Table 10.1    Summary of Clarificative evaluation (Form B)**

| Dimension | Properties |
|---|---|
| Orientation | Clarification of program design including explication of program delivery |
| Typical issues | • What are the intended outcomes and how is the program designed to achieve them?<br>• What is the underlying rationale for this program?<br>• What program elements need to be modified in order to maximise the intended outcomes?<br>• Is the program plausible?<br>• Which aspects of this program are amenable to a subsequent monitoring or impact assessment? |
| State of program | Developmental |
| Major focus | All program elements |
| Timing (vis-à-vis program delivery) | Can be used to develop program *ab initio* but more likely to be during delivery, with particular relevance during early stages of program delivery |
| Key Approaches | • Evaluability assessment<br>• Logic/theory development<br>• Accreditation |
| Assembly of evidence | Generally relies on combination of document analysis, interview and observation. Findings include program plan and implications for the organisation. Process can lead to improved morale among program providers. |

are needed. The evaluator has a part to play in the planning processes. This can be achieved through the use of Approaches that fall within the Clarificative evaluation Form (Form B). Note that in a previous edition of this book, this Form of evaluation was labelled as Design evaluation.

Clarificative evaluation leads to better policy and program planning and explicit program designs. Over the past decade, interest in this Form of evaluation has burgeoned as organisations and government agencies have looked for support to overcome barriers to more effective program development.

*Clarificative evaluation* is concerned with:

• description of programs;

- analysis of the logic or theory of programs;
- plausibility of program design;
- consistency between program design and implementation; and
- providing a basis for subsequent program monitoring or impact evaluation.

Program clarification has a strong formative purpose. Normally, the evaluator works closely with program management and deliverers to conceptualise and describe the characteristics of a program and, in some cases, to provide validation of its quality. Table 10.1 sets out the basic features of Clarificative evaluation in terms of the key dimensions of the Form.

## KEY APPROACHES TO CLARIFICATIVE EVALUATION

Evaluative processes which lead to program specification have evolved over time. In the past, inadequacies in the specifications of many social and educational programs emerged when evaluators were asked to carry out traditional outcome evaluations of these programs. Evaluators in these circumstances found that they were asked to evaluate 'non-events'—programs with little or no documentation. Sometimes programs existed with vague goals which provided little direction for those responsible for program delivery. From the point of view of evaluators undertaking impact evaluations, there was little or no basis for developing outcome measures, required as the basis for collecting information about impact to serve accountability purposes.

In the early 1970s, Wholey (1983) and others, working as internal evaluators across departments of the United States Government, developed procedures designed to overcome these deficiencies. These included efforts to improve the quality of program design and to provide a firmer basis for subsequent outcomes evaluation. These efforts aimed to:

- identify the 'real' goals or intentions of a given program as distinct from the stated ones, as the basis for management of that program;
- identify unrealistic goals that were unachievable through the program and for which managers could not be held accountable;
- obtain consensus about goals held by different program providers;
- elaborate the program through attention to how it worked in practice as a way of making the program more plausible to policy-makers;
- identify various perceptions among managers and site-level

providers about the program in an attempt to identify the underlying program logic.

An outcomes evaluation could not take place until the evaluator worked with program management to clarify what had been learned in the design stage. The evaluator presented a model of the program: 'that portion of the program which is currently manageable in terms of a set of realistic program objectives and agreed on program performance indicators' (Wholey, 1983). Thus the evaluator identified those aspects of the program which were amenable to rigorous evaluation designs for which 'measurable' data was available. Effectively this meant that those aspects not amenable were not included in the evaluation design.

## EVALUABILITY ASSESSMENT

Partly because of the emphasis on identifying measurable outcomes, the Approach developed by Wholey is now known as *evaluability assessment*, or EA (Rutman, 1980). Evaluability assessment continues to be a key Approach to Clarificative evaluation. However, EA devotees have modified the outcomes emphasis, towards a greater weight on design clarification as an end in its own right. There is now less emphasis on the clarification as a precursor to carrying out an impact evaluation. There has also been an orientation towards more involvement of stakeholders in the EA process.

The primary purposes of EA are to:

- refine program theory—that is, the underlying cause and effects relationships and functional aspects (resources and activities) with indicators of evidence for determining when planned activities are implemented and when intended and unintended outcomes are achieved; and
- identify stakeholders' awareness of and interest in a program—that is, their perceptions of what a program is meant to achieve, their concerns about program progress, perceptions of resource support and interests in evaluative information (for a variety of purposes). Stakeholders include all interested parties—for example, those providing resources, program managers and program deliverers.

There is now a strong process element in EA which leads to increased program commitment. Midge Smith (1989b) reports that, after undertaking six major EAs in cooperative extension services such as master gardening programs and water conservation studies, one of the changes from the original conceptualisation of the process was the intense involvement of the program staff in every step. That change resulted in what I perceive as being one of the most important outcomes of the Cooperative Extension Services' EAs, *change in team member attitudes, knowledge and skills about evaluation and programming.* (Smith, 1989b, author's emphasis)

Smith goes on to note that, when a program is being planned, the first of the two purposes described above is the end point of the EA—that is, the outcome is a comprehensive program description. However, when the focus is an existing program, an effective EA will lead to a clarification of design and an increased commitment to the implementation of the design. Policy-makers and program planners should thus be interested in evaluations which follow approaches suggested by Smith.

## PROGRAM LOGIC (OR PROGRAM THEORY)

Consequent to the work in EA, there has been an emphasis on the roles of evaluators in the construction and testing of program logic, or program theory. These terms tend to be used interchangeably. In view of the increasing acceptance of the term 'evaluation theory' (see, for example, Shadish et al. (1991)), we will use the term 'program logic' here. This serves to maintain a clear distinction between concepts that underlie current thinking about evaluation and program design respectively. According to Chen (1990), logic (theory) in this sense is defined as 'a set of interrelated assumptions, principles, and/or propositions to explain or guide social actions'.

Central to program logic is the nature of program causality, the ordering of events in such a way that the presence of one event or action leads to, or causes, a subsequent event or action. In programmatic terms, one could ask whether mechanism X causes outcome Y. While philosophers tell us that we can never be certain that X causes Y, it seems that unless we think in a causal fashion, there is no basis for developing interventions of any kind. Causal thinking is the fundamental basis for program planning.

The development of a means–ends hierarchy is an essential element of program logic. Patton (1997) and others have recommended the construction of a chain of objectives, the links between them implying the existence of actions where an objective at one level must be attained before the next can be accomplished. This notion of a program hierarchy is useful in that it largely does away with the often-unhelpful distinction between outputs

194

and outcomes which appear in some branches of the strategic planning literature. In terms of clarifying program logic, Patton recommends that evaluators use techniques that are inductive, pragmatic and highly concrete. He sees the development of program logic as an end in itself, in the same way that later proponents of EA have. For example, Patton says:

> At times, helping program staff or decision makers to articulate their programmatic theory of action is an end in itself. Evaluators are called on, not only to gather data, but also to assist in program design. Knowing how to turn a vague discussion of the presumed linkages between program activities and expected outcomes into a formal theory of action can be an important service to the program . . . On many occasions then, the evaluation data collection may include discovering and formalising the program's theory of action.

This is fundamental to the Clarificative Form of evaluation.

Likewise, Chen (1990) and his colleagues argue that evaluators should be engaged in program logic development: the creation of a model of how a given program should work, the explication of the how and why. This involves recognition of crucial patterns and the development of a comprehensive framework in which these patterns are included. Chen distinguishes between two phases of evaluator action: normative and summative. In the normative phase, the program's logical structure is developed. In the summative phase, the model is tested in some way by empirical means.

We are mostly concerned in the Clarificative Form with the normative phase, in which the logic is developed and evaluators assist stakeholders in identifying, clarifying or developing goals or outcomes. 'Causal theory specifies the underlying causal mechanisms which link, mediate or condition the causal relationship between the treatment variable(s) and outcome variable(s) in a program' (Chen, 1990).

Stakeholders are consulted to determine their assumptions and expectations, along with an analysis of documentation supporting the program. The evaluator constructs a tentative model in which discrepancies are highlighted and, once these are resolved, a formal program model is produced. Thus there are similarities with EA and with Patton's (1997) methods described above.

But Chen (1990) departs from the high reliance on stakeholders' views because he maintains that they may not enable the clearest articulation of the complexity of the program's causal links. Chen likes to use social science theory to bolster information collected from stakeholders. This means gathering what is already known about the social or educational phenomenon under review. This is the use of the research review Approach within the Proactive Form, and is an illustration of how different Approaches can be used in conjunction. An example would be to review the literature on staff development to ensure that a given training program is well grounded in addition to consulting with the program providers to include characteristics of the setting in the program design. Thus the evaluator brings his or her training and knowledge of the relevant research base to bear on the problem and constructs a model based on several sources. For some evaluators, reliance on social science theory would be attractive in itself; however, in practice, we see the combination of information from research reviews and from stakeholders—particularly those actually providing the program—as most effective.

The process deals with program goals which are important in legitimising the program. It draws together the stakeholders and helps them understand resource requirements, and establishes where possible a conceptual base for the program from an external frame of reference. In addition, Chen (1990) is interested in developing criteria for establishing program effectiveness, also an aim of Clarificative evaluation.

More recently, Weiss (1996) undertook a review of the use of program logic in evaluation practice. She makes an interesting distinction between program delivery and mechanisms that intervene between program delivery and the attainment of outcomes. These mechanisms are the responses to program delivery. She cites an example of a contraceptive counselling service.

> If contraceptive counselling is associated with reduction in pregnancy, the cause of the change might seem to be the counselling. But the mechanism isn't the counselling; that is the program activity, the program process. A common assumption would be that the mechanism is the knowledge that the counselling provides. But knowledge might not be the operating mechanism. It might be that the existence of the counselling program helps to overcome cultural taboos against family planning; it might give women confidence and bolster their assertiveness in sexual relationships; it might trigger a shift in the power relationships between men and women. These or any of several other cognitive/affective/social responses would be the mechanisms leading to the desired outcomes.

Weiss makes an important point that full explication of a program should involve program logic in terms of mechanisms and details about delivery—how the program is to be implemented. She describes evaluations which include both as *theories of change (TOC) evaluations*. It should be noted that in program clarification we are concerned with implementation as much as with mechanisms expressed in one way or another, which is consistent with the Weiss view. Clearly some of these mechanisms must reside within the implementation and some in the ways in which participants react to the implementation process. This is a rich area for further evaluation research.

It should also be noted that the development of program logic can provide a means by which the program can be both clarified and monitored over time.

Funnell (1997) has developed a framework that includes:

- hierarchy of outcomes;
- program activities and resources;
- factors within program control; and
- factors outside program control.

Components of the 'monitoring' element include, for each level of the hierarchy:

- success criteria and standards for activities and outcomes;
- performance information; and
- judgments/interpretations.

Funnell's work is among the most advanced in terms of its contribution to helping organisations deal with the practical problems of program delivery. Her work is also an example of two evaluation Forms, Clarificative and Monitoring, being used together.

---

**Example 10.1 Identifying important components and gaps in programs**

Program clarification can be useful for clarifying new programs and including those not involved in tangible service delivery. Funnell's program logic Approach was used with an organisation that promotes standards-based school reform at the state and national levels. An evaluation team, working with senior management, developed a framework which included ultimate intended outcomes of the program, how the program's activities were intended to lead to them, and the important intermediate outcomes. In addition, the evaluation team identified factors which could influence the achievement of each outcome, and what the program was currently doing to achieve them. This analysis helped the program administrators to identify gaps in their program logic and to recognise the importance of particular program activities. (Rogers & Huebner, 1998)

## ACCREDITATION

Accreditation is a third and very practical procedure or Approach to program clarification. This usually involves external agencies composed of experts in the field who act to validate the plans of the agency under review.

Accreditation had its genesis in the need for professional bodies to offer or sanction professional training for its members. Accreditation is thought of as the process of professionals judging the worth of fellow professionals. In more recent times, the notion has been extended to allow for an external group to undertake the judgment of an agency in order that the public may have confidence that the work of the agency is up to standard. Accreditation can be thought of as a type of quality assurance. The adoption of the ISO 9000 accreditation procedures, for example, involves the management of organisations defining and describing their policies and programs with a view to ensuring that they meet the standards of quality inherent in the ISO 9000 framework.

Accreditation not only involves actual programs, but also the ways in which the agency offering the programs is organised. In the accreditation process, it is common for an accreditation board to require modifications and clarifications to programs. The major reason for including accreditation here is that its major leverage is to ensure that policies and programs are 'up to date'. Negotiation between the accreditation board and agency management and staff generally leads to more revised and more explicit program descriptions. It is rare for accreditation to be concerned directly with program implementation. Relative to the other Approaches in this chapter, program designs that result from accreditation are likely to be far less systematic, with less attention to empirical data collection and analysis in the process of clarifying the policies and programs under review.

## CLARIFICATIVE EVALUATION: TRENDS AND CASE STUDIES

### Assembling evidence

Table 10.1 provides a summary of ways in which data management can be carried out in Clarificative evaluation. There is high reliance on the collection of information which will assist the evaluator to construct a plausible program plan and to lay out findings in ways that are readily understood by program managers and deliverers. Major sources of information are documentation, interviews and observations. Visits to the program site are essential.

Clarificative evaluation studies:

- should take into account the ideas that have been developed by theorists who have developed the principles of the key Approaches;
- involve the evaluator in a creative exercise involving the synthesis of information from a range of sources;
- should include, as a product of the evaluation, an articulated program plan and an indication of their implementation potential.

As we have indicated, a key Approach is evaluability assessment (EA). A number of methodologies have been suggested for undertaking EAs. Smith's (1989b) contribution is the most comprehensive and recent, and is summarised below.

1 *Determine purpose, secure commitment, and identify evaluation team members.*
An evaluator with experience in EA should be a key member of the evaluation task team which should be composed of members of the organisation responsible for the program. Time is needed for the evaluation team to commit themselves to the program. A key task of the evaluation team is to identify the stakeholders and key influential decision-makers. Then the team needs to meet stakeholders and other influentials to explain the EA process.

2 *Define evaluation boundaries of program to be studied.*
There is no hard and fast rule for defining the boundaries of the program. Smith suggests two factors should be taken into account: the importance of the program and decisions likely to be made. EAs should only be undertaken on a major program, not an isolated one-day event. Similarly, evaluators may need to ask decision-makers how an EA would be useful in decision making before they decide to put resources into the evaluation effort. If the findings are not likely to make a difference, the EA should not be undertaken.

3 *Identify and analyse program documents.*
Document analysis is central to the EA process. This includes legislation, hearings, debates, reports, policy statements, memoranda, research syntheses, program guidelines and resource statements. Smith counsels to read documents with care.

Conflicting documentary statements regarding what is intended and what is being accomplished may point to confusion among program personnel who read these documents and those who produce them. Two other suggestions are:

1   note the purpose of each document: publicity handouts may contain mostly rhetoric whereas internal materials probably deal more with reality, albeit political; and

2   identify quoted notes so that documents can be referenced and located later on.

4 *Develop and clarify program theory.*
The approach is to develop a model closest to that which mirrors the reality of the implementation. Essentially the exercise is the identification of the most critical, and to some extent general, elements of the program. Extensive consultation is necessary between members of the evaluation team and key program staff. The exercise is best completed by involving those who have a close working knowledge with what the program is like in the field, perhaps representing different levels of implementation. Smith (1989b) notes that program staff who form part of the evaluation team are those most likely to benefit from developing the theory, and thus it is important for them to be involved as much as possible in the exercise. Once the model has been developed, it should be returned to selected program staff for validation.

5 *Identify and interview stakeholders and describe their perceptions of the program.*

6 *Identify stakeholders' needs, concerns and differences in perceptions.*
Here the aim is to collect information concerning knowledge and opinions about the program from the stakeholders. The major aim is to identify the awareness of and interest in the program. Information is generally collected by interviews and usual canons of data collection and analysis related to interviews apply. The key issues in these sections are to compare stakeholders' perceptions of the program with the program model, to validate any differences with more data, and to present an interim report on the findings to the primary client and other stakeholders.

7 *Determine plausibility of program model.*
Plausibility is defined as the existence of necessary and sufficient conditions for a program to succeed. Components of a successful program are:

•   a clear intention to bring about outcomes in participants;
•   activities sufficient in quality and quantity to bring about the expected outcomes;

200

- sufficient resources to implement these activities.

Judgments of program staff and other stakeholders should be used to work towards a plausible program. Interviews and group meetings are vehicles for determining whether the above conditions apply. When the goal of the EA is to plan a program, the question is one of intent; when the program is in action, the EA is used to work towards a plausibility of action.

8 *Draw conclusions and make recommendations.*

Smith notes that conclusions are made throughout the EA, and that generally clients want recommendations to be made. As with all evaluations, she recommends that conclusions should be drawn with the best possible backup information.

9 *Plan specific uses for utilisation of findings of the study.*
Five possible decisions are possible. These are to decide to;

- stop the program, if it has not yet been implemented;
- change the program, if it has been implemented;
- undertake an outcomes evaluation, if the program as implemented is faithful to the refined program plan;
- take no further action;
- take no notice of the findings of the EA.

It is the responsibility of the evaluator to come up with the product, on the basis of the evidence that has been assembled and analysed. Coming up with a plausible program plan, whether it be in the form of a flow diagram, program logic or a written description, requires a combination of analytical and developmental data management skills.

## Products of Clarificative evaluation

Fundamental to Clarificative evaluation is the portrayal of the design or plan of the program under review in the evaluation findings. It is up to the evaluator, in conjunction with the clients, to determine ways in which the design will be reported. A variety of formats exist, ranging from Boolean diagrams to extensive prose descriptions. The evaluator is encouraged to be creative in the use of these formats. Some examples follow.

### Line diagrams

Clients may require only a rough conceptualisation of a program as a line diagram, shown in Example 10.2.

## Example 10.2 The Job and Course Explorer (JAC) program

Job and Course Explorer (JAC) was a program designed to provide advice to young people about jobs and further study after secondary school. A major feature of JAC is a comprehensive data base of jobs and post-school courses. One aim of an evaluation of JAC was to identify the program logic of the JAC program as it had evolved over time. A round of visits to schools and employment agencies suggested that JAC in practice operated in the following ways:

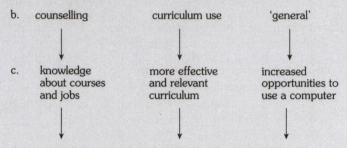

a. central policy development and resource production

b.   counselling              curriculum use           'general'

c.   knowledge about courses and jobs     more effective and relevant curriculum     increased opportunities to use a computer

d. increased linkage between formal secondary education and requirements of the labour market and further education

A primary goal was to outline how a policy was being implemented at different site types (libraries, schools, prisons, etc.). The evaluation not only developed a conceptual model of implementation, but also described the relative importance of the major arms or activities, and assessed their effectiveness in achieving the overall goals of the JAC initiative. The development of what became the beginnings of a program logic arose from visits to sites. The approach is consistent with the development of a grounded theory (Glaser & Strauss, 1967), and the use of investigatory methods of data management (Smith, 1992).

### Flow diagrams

Many studies include flow diagrams in their reports, using them as a basis for discussion. Figure 10.1 shows a program logic as a series of if/then statements, used as the basis for planning the development of a water conservation program in the United States (Smith, 1989a).

**Figure 10.1   Program logic for a water conservation program**

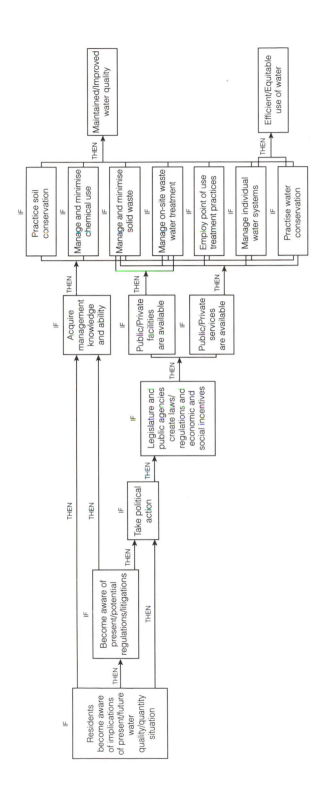

**Figure 10.2  Program logic for an innovatory rehabilitation program**

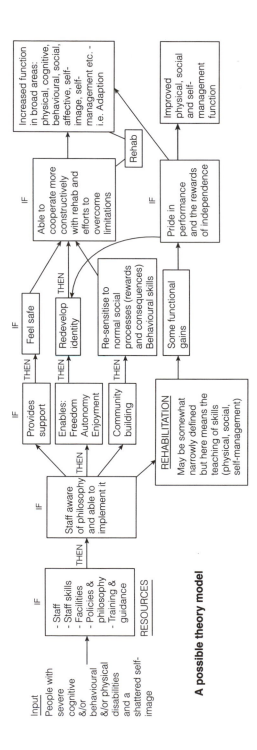

A possible theory model

Figure 10.2 describes the logic of a rehabilitation intervention for people who incurred serious head injuries as a result of road trauma. Batterham (1991) developed the logic to assist management and staff providing the service to clarify the program plan, regarded as innovatory in rehabilitation care. Some of the model linkages highlight the more innovative approaches to rehabilitation, with those in the middle blocks representing support, autonomy and community building. Batterham remarks that:

> this model assumes that many head injured people can run up against a wall of behavioural and self image problems that slow or halt functional progress. Traditional rehabilitation approaches (represented by the lower line on the model) would have abandoned these patients when progress halted due to these problems.

### Objectives hierarchies

Another way in which a program can be represented is through an objectives hierarchy. A hierarchy represents a chain of objectives (or outcomes) in such a way that any one objective in the chain is the outcome of the attainment of the previous objective and, in turn, needs to be attained before the next objective in the hierarchy can be reached.

In Example 10.3, an outcomes hierarchy for a family welfare program titled Shared Action is outlined. A feature of this program is that it has nested projects located within it. The nature of each project is determined by providers, so their logic is dependent on the actual projects selected. The program logic was developed by an external evaluation working closely with providers at the commencement of the program.

Example 10.4 is a more complex hierarchy. It depicts an innovative school curriculum based on individual student use of notebook computers in the classroom. This curriculum was introduced as a pilot at one year level, Year 5, for students about 10 years of age, before being considered for use more widely across the school. Note that in addition to the objectives, Example 10.4 contains a set of underlying assumptions. One can think of them as providing a rationale for the relevance of each objective.

In this study, evaluators were invited into the school where the expectation was that they would perform an impact evaluation of the Year 5 notebook program. However, in common with many similar situations, it became clear that there was a need to conceptualise the program, rather than to be concerned, at an early stage of implementation, with student outcomes. This objectives hierarchy was developed and reported to the school. This provided explicit direction for the implementation of the notebook curriculum over the next three years across other grade levels, and a framework by which the curriculum could be monitored. In this evaluation, a flow diagram was *also* constructed and is presented as Figure 10.3.

Writing about this study, we said:

> [Figure 10.3] identifies the full range of program consequences and, in addition, places the program within the context of the total school system. Comparisons between this information and program documentation showed that the school had failed, in its initial planning, to anticipate the consequences of the program for: work that was already being done in specialist computer classes which continued during the trial; existing methods of student assessment and reporting which were standardised for Years 5, 6 and 7; and communication between teachers from different campuses. (Owen & Lambert, 1995)

Inclusion of implications for the school as a whole appear in the lower part of Figure 10.3. This reflects the more general conclusion that the introduction of an innovation into an organisation has implications for the organisation as a whole, and that evaluations should be sensitive to this fact. Merely providing findings about the program without attending to organisational consequences often leaves decision-makers with less than a satisfactory level of information about what action to take.

### Descriptive product

By comparison, Example 10.5 provides a description of a scenario in which Clarificative evaluation was undertaken to develop policy and disseminate it to users. The focus of the study was again an innovation known as Enterprise Education. In this case, the audience for the report comprised principals and staff of rural schools who were served by a state-level agency called the Country Education Project. We decided that the most effective style of reporting to schools was a simple short-prose style. Thus no diagrams were used to outline the essential features of the program. The report included some key elements of program design in prose form: objectives, implementation and rationale. Again mindful of the interaction between program innovation and organisational change, we included a section titled 'Integrating Student Enterprise into the School Curriculum'. The outcome was a consolidated Program Plan (big P because this could be thought of as a macro program which has been synthesised out of ten innovatory small programs). This study is consistent with what Weiss (1996) has labelled a 'theory of change' evaluation.

**Example 10.3 Program logic: shared vision**

| Program logic | Program assumptions | Project A | Project A assumption | Project B | Project B assumption | Project C | Project C assumption | Evaluative questions | Data management (monitoring) | Data management (impact) |
|---|---|---|---|---|---|---|---|---|---|---|
| | | | | | | | | What is the initial level of wellbeing of families associated with the sites chosen? | | Sample of families from site population. Choice of repondents. Choice of instrument to assess level of wellbeing at start of project. Need instrument which has face validity. (Scott Clarke?) |
| Develop program guidelines which set out the Shared Action vision | Core program staff need to have a clear understanding of the way Shared Action will work in advance of involving others in the program. | | | | | | | Have the guidelines been made clear to the satisfaction of the Advisory Committee? Has a brochure been developed? | For this and all following questions, evaluation designed to check progress and provide the basis for providing an account of the project. Data management to rely on diaries and records. Possibility of support from local sources. | |
| Provide guidelines of Shared Action to school principal/council | Schools are the most appropriate sites for locating the program in the community, to access these sites, permission must be obtained from those with responsibility for the school. | | | | | | | Has a rationale for the selection of sites (schools) been developed? Have the sites been approached and the vision of the program outlined? Have the sites agreed to participate and under what conditions? What have we learnt from the program so far? | See above | |

| | | | |
|---|---|---|---|
| Set up local planning committee and inform them of potential benefits of Shared Action | Local involvement in the program must be built in from the start to ensure long-term commitment to the program and to maintain it once the temporary system is withdrawn | How was the committee set up? What was their initial reaction to the program? | See above |
| Undertake neighbour-hood assessment consistent with Shared Vision rationale | Selected projects must respond to the perceived needs at each site in addition to being consistent with the Shared Action vision. | How was the assessment conducted? | See above |
| Identify priorities for Shared Action projects (at each site) | The program will have maximum impact if available resources are directed towards a small number of priorities consistent with the Shared Action vision. | How were the priorities arrived at? How did the core staff ensure that these priorities were consistent with the Shared Action vision? What have we learnt from the program so far? | See above |

| Activity | Assumptions / Notes | Plan project A (e.g. creation of family support clusters). | | Plan project B (e.g. working with children at risk). | <Add assumptions for project B> | Plan project C (e.g. community knowledge dissemination). | <Add assumptions for project C> | Questions | |
|---|---|---|---|---|---|---|---|---|---|
| Plan site Shared Action projects in conjunction with local planning committee | Each project must have sufficient structure in advance in order for key players to have shared understandings of its intentions. | Plan project A | At-risk parents often lack social supports. If a family lives in a neighbour-hood where resources are scarce and social isolation is common then they are more likely to be at risk. | Plan project B | | Plan project C | | How were the projects set up? What were the key roles for program staff? | See above |
| Identify services, organisations and informal supports for each Shared Action project | The major role of core program staff is not to provide services direct, but to organise, coordinate and provide support for existing service providers. | Identify key themes, provide substantive input, identify providers, maintain project. | | Identify key themes, provide substantive input, identify providers, maintain project. | | Identify key themes, provide substantive input, identify providers, maintain project. | | How did the core staff encourage other providers to participate in each project? What were the benefits of each project? What were the problems in implementation of each project? What have we learnt from the program so far? | See above |
| Encourage adoption of Shared Action principles in communities | Shared Action is a temporary system with a finite life. The objectives of the program can be institutionalised at the sites if core staff can assist site planning committee to integrate the Shared Level vision into site level programs. | | | | | | | What strategies were successful in transferring the key elements of the program to sites? Under what local conditions was this possible? What are the implications for existing family support services? | See above |

| | | | | | |
|---|---|---|---|---|---|
| Assist sites to mount new projects consistent with the vision which will be implemented without program support | Local communities may need support from Shared Action at the outset to mount their own shared action program. | | Was it possible for sites to plan projects with fewer resources? To what extent were new projects implemented? On reflection of the program as a whole, what have its benefits been? What have its failures been? Has it achieved its objectives? | See above | Sample of families from school population. Choice of respondent. Use of instrument to assess level of wellbeing at conclusion of project. Use of initial instrument with modified wording. |
| | | | What is the final level of wellbeing of families associated with the sites chosen? Has the program made a difference? What factors made the difference? | See above | |

# Example 10.4 An objectives hierarchy for the notebook computer initiative

| Hierarchy of objectives | Underlying assumptions |
| --- | --- |
| **III. Ultimate objectives** | |
| 15. To enhance students' ability to participate and contribute in a rapidly changing technological world. | Individuals who can participate in and contribute positively to the society at large will have a greater sense of personal control and lead more fulfilling lives. |
| 14. To create a more rewarding teaching/learning environment. | Computer use enhances the quality of the classroom teaching/learning environment. |
| 13. To integrate notebook computer use into the curriculum (i.e. to crate a notebook curriculum). | Learning opportunities will be enhanced if computer use is integrated into the curriculum, not just regarded as a specialist, 'add on' skill remote from daily work. |
| 12. To enhance awareness of the capability of computer technology. | All students require computer skills. (For girls in particular, it is important to learn to use the computer as a tool at an early age, and preferably to secondary school level.) |
| **II. Intermediate objectives** | |
| 11. To provide more opportunities for students to learn independently at their own pace using their own learning materials. | Teachers should adopt a constructivist approach to curriculum, one where some of the knowledge is built by the learner, so not all is supplied by the teacher. |
| 10. To develop data manipulation/ research skills that can be applied to their own learning. | Students require strong data manipulation/research skills in order to pursue their learning. |
| 9. To enhance creative problem-solving skills. | A high level of proficiency in programming is required to develop higher-order problem-solving skills. |
| 8. To develop a strong level of proficiency in programming. | |

211

| Hierarchy of objectives | Underlying assumptions |
|---|---|
| *I. Immediate objectives* | |
| 7. To increase the level of cooperation between students (in particular the propensity of more able students to work with others of less ability). | The portability of computers combined with the printed word facilitates and promotes a high level of interaction between students. |
| 6. To enhance the acquisition of skills in literacy, wordprocessing and creative writing. | The ability to edit, to present work more clearly and to reflectively share written work via computer screens and classroom monitors enhances basic literacy and creative writing skills. |
| 5. To develop skills of instructing and controlling the computer (e.g. basic programming) | The ability and willingness to apply the computer to learning situations depends upon level of keyboarding and programming skill. |
| 4. To develop proficiency in basic keyboarding skills. | Proficiency in keyboarding, and in particular touchtyping skills, is fundamental to efficient computer use. Bad habits developed in poor initial training are difficult to rectify later. |
| 3. To inform students about how to care for the computer, and the rules for handling/storage of computers and related hardware. | Rules and procedures for handling hardware and software in the classroom are fundamental to effective and efficient use. |
| 2. To provide teachers with an understanding of how notebook computers and related software can be used to enhance the curriculum in core subjects (English, Humanities, Science and Maths). | Beyond personal mastery of the hardware and software, teachers need to learn how to integrate the innovation into classroom practice to enhance learning. |
| 1. To provide teachers with the basic skills related to personal mastery of the notebook computer and related hardware. | Personal mastery of the technology by teachers is a necessary prerequisite to successful introduction into the classroom. |

Source: Owen, J.M. & Lambert, F.C. (1995) *Evaluation*, 1(2), 237–50.

Another feature of this study was that the evaluators cooperated with policy developers in determining the style of reporting and with dissemination strategies (Owen & Andrew, 1989). This example suggests a further use of Clarificative evaluation, over those suggested by others—namely, the dissemination of a program in a clarified state to a range of sites not yet using a program.

---

**Example 10.5 Development of principles of Enterprise Education**

The Country Education Project is an agency designed to improve the quality of education in rural areas of Australia. Heavily committed to community participation, the CEP has a history of encouraging innovative programs in schools and in the small communities serviced by the schools.

An initiative supported by the Victorian CEP was to provide seeding for the development of Student Enterprise programs in a small number (about ten) of the 300 individual rural schools across the state. These programs involved students planning and implementing small business ventures as part of the curriculum in the middle years of secondary school (Years 9–10).

Towards the end of the first year of operation of these trial programs, an evaluation was commenced which aimed to develop documentation on Enterprise Education. The purpose of the evaluation was to synthesise Enterprise Education principles and a program plan from the practice of these innovatory programs.

The plan could then be used as a basis for the adoption and implementation of Enterprise Education in rural schools which were not participants in the trial phases to develop their own programs.

An evaluation team followed many of the principles suggested by Smith (1989b). In addition to analysis of documentation, visits were made to the sites where Enterprise Education was trialled. Teachers, community representatives and students were interviewed. In addition, a literature search was undertaken.

The evaluators drew up some tentative principles of Enterprise Education which were synthesised from the best of the innovative practice. Key players, teachers and representatives of the CEP executive were asked to comment on

---

the developed principles. As a result of these procedures, a final plan was developed. The plan was organised around seven elements of Enterprise Education:

1 Selection of a team and working together;
2 Creative thinking;
3 Planning the enterprise;
4 Getting underway;
5 Implementing the plan;
6 Monitoring procedures;
7 Modifying procedures.

In addition, the evaluation identified issues associated with the successful introduction of Enterprise Education into a rural secondary school. These included the following:

- Student Enterprise should not be seen as an 'extra', outside the mainstream of school curriculum. Enterprise projects to become embedded in the school curriculum need:
  - strong commitment on the part of teachers and school principals;
  - cooperation with the local community, and initiative and entrepreneurship in developing and sustaining programs;
  - continuous evaluation leading to ongoing staff development and adaptation to student needs;
  - significant departures from traditional schooling in response to individual student needs in a pluralistic society.

- The implementation of Student Enterprise projects requires a shift in pedagogy, from an emphasis on directed teaching to one of enabling students to learn. At the same time, teachers must be clear about the skills students will acquire. A review of Enterprise programs concluded that: 'A great deal of present practice in what might be termed enterprise skill development is not accountable for the skill formation of learners. Too many workers with young people . . . focus on broad generalities such as personal development, self esteem and empowerment and do not pay enough attention to identifying skills and discussing their relevance to the personal and career objectives of the young people'.

- There is a fine line between too much assistance and too little help from teachers and others. On the one hand, Enterprise Education is designed to foster self-initiative, and thus it is inappropriate for teachers to use 'lock-step' approaches. On the other hand, there is no doubt that teachers need to set up structures to facilitate the processes. Without them, projects can flounder. At least one 1989 CEP project almost came to grief due to lack of assistance at crucial times in the implementation of the project.

- Enterprise skill development should not be seen as the only way of organising learning. However, it is an important strategy for preparing students for the realities engendered by a rapidly changing society and associated employment conditions.

- Most students carrying out a CEP Enterprise project found that it was harder than they had expected. More that one team reported that the project was 'not as easy as we thought it would be'. It is clear that Enterprise projects were no soft option, requiring intellectual and other skills at least on a par with more traditional school subject work.

- School-level evaluations showed that learning management and organisational skills were major outcomes of the innovatory projects. These included: time management, teamwork, communication, problem-solving, budgeting and marketing, and working and negotiating with a range of people. It was through the acquisition of these skills that, at the conclusion of their projects, students had gained confidence and pride in their achievements.

As we have seen, Accreditation is another Approach which is oriented towards program clarification. It is widely used across a range of disciplines and areas to provide assurance to the public and to government that standards appropriate to the area are being upheld. For example, in the area of higher education in the United States, the National Council for the Accreditation of Teacher Education (NCATE) has the responsibility to ensure that the quality of college-based programs designed to prepare teachers to work in schools is adequate. Similarly, the National Association for the Education of Young Children (NAEYC) accredits child-care centres across the United States and there is evidence that these procedures have improved the quality of child care across the country.

**Figure 10.3  Program logic statement informed by the evaluation: adding a system perspective**

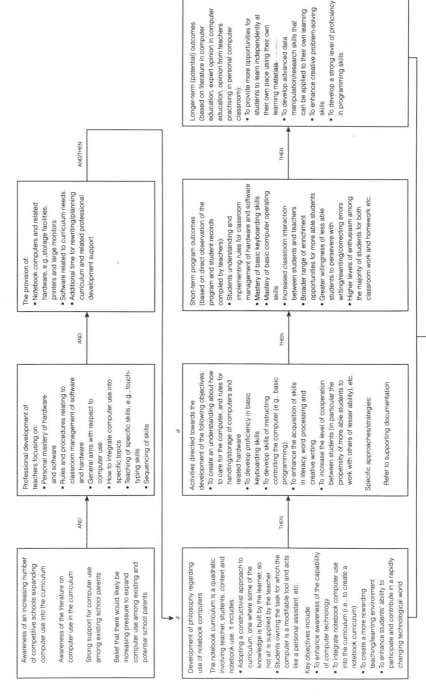

Awareness of an increasing number of competitive schools expanding computer use into the curriculum

Awareness of the literature on computer use in the curriculum

Strong support for computer use among existing school parents

Belief that there would likely be increasing pressure to expand computer use among existing and potential school parents

IF

Professional development of teachers focusing on:
- Personal mastery of hardware and software
- Rules and procedures relating to classroom management of software and hardware
- General aims with respect to computer use
- How to integrate computer use into specific topics
- Teaching of specific skills, e.g., touch-typing skills
- Sequencing of skills

AND

The provision of:
- Notebook computers and related hardware, e.g. storage facilities, printers and large monitors
- Software related to curriculum needs.
- Additional time for rewriting/planning curriculum and related professional development support

AND/THEN

Development of philosophy regarding use of notebook computers

The notebook curriculum is a quadratic involving teacher, students, context and notebook use. It includes:
- Adopting a constructivist approach to curriculum, one where some of the knowledge is built by the learner, so not all is supplied by the teacher
- Students owning the task for which the computer is a modifiable tool and acts like a personal assistant, etc.

Key objectives include:
- To enhance awareness of the capability of computer technology
- To integrate notebook computer use into the curriculum (i.e. to create a notebook curriculum)
- To create a more rewarding teaching/learning environment
- To enhance students' ability to participate and contribute in a rapidly changing technological world

IF

Activities directed towards the development of the following objectives:
- To create an understanding about how to care for the computer, and rules for handling/storage of computers and related hardware
- To develop proficiency in basic keyboarding skills
- To develop skills of instructing controlling the computer (e.g., basic programming).
- To enhance the acquisition of skills in literacy, word processing and creative writing.
- To increase the level of cooperation between students (in particular the propensity of more able students to work with others of lesser ability), etc.

Specific approaches/strategies:

Refer to supporting documentation

THEN

Short-term program outcomes (based on direct observation of the program and student records compiled by teachers):
- Students understanding and implementing rules for classroom management of hardware and software
- Mastery of basic keyboarding skills
- Mastery of basic computer operating skills
- Increased classroom interaction between students and teachers
- Broader range of enrichment opportunities for more able students
- Greater willingness of less able students to persevere with writing/rewriting/correcting errors
- Higher levels of enthusiasm among the majority of students for both classroom work and homework etc.

THEN

Longer-term (potential) outcomes (based on literature in computer education, expert opinion in computer education, opinion from teachers practising in personal computer classroom):
- To provide more opportunities for students to learn independently at their own pace using their own learning materials.
- To develop advanced data manipulation/research skills that can be applied to their own learning
- To enhance creative problem-solving skills
- To develop a strong level of proficiency in programming skills

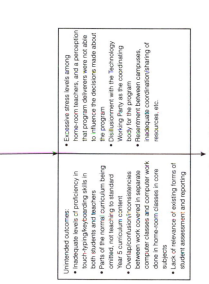

**Unintended outcomes:**

- Inadequate levels of proficiency in touch-typing/keyboarding skills in both students and teachers
- Parts of the normal curriculum being omitted, not teaching to standard Year 5 curriculum content
- Overlap/confusion/inconsistencies between work covered in separate computer classes and computer work done in home-room classes in core subjects
- Lack of relevance of existing forms of student assessment and reporting
- Excessive stress levels among home-room teachers, and a perception that program deliverers were not able to influence the decisions made about the program
- Disillusionment with the Technology Working Party as the coordinating body for the program
- Resentment between campuses, inadequate coordination/sharing of resources, etc.

Implications for the total school scheme

**Broader curriculum implications:**

- How and when should keyboarding be introduced to students? (i.e., is Year 5 the most appropriate year for this basic skill building?)
- What is the rationale for continuing to offer separate specialist computer classes at the Year 5 level? If they are continued what should the content be?
- If continuity of classroom experience is important for mastering basic computer operating skills, what changes might avoid Year 5 classroom being a floating population in the introductory stages of computer use (i.e., implications for time-tabling music and sport, remedial instruction, enrichment, etc.
- Given the different skills and content embodied in the notebook computer curriculum, what methods of student assessment and reporting are most suitable? How will these relate to the reporting at other levels?

**Implications for professional development and support:**

- Should teachers receive more hands-on experience with hardware and software before tackling the program in the classroom?
- In light of the double burden this innovation imposes, what additional types of support can be given to teachers? What changes in institutional structure are necessary to ensure this support is there when needed?

**Implications for institutional structures:**

- How effective is the Technology Working Party and its current mode of operation in responding to the implementation demands of the program? Would alternative institutional arrangements be more responsive to the needs of teachers?
- Should a projects officer be given responsibility for the daily management and coordination of the program, and a small subcommittee formed to report to the Technology Working Party on matters relating to the notebook curriculum and resources required for its implementation?

## CONCLUSION

This chapter has outlined the basis for Clarificative evaluation and some key Approaches to practice consistent with the need to help make explicit the logic of their programs. It is important to emphasise the legitimacy of Clarificative evaluation as evaluation. But, given the fact that Clarificative evaluation is novel to some, it is often up to the evaluator to point out the salience of a Clarificative evaluation. More than once, program managers have approached us with a perceived need to undertake an Impact evaluation. Through discussion, it has become apparent that there would be far greater benefit if the resources available for an Impact evaluation could be directed towards an evaluation of a more formative nature, leading to a clarification of the design of the program for which they are responsible.

There is no doubt that program managers and deliverers value having a sound basis for their programs. While program staff can sometimes develop a workable program design alone, an evaluator with strong analytical and creative skills can often provide a program design which more accurately and comprehensively represents its intentions and implementation characteristics.

## REFERENCES

Batterham, R. (1991). 'Are Clinical Indicators Bullies?' Unpublished paper for the Graduate Diploma in Evaluation, The University of Melbourne.

Brinkerhoff, R. (1989). 'Evaluating Training in Business and Industry'. *New Directions in Program Evaluation*, 44 (Winter), 5–19.

Chen, H. (1990). *Theory Driven Evaluation*. Newbury Park: Sage.

Funnell, S. (1997). 'Program Logic: An Adaptable Tool for Designing and Evaluating Programs'. *Evaluation News and Comment*, 6 (1), 5–17.

Glaser, B. & Strauss, A.L. (1967). *The Discovery of Grounded Theory*. Chicago, IL: Aldine.

Owen, J.M. & Andrew, P.F. (1989). *Student Enterprises: Learning by Doing* Melbourne: Centre for Program Evaluation, The University of Melbourne, for the Country Education Project.

Owen, J.M. & Lambert, F.C. (1995). 'Roles for Evaluation in Learning Organisations'. *Evaluation*, 1 (2), 259–73.

Patton, M.Q. (1997). *Utilization Focused Evaluation*. 3rd edn. Thousand Oaks, CA: Sage.

Rogers, P.J. & Huebner, T.A. (1998). 'Using Program Theory for Organisational Learning and Formative Evaluation'. Paper given at the annual conference of the Canadian Evaluation Society. St Johns, Newfoundland.

Rutman, L. (1980). *Planning Useful Evaluations*. Beverly Hills, CA: Sage.

Shadish, W.R., Cook, T.D. & Leviton, L.C. (1991). *Foundations of Program Evaluation*. Newbury Park: Sage.

Smith, M.F. (1989a). 'Evaluability Assessment of the Maryland Water Quality/Quantity Program'. Personal communication from the author.

Smith, M.F. (1989b). *Evaluability Assessment: A Practical Approach*. Norwell, MA: Kluwer.

Smith, N.L. (1992). 'Aspects of Investigative Inquiry in Evaluation'. *New Directions in Program Evaluation*, 56 (Winter), 3–13.

Weiss, C.H. (1996). 'Theory Based Evaluation: Past, Present and Future'. Paper presented at the annual meeting of the American Evaluation Association, Atlanta, CA.

Wholey, J. (1983). *Evaluation and Effective Public Management*. Boston, MA: Little, Brown.

# 11

# Interactive Evaluation

## INTRODUCTION

The control of providers over program development and delivery is fundamental to Interactive evaluation. This Form assumes that people at the local level can create effective solutions to situational concerns. Some time ago, Ronald Havelock (1971) developed a set of innovation and change models, one of which was the Problem Solving Model. The model describes an organisational setting where those responsible for a given problem have the ability and inclination to deal with that problem. If outsiders are involved they are involved on the terms set by providers—that is, outsiders are not there to hand down knowledge. The model is thus predicated on the adequacy of local expertise to deal with local problems and to recognise the need for outside assistance when it is needed. In such a scenario, there is an assumption that external knowledge—and in particular accumulated research-based knowledge—is of lesser relevance than 'local' knowledge. Thus external policies and directives do not play a major role in shaping program delivery and associated evaluative procedures. The evaluator is employed to provide input and, in some cases, support the agenda of the local practitioners.

Participants play a major part in setting goals and in organisational and program delivery, and evaluation efforts are influenced strongly by those who are 'close to the action'. Consistent with this is a view that each program initiative is 'new'—that is, it can be regarded as an innovation from the perspective of those involved in its delivery. Programs which are consistent with this view:

- attempt to address problems that have not been subject to program intervention before; and/or
- employ program structures or processes that are unique, at least from the point of view of the program staff.

Typically, program objectives and delivery are evolving rather than preordinate, sometimes not fully explicit, and thus open to debate. Those directly involved might expect to come to a steady state in terms of general direction over a period of time, but continue to reserve the right to use new or alternative strategies to achieve program goals—that is, there is ongoing adaptation and responsiveness.

Program delivery can be idiosyncratic and there is little, if any, regard for consistency of treatment, uniform implementation or outcomes. In some areas, there is government support for this approach to problem-solving, based at least partly on an ideological position that there should be local control over decisions that affect the local community.

---

**Example 11.1 Landcare**

This has been a position adopted by the Department of Agriculture in Australia as part of a national Landcare policy. Landcare aims to reduce the deleterious effects on the rural environment by encouraging farmers and others employed on the land to adopt programs that address local concerns— for example, erosion due to excess land clearance, raising of the water table and increased salinity, and spread of noxious weeds. Rural communities are given limited resources to apply to problems that arise in their region. Devolution of responsibility of this nature has been found to be successful due in no small part to the commitment of local people, and the additional resources they bring to the program in terms of time, travel and use of their own materials, resources which would otherwise have to be provided by government.

---

The problem-solving perspective is also consistent with the more recent literature on developing a culture of learning within organisations (Schein, 1985), and the broader need for continuous relevant knowledge for decision-making in social, political and economic spheres of endeavour (Sowell, 1996). This has led to a burgeoning interest in integrating evaluation into the day-to-day processes of organisations that adopt a commitment to systematic examination of what they do and how they might become more effective and efficient (Rowe & Jacobs, 1996). We see an increasing need for trained evaluators to provide timely information for organisational decision-making at all levels, from formal and informal leaders to those working on the 'shop floor' (Owen & Lambert, 1998).

*Interactive evaluation* is concerned with:

- the provision of systematic evaluation findings through which local providers can make decisions about the future direction of their programs;
- assistance in planning and carrying out self-evaluations;
- focusing evaluation on program change and improvement, in most cases on a continuous basis; and
- a perspective that evaluation can be an end in itself, as a means of empowering providers and participants.

Interactive evaluation has a strong formative purpose. Table 11.1 sets out the basic features of the Interactive Form. Five Approaches to evaluation are included within the Form. Note that in a previous edition of this book, this Form of evaluation was labelled Process evaluation.

## KEY APPROACHES TO INTERACTIVE EVALUATION

While Interactive evaluation can focus on all aspects of program delivery, there is a concentration on program delivery and implementation—that is, on process variables. This can also include the processes used by the organisation to support (or retard) the program. There is far less concern for determining outcomes through a formal 'end of program' analysis, because key stakeholders never expect their program to be constant for sufficient time to make a traditional Impact evaluation (Form E) meaningful or useful. Instead, program providers want evaluations which will support change and improvement.

Typically, a trained evaluator provides a direct service to program providers based on his or her expertise, working in close contact and providing a range of inputs and advice. The evaluator may be asked to observe what is happening, to help participants make judgments about the success or otherwise of a given strategy or program initiative, with a view for future planning. In some Approaches, the evaluator can be thought of as an extension of the program team, helping to make decisions about program direction. In addition to collecting and analysing information, the evaluator might assist decision-makers in setting directions and, in some cases, actually assisting with change and improvement strategies. The essential characteristics of the major Approaches are now discussed.

**Table 11.1   Summary of Interactive evaluation (Form C)**

| Dimension | Properties |
|---|---|
| Orientation | Improvement of program already being delivered |
| Typical issues | • What is this program trying to achieve?<br>• How is this service going?<br>• Is the delivery working?<br>• Is delivery consistent with the program plan?<br>• How could delivery be changed to make it more effective?<br>• How could this organisation be changed to make it more effective? |
| State of program | Under initial implementation, or subject to continuous review and improvement |
| Major focus | Major focus is on delivery but findings could influence changes in program plan and thus affect outcomes |
| Timing (vis-à-vis program delivery) | During delivery |
| Key Approaches | • Responsive<br>• Action research<br>• Quality review<br>• Developmental<br>• Empowerment |
| Assembly of evidence | Relies on intensive onsite study, including observation and interview. Extent to which data collection is systematic depends on Approach. Providers may also be involved in the evaluation to varying extents, from total responsibility to conclusion drawing. |

## RESPONSIVE EVALUATION

Robert Stake (1980) is the theorist most associated with this term, and with methodological approaches consistent with this Approach. An evaluation is responsive if:

- it orients more directly to program activities than to program intents;
- it responds to audience requirements for information;
- the different value perspectives of the people at hand are referred to in reporting the success and failure of the program.

Stake has used these principles to structure his fieldwork. It is noteworthy that he is an external evaluator: in structural terms, he is an 'outsider'. He prefers to immerse himself at the evaluation site, negotiate the boundaries of the study, base data collection on observation, and write extensive case study reports. Interpretation and discussion of these reports and other more informal means of reporting are designed to help practitioners reach new understandings by placing their existing craft knowledge alongside the findings of the evaluation. This is referred to as 'naturalistic generalisation'. Stake assumes that this will lead to improved practice. The instrumental use of responsive evaluation has not been well documented, however, and we would value examples of how practitioners translate evaluation findings into decision-making. For other evaluators adopting this Approach, there are related questions. Does the evaluator help clients work through the implications of the case analysis? Does one provide summaries for those too busy to read an entire case report? Does the evaluator have 'the right' to indicate action implied by the findings of the study?

Stake's approach is orientated towards client understanding. This is a legitimate evaluation role (see Chapter 6), in that Responsive evaluation leads to enlightenment of stakeholders from which they can make decisions about program change. This Approach provides an illumination of issues from the perspective of someone with knowledge of the context in which the evaluation is set.

## ACTION RESEARCH

Action research is a second Approach used in the context of site-level improvement and local control. What is action research and how does it link to the needs of practitioners and, more generally, to Interactive evaluation? Action research had its beginnings in the search for local-level solutions to on-the-job problems. Lewin (1946) wrote about its use in areas such as race relations and community housing more than half a century ago.

Orton (1992) defines action research as:

> a collaborative research, centred in social practice, which follows a particular process, espouses the values of independence, equality and cooperation, and is intended to be a learning experience for those involved, to produce a change for the better in the practice and to add to social theory.

Wadsworth (1991) views the process as a cyclic one involving the following components:

- *reflection on current action.* Every now and then, site-level practitioners notice a discrepancy between what they do and/or experience and what they expect to be happening.
- *design.* In this stage, practitioners make explicit the problem and set out to answer questions associated with the problem. At this stage it is also important to identify whose problem it is. A critical reference group should be set up at this stage composed of those with a stake in the enquiry.
- *fieldwork.* This is the stage when data are collected. Emphasis is placed on the meanings of the object of the enquiry from the perspective of each of the critical reference group members.
- *analysis and conclusions.* The fieldwork allows the generation of insights which lead to understandings not previously thought of. There is an emphasis on understanding the meaning of the action. Conclusions, explanations and even theories are generated.
- *planning.* It is now possible to consider changes and options for improved practice. Imaginative but realistic recommendations can be made and put into practice. These are well grounded in past practice and the experience of learning from it.

A fundamental feature of action research is that it concentrates on evaluating implementation of a possible *solution* to a site-level problem. Kemmis (1985) describes four 'moments' of action research as follows:

- Develop a plan of action to improve what is already happening.
- Act to implement the plan.
- Observe the effects of action in the context of which it occurs.
- Reflect on these effects as a basis for further planning, subsequent action, and so on, through a succession of cycles.

Kemmis is specific about the order of these phases. The plan is constructed action and by definition it must be prospective and forward-looking. This can include the trialling of an innovatory practice from outside the immediate experience of the practitioner. For example, in a teaching situation, this could involve the introduction of group techniques where the practitioner is accustomed to didactic styles of teaching. Consistent with the Interactive Form, an important aspect of action research is that the innovation would not be imposed; it would be introduced on the basis of an expressed need of the practitioner to adopt approaches more conducive to the content matter or students in the class. This view is supported by others. For example, Brown (1990) states:

> at the core of the notion of group self-evaluation lies the concept of action research; a recurrent cyclic approach to planning, action, observing the outcomes, reflecting on them and replanning on the

basis of what has been understood. For those who engage in it, it provides the prospect of enhanced understanding leading to improved performance. It is essentially a simple idea and one which has a natural appeal for people in new circumstances or engaging in new activities.

In summary, Action Research emphasises the prospective. In some work we have undertaken in the context of organisational improvement, there has been a tendency to first ask questions about the *current* situation with a view to analysing data on how this situation can be improved. In this scenario, for example, a trainer might wish to know how he or she spends his or her time in a typical staff development activity with a view to eliciting suggestions about how to manage his or her time more effectively. Then, in a second stage of the evaluation, the trial of an innovation—say, a new method of time management—following from the review would be monitored. For the practitioner, this would be seen as a logical follow-up within the one development and improvement process. The first stage is more in keeping with Responsive evaluation, in that it examines the status quo rather than focusing on an introduced stategy or solution.

## QUALITY REVIEW (INSTITUTIONAL SELF-STUDY)

Quality reviews usually take place within an organisational system in which individual agencies are responsible for program delivery within broad policy directives. Reviews would be the responsibility of, say, each manager in a chain of hotels, or the principal of each school within a school district. This Approach could also apply within one organisation in which there are logical sub-groups—for example, to all wards in a large public hospital.

The major propositions which underlie the quality review are that:

- an organisation or organisational system provides guidelines for self-evaluation and improvement;
- effective agency-level development is enhanced by the implementation of these system-level guidelines to support local problem-solving; and
- all agencies are expected to undertake such processes within a given time span (Cuttance, 1994).

This implies a need to develop a 'culture of evaluation' whereby evaluation becomes a way of thinking which permeates every kind and level of daily action. To help achieve this, Wadsworth (1991) suggests a number of opportunities for developing a comprehensive program of in-built evaluation:

- *daily informal personal reflection.* Good practitioners intuitively reflect on their teaching practices and modify them accordingly on a day-to-day basis.
- *weekly reviews.* These might involve making special diary notes on the progress of particular students, reviewing the week's diary to reflect on priorities and time management issues, or arranging informal discussion time with colleagues to discuss facets of program operations.
- *special effort evaluations* of particular aspects of practice. These will be evaluations which respond to the immediate concerns of those involved in program activities. For example, there may be some concern that the program is not satisfactorily reaching those who need it most. This might prompt an investigation of current strategies for reaching the target group, and might in the initial stages lead to an evaluation of the program newsletter.
- *monthly collective problem-pooling sessions.* Such sessions could provide a forum for raising new issues, identifying those issues clearly in need of action, or tabling contentious issues for further discussion and/or research.
- *annual 'what-have-we-achieved?' and 'where-are-we-heading next year?' workshops.* This might involve reports from individuals reflecting on the program over the year, brainstorming sessions about future program development and identifying action that needs to be taken.

In the most effective quality reviews, a small number of areas for evaluation are identified by each agency. These are the ones that would repay greatest return for further development. In doing so, agencies might address factors such as:

- factors enabling current successful programs;
- factors impeding current performance;
- areas of development necessary to meet emergent needs of clients in the future;
- effectiveness of system-level services provided by the system to the agency.

It is generally assumed that quality reviews can be undertaken by program staff and are often added to their workloads without assistance from the organisation except for staff training and the provision of manuals for guidance. Expertise in the form of experienced evaluators is generally not available. Experience in the use of quality reviews suggests that they tend to impose unrealistic burdens on staff, who are rarely in a position to refuse to cooperate. There is also usually a tension between an improvement-focused agency effort and a requirement to inform the system-level authority of the findings of the evaluation. Nevertheless, there are instances where agencies have grasped the autonomy to make changes and improvements based on the review process.

## DEVELOPMENTAL EVALUATION

This Approach has been championed by Patton (1996) in the United States and Cousins (Cousins and Earl, 1992) in Canada and requires the ongoing commitment of a key adviser with evaluation expertise.

Developmental evaluation involves evaluation processes, including asking evaluation questions and applying evaluation logic, to support program, project, product and/or organisational development. The evaluator is part of a team whose members collaborate to conceptualise, design and test new approaches in a long-term ongoing process of continuous improvement, adaptation and intentional change. The evaluator's primary function with the team is to elucidate team discussions with evaluative questions, data and logic, and to facilitate data-based decision-making in the developmental process (Patton, 1996).

By contrast with quality review, the evaluator is constantly available for assistance with almost any aspect of concern to the organisation. Compared with the Responsive Approach, the evaluator is likely to spend less time in data collection and analysis, and more time in assisting others to undertake systematic enquiry. Some see the role of the evaluator as described above—more like an organisational development consultant. We have argued earlier in this book that the roles of evaluator and supporter of organisational change are becoming fuzzier. Patton (1996) may be pointing the way to the future in which the evaluator profession will accept that the provision of timely advice to managers and program providers based on evaluation expertise, broadly rather than narrowly defined, will represent the new orthodoxy.

## EMPOWERMENT EVALUATION

Of the Approaches that are associated with Interactive evaluation, the one that has attracted the most controversy is Empowerment evaluation. From the time when he was president of the American Evaluation Association in 1993, David Fetterman has disseminated principles of empowerment and their use as a basis for evaluation. Self-determination, defined as the ability to chart one's own course in life, is a basic tenet of Empowerment evaluation. Organisations and individuals must be able to find ways to bring relevant information to bear on problems and find solutions.

Key tenets of empowerment are as follows.

- The most meaningful changes are those that occur in the people themselves and that reflect an increased capacity for initiating and carrying out social change.
- The definition of human capacity is more concerned with self-sufficiency, self-determination and empowerment, than with changes that can be statistically measured.
- Success is measured by the extent to which people are able to identify their own problems and form a consensus to propose appropriate solutions.
- Change occurs best when greater emphasis is placed on the process for change while maintaining a focus on the results of change (Dugan, 1996).

Fetterman is just as concerned with the notion of empowerment as with the roles of evaluation (Fetterman et al., 1996). He suggests that, in practice, empowerment involves program staff, participants and evaluators in:

- collaborating to come to a consensus about their mission, vision and expected results;
- taking stock of what they already have and using this as a baseline to plan for the future; and
- using evaluation as a tool to develop strategies linked to the attainment of specific goals.

The Empowerment evaluation Approach:

- is designed to create a 'folk culture' of evaluation;
- is a mechanism used to create and drive a learning organisation;
- is not mutually exclusive to more traditional Impact evaluation undertaken by external evaluators; and
- can be fostered by experienced evaluators through the following:
  - training others to acquire evaluation skills
  - acting as facilitators or coaches to help others conduct evaluation
  - undertaking illuminative evaluations in conjunction with practitioners, and
  - acting as advocates for disadvantaged groups (Fetterman, 1994).

In practice, the role of the evaluator generally spans a range of roles associated with program planning and delivery, in addition to those more often associated with evaluation practice. There is an implication that the evaluator will be committed to the organisation for a period of time, during which there is an expectation that more of the major programmatic and evaluative decisions will pass to program staff and participants.

# INTERACTIVE EVALUATION: TRENDS AND CASE EXAMPLES

Evaluation practitioners often borrow principles and concepts from across the major Approaches. In this section we present a range of case study examples of good practice which illustrate trends in Interactive evaluation.

## Response to client agendas

Evaluators are expected to respond to the concerns of clients in evaluation. However, in Interactive evaluation, it is likely that the evaluator would be especially attuned to the needs of clients, and adopt a close 'psychological proximity' in dealing with all aspects of the evaluation process.

### Example 11.2 Country Education Project (CEP)

The Country Education Project (CEP) successfully applied for a grant to fund professional development programs for teachers in rural centres in two states. While the programs in each state differed in detail, they had the following common elements:

- focus on the teaching of literacy, involvement of a defined cluster of schools in a rural area;
- involvement of staff from a rural university;
- release of teachers from classes to take part in a meaningful professional development activity;
- support from a coordinating agency with interests in rural education for schools and the community.

The program was initially offered at two sites.

In the planning stage, evaluators who had considerable empathy with the philosophy of the CEP were asked to undertake the evaluation. A second reason for choosing these evaluators was that they had a strong conceptual knowledge of professional development. The clients were sure that the evaluators would provide plausible conclusions which could be used to refine the program. Following observations and interviews at the sites, a discussion paper was prepared by the evaluators. This was the basis of a series of meetings at which changes to the program for subsequent implementations were decided. (Johnson & Owen, 1995)

## Ongoing support over time

In Chapter 4, we argued that evaluators must develop social interaction skills to undertake effective evaluations. The need for social skills is particularly relevant within this Form because of the nature of evaluator–program provider interaction. For evaluators to be effective, they must find ways for their findings to provide leverage in program decision-making. Now, there is some variation in the extent to which evaluators working in this Form see their role in the program change process. As we have seen, evaluators using the Responsive Approach would say that their major role is an educational one. This is to lay out the organisational and programmatic situation, often presented as an extensive case study which portrays this situation in detail. This provides a starting point for program providers and other stakeholders to engage in a 'dialectic' about the current worth of the intervention. This implies a 'point-in-time' reporting strategy, leaving program providers responsible for change based on the results of the discussion (and, presumably, debate). By comparison, others take the view of Interactive evaluation as ongoing and this implies communicating findings to stakeholders on a regular basis. The task of the evaluator is one of:

> informing and developing the understandings of those associated with the program. [The evaluator] may report frequently rather than just towards the end of the evaluation, so that the perspectives of participants and audiences can be engaged more or less continually rather than in a single confrontation of perspectives. The recurring reports of the evaluator can be regarded as a conversation which develops the points of those it engages. (Kemmis, 1986)

### Example 11.3 The Girls and Mathematics and Science project (GAMAST)

GAMAST was a nationally commissioned project designed to increase participation of girls in mathematics and science subjects in schools and other educational institutions. The project had two major phases. In the first, extensive research was undertaken by the project staff and ideas and strategies based on this information were tried out in a small number of cooperating schools. The objective was to determine which of these strategies could be used for professional development, given restrictions imposed by the day-to-day realities of school operations. The second phase involved the compilation of strategies found to be workable and their dissemination.

The project staff were committed to formative processes as an essential element of the first phase. It was necessary for them to argue strongly for such a component to be built into project funding because government administrators commissioning the project were unfamiliar with benefits which could flow from the use of evaluation for developmental purposes. Finally, 9 per cent of the total budget was allocated for this purpose.

The evaluators worked in a cyclical mode of issue-setting and evaluation. At the beginning of each cycle, a meeting of staff and evaluators decided on an issue for attention. Evaluative feedback was brought to each following meeting for discussion to enable project staff to plan the next round of action. Over a period of just under a year, the evaluators were able to address a range of problems which arose over the life of the project. The success of the evaluation relied heavily on a high degree of interaction and trust between project staff and evaluators and the ability of the evaluators to tackle issues which arose at short notice. In addition to informing action, the evaluation facilitated the accumulation and consolidation of ideas that worked and thus it made a major contribution to the final products of the project. (Owen & Hurworth, 1988)

## Interactive evaluation and organisational change

In practice, the use of ongoing reporting to influence change has its challenges. While laying out findings to staff may merely involve setting up a meeting at which these can be presented, it is more difficult to get staff to focus on the implications of the findings for their collective practice.

### Example 11.4 Saturn School

Preskill (1992) reports on a case study of an internal evaluation at Saturn School in Minnesota in the United States that adopted an innovatory program in which the roles of teachers, pupils and the parent community were redefined. Among other features, the curriculum of the school was developed from the information gathered from teachers and students.

232

The curriculum was changed every ten weeks. Preskill was employed as 'neutral force' evaluator to document the implementation of the curriculum and to provide systematic feedback to assist in its development. While her role as a documentor was appreciated, Preskill became frustrated with her influence on decision-making.

> As time went on into the second year . . . I became frustrated by my seeming inability to positively affect the school. I was sitting on so much data—information from all perspectives that seemed to be sealed within individuals or small groups of people. I increasingly felt ineffective in my ability to do what I had hoped—to provide ongoing information to the teachers and other staff about how things were going and to help them implement their mission more effectively.

On the basis of this experience, Preskill believes that organisations need to adjust their perspectives on organisational learning in order to use evaluation findings effectively. She notes that while individual teachers and others continually learnt from the evaluation and used the evaluator in many different ways, the organisation as a whole was unable to develop a process where the staff could collaboratively reflect on the findings and apply them to the issues and problems associated with the innovation. Preskill analyses this in terms of the need for organisations to develop structures within which evaluation can be used to restructure organisational norms, strategies and assumptions, known as 'double-loop' learning.

The implication for evaluators is that they need to be competent in facilitating group work and managing conflict. We have found from our practice that it is essential that the findings of the evaluation can provide a neutral force when there are existing and competing positions within an organisation. In these situations, it is essential that all parties have absorbed the findings of the evaluation. Thus the evaluator must be prepared to give time to dissemination—in particular, to face-to-face dissemination. This often provides a means by which the organisation can go forward on the basis of the input from the 'third party'.

## Practitioner-led evaluation

Another issue is the extent to which stakeholders and clients should and do become involved in evaluation. While individual theorists have addressed this issue, it is only now that syntheses of these ideas are beginning to appear (Alkin et al., 1998). In Interactive evaluation, the most likely clients will be those responsible for program delivery, including the local program manager or leader, and in some cases, program participants. In highly participatory site-based evaluations, these clients could be involved in all phases of the evaluation: negotiating the key questions, collecting and analysing evidence and reporting to colleagues.

For example, as part of a commitment to local control over schooling, Brennan and Hoadley (1984) suggest that evaluation could be used for the following reasons:

- The school council might want to revise and update the school policy so that it meets current needs.
- Students may feel that the curriculum and organisation of the school are not adequately preparing them for adult life.
- One group of teachers may want to introduce a change which will impinge on other areas of the school.
- There is a change of policy (e.g. from the Minister) necessitating a new look at the school's practices and priorities.

Whatever the object of the evaluation, it is clear that self-evaluation is action focused and orientated towards innovatory practice.

> Action is the primary purpose of evaluation-improved school practice. School life does not stop because people undertake evaluations, nor should it. We have to try things out, check to see how they are working and modify further practice in the light of this evaluation. (Brennan and Hoadley, 1984)

Anecdotal evidence suggests that schools respond favourably to these principles. However, recent public spending cuts have led to a severe reduction in external consultancy support. Despite this, there are cases of good local evaluation practice. The extent of commitment and quality of practice within school-level evaluation has surprised some evaluation theorists. For example, McLaughlin (in Alkin, 1990) makes the following comment about school-level evaluation as practised in Australia:

> [Practitioner-led evaluation], I think that's a fantastic way to go and in fact I have seen it work. But what seems to have gone along with it is, in addition to responsibility for evaluation, the authority to act on the results. That is not seen to be as an empty 'formal' kind of exercise. And I'm thinking particularly of schools I've seen in Australia, in which I was blown away with the really hard-nosed look they were taking at their own school. I thought, God, how did this

happen? They were asking tough questions. When I asked them about that, it turned out that they also had the power to make changes—they could make their schools better, based on the results. They worked with outside evaluators. They did a school-based review every two years. And it was really tough nosed.

While there has been enthusiastic system-level support for site-level evaluation in education, this has not always been matched in schools themselves, as teachers find that additional work burdens accrue with only limited support from Education Departments. Wise school administrations have limited the number and scope of their formal evaluation work, concentrating on perhaps one major and a small number of minor evaluations a year and heeded advice to use outsiders in a supporting role. Case studies of effective use of outsiders are emerging.

### Example 11.5 Critical friend in self-evaluation

Telford (1991) describes one case in which a 'critical friend' took part in an evaluation of an elementary school mathematics program.

The [school staff] referred to the external evaluator as a critical friend. The critical part takes into account objectivity, being rigorous, and avoiding things that seemed too hard. The friend component specifies that the external evaluator be someone whose thinking is along similar lines, who has a similar philosophy and knows the direction of the school. Selection of a compatible critical friend is essential to the success of a useful evaluation as it brings a mutual understanding of the issues at hand. 'Hot-shot' evaluators who see themselves as those 'hired sages' or 'visiting philosophers' are avoided.

### Organisationally integrated evaluation

There is a growing evidence of a need for an external evaluator with appropriate skills to be involved in effective evaluations within the Interactive Form. In addition to bringing a critical perspective, the external evaluator may be employed as a coordinator of the effort, for staff training and in areas where technical and methodological skills are needed (Cousins & Earl, 1992). However, as we saw earlier, in the empowerment approach the evaluator could be called on to do more that coordinate the evaluation.

In a project built around the provision of support groups designed to prevent or delay the use of drugs by young people, Dugan (1996) developed a five-stage model to evaluate these programs. The stages were:

- organising for action;
- building the capacity for action;
- taking action;
- refining the action;
- institutionalising the action.

Dugan undertook the following roles as a trained evaluator: facilitator, mentor, advocate, trainer, coach and 'expert'. Dugan documented the proportion of time devoted to these tasks at each stage. For example, facilitation occupied 20 per cent of her time in the organising for action stage, and 40 per cent in the 'building for capacity' and 'taking action' stages. Providing expertise grew from a small proportion in stage one (10 per cent) to 50 per cent in 'refining the action' stage. While this example was developed within the empowerment Approach, it could just as easily have been classed as action research. In fact, when Rowe & Jacobs (1996) undertook a similar study in a local evaluation of a Native American community, they regarded it as an action research study. However, both would subscribe to the following propositions:

- Evaluation is something that ordinary people can be involved in.
- Evaluation is guided by three tenets: it should be participatory, as systematic as possible and at the same time use simple methodologies.
- Evaluation should strive to address key issues, not prove hypotheses.
- Findings that have the potential to transfer benefits from one situation to another should be described in simple lessons-learned statements.
- People 'on the ground' not agencies or experts, are responsible for their own development. (Dugan, 1996)

There is, not surprisingly, an overlap in the methods used and the assumptions made about action across the Approaches in the Interactive Form.

## CONCLUSION

The role of the 'expert evaluator' is an issue within Interactive evaluation and varies from Approach to Approach. While we see the advantages of the involvement of program providers in the evaluation process, there is a need for someone to provide expertise if the findings of evaluation are to provide high-quality information in program decisions.

Generally, we would expect that those interested in using Interactive evaluation in organisations and agencies would consider carefully how much evaluation expertise will be needed. They should also build evaluation into organisational arrangements from the moment a program is initiated by allocating resources, and setting up guidelines to direct evaluative processes and feedback. Managers and others need to be involved so that evaluation findings can be used in program change, often on an ongoing basis. There is also the issue of evaluation questions, which we have argued are central to the evaluation process. We urge key players to base their questions on criteria raised by program deliverers and recipients, and to use program recipients as sources of data and, where appropriate, in the assembly of evidence and its analysis. These questions should be of an organisational nature, in addition to questions about the program, and address proactive questions, of the 'what if' kind, to aid in decision-making about future directions.

## REFERENCES

Alkin, M.C. (1990). *Debates on Evaluation*. Newbury Park, CA: Sage.

Alkin, M.C., Hofstetter, C.H. & Ai, X. (eds). (1998). 'Stakeholder Concepts in Program Evaluation'. In A. Reynolds & H. Walberg (eds), *Evaluation for Educational Productivity*. Greenwich, CN: JAI Press.

Brennan, M. & Hoadley, R. (1984). *School Self Evaluation*. Melbourne: Education Department of Victoria.

Brown, L. (1990). 'Self-evaluation for System Management'. In L. Brown (ed.), Melbourne: Office of Schools Administration, Ministry of Education, pp. 1–9.

Cousins, J.B & Earl, L.M. (1992). 'The Case for Participatory Evaluation'. *Educational Evaluation and Policy Analysis*, 14 (4), 397–418.

Cuttance, P. (1994). 'Quality Systems for the Performance Development Cycle of Schools'. Paper presented at the International Conference on School Effectiveness and Improvement (ICSEI), Melbourne, January 1994.

Dugan, M.A. (ed.) (1996). *Participatory and Empowerment Evaluation: Lessons Learned in Training and Technical Assistance*. Thousand Oaks, CA: Sage.

Fetterman, D.M., (1994). 'Empowerment Evaluation'. *Evaluation Practice*, 15 (1), 1–15.

Fetterman, D.M., Kaftarian, S. J. & Wandersman, A. (1996). *Empowerment*

*Evaluation: Knowledge and Tools for Self-Assessment and Account-ability*. Thousand Oaks, CA: Sage.

Havelock, R.G. (1971). *Planning for Innovation through Dissemination and Utilization of Knowledge*. Ann Arbor, MI: Center for Research on Utilization of Scientific Knowledge.

Johnson, N.J. & Owen, J.M. (1995). *The Rural Professional Education Program: An Evaluation*. Prepared for the Country Education Project (Inc): Melbourne, Vic.

Kemmis, S. (1985). *The Action Research Planner*. Geelong: Deakin University Press.

Kemmis, S. (1986). 'Seven Principles for Program Evaluation in Curriculum Development and Innovation'. In E.R. House (ed.), *New Directions in Educational Evaluation*. London, UK: Falmer Press, pp. 117–30.

Lewin, K. (1946). 'Action Research and Minority Problems'. *Journal of Social Issues*, 2 (4), 41–56.

Orton, J. (1992). 'Notes for a graduate course in Action Research'. Draft Paper. Melbourne: Faculty of Education, The University of Melbourne.

Owen, J.M. & Hurworth, R.E. (1988). *Roles for Evaluators as Critical Friends: An Evaluation of the Girls and Mathematics and Science Program*. Centre for Program Evaluation, The University of Melbourne.

Owen, J.M. & Lambert, F.C. (1998). 'Evaluation and the Information Needs of Organisational Leaders'. *American Journal of Evaluation*. In press.

Patton, M.Q. (1996). 'A World Larger than Formative and Summative'. *Evaluation Practice*, 17 (2), 131–44.

Preskill, H. (1992). 'Riding the Roller Coaster of Educational Reform: The Ups and Downs of Evaluation Practice'. Paper presented at the annual meeting of the American Evaluation Association: Seattle WA. November 1992.

Rowe, W. & Jacobs, N. (1996). 'Principles and Practice of Organisationally Integrated Evaluation'. Personal communication, August.

Schein, E.H. (1985). *Organisational Culture and Leadership*. San Francisco, CA: Jossey-Bass.

Sowell, T. (1996). *Knowledge and Decisions*. New York: Basic Books.

Stake, R.E. (1980). 'Program Evaluation, Particularly Responsive Evaluation'. In W.B. Dockrell & D. Hamilton (eds), *Rethinking Evaluation Research*. London: Hodder & Stoughton.

Telford, H. (1991). 'Responsive Evaluation for Development in Self Managing Schools'. Unpublished coursework requirement, Doctor of Education, Faculty of Education, The University of Melbourne.

Wadsworth, Y. (1991). *Everyday Evaluation on the Run*. Melbourne: Action Research Issues Association.

# 12

## Monitoring Evaluation

### INTRODUCTION

A distinctive feature of Monitoring evaluation is its relation to Program[3] management within an agency or organisation. The evaluation objective is to provide information to ensure that Programs are working, and that they contribute to the success of the organisation. The Monitoring Form is generally associated with the allocation of resources and a need to show that they are being used wisely. Monitoring evaluation is often part of the total quality management and quality assurance thrusts. In the public sector, there has been an upsurge in the incorporation of evaluation for both decision-making and accountability purposes in government departments and public utilities, such as hospitals and community care centres. Quality assurance is motivated by the need for governments to be seen to deliver high-quality services at minimum expenditure of funds—that is, to assure voters that there is efficiency in spending from the public purse.

*Monitoring evaluation* is concerned with:

- the use of articulated Program plans which provide specific directions for Program delivery;
- checking that the delivery and outcomes specified are 'on-track';
- developing management information systems that can provide responsive, valid and useful information for assessing Program delivery and outcomes;
- developing mechanisms by which Programs can be finetuned on the basis of the findings provided.

---

[3] For simplicity, Program rather than program will be used in this chapter, as the emphasis in Monitoring evaluation is on mega and macro programs.

**Table 12.1    Summary of Monitoring evaluation (Form D)**

| Dimension | Properties |
|---|---|
| Orientation | Assessing Program processes and outcomes, for finetuning and to account for Program resources |
| Typical issues | • Is the Program reaching the target population?<br>• Is implementation meeting Program objectives and benchmarks?<br>• How is implementation going between sites?<br>• How is implementation now compared with a month ago?<br>• How can we finetune this Program to make it more efficient?<br>• How can we finetune this Program to make it more effective?<br>• Is there a Program site which needs attention to ensure more effective delivery? |
| State of program | Settled, Program plan is in place |
| Major focus | Delivery and outcomes |
| Timing (vis-à-vis Program delivery) | During delivery |
| Key Approaches | • Component analysis<br>• Devolved performance assessment<br>• Systems analysis |
| Assembly of evidence | Relies on the meaningful use of valid performance measures to produce performance information. In some cases this will be in the form of quantitative indicators. Systems approach relies on the availability of a management information system (MIS) which includes the capacity to develop the indicators. |

Features of this Form are included in Table 12.1. Note that, in a previous edition of this book this Form of evaluation was labelled Evaluation in Program Management.

## KEY APPROACHES TO MONITORING EVALUATION

An analysis of existing patterns of Program management suggests three major Approaches within this Form of evaluation:

• component analysis;

- devolved performance assessment; and
- systems analysis.

## Component analysis

In this Approach, senior management select a component of the Program for systematic analysis and review, and assess that component both in terms of its own objectives, and in terms of its contribution to the mission and overall goals of the Program.

In this Approach, the selection of the component for intensive study is made on the grounds of concern—for example, the component appears to be running poorly, or its outcomes are not as expected, or the component is a new or high-cost intervention that must be justified to the funding agency. The organisation's internal evaluation unit is directed to concentrate its energies on this component for a defined period.

Key assumptions underlying this approach are that senior management:

- has sufficient overview of the organisation to be able to identify a component for attention;
- has the power to direct the evaluation unit to address the issue;
- is a major audience for the evaluation findings.

An impressive instance of this Approach involved a special unit within the Department of Health and Human Services (DHHS) of the US Government. The evaluation unit, the Office of Analysis and Inspections (OAI), had the authority to evaluate any component Program funded by DHHS with a view to identifying inefficiencies and suggesting changes in its operation. The OAI reported directly to the Office of the Inspector General of the DHHS (Mangano, 1989).

Some education systems encouraged individual schools to concentrate on the evaluation of one component of their total curriculum. These 'major' evaluations were expected to involve the systematic collection and analysis of information on an area of the Program in need of review—for example, the mathematics curriculum. As the body responsible for the governance of the school, the school council, in association with the school principal, was responsible for the selection of the component to be evaluated, and received the evaluation findings (Telford, 1991).

## Devolved performance assessment

A second Approach is for senior management to encourage all components of a Program to assess their performance on a regular basis. Senior management receives these reports and, using appropriate criteria, makes judgments on the contribution of each component to the mission and overall goals of the organisation. Decisions about changes to one or more components are made in the light of these judgments.

In this approach, senior management is expected to provide guidelines and resources for undertaking component evaluations, and principles for judging the relative contributions of each component, should this be necessary. In this approach, field staff may be expected to implement the evaluation of the component in which they are located, perhaps with assistance from a central evaluation unit.

The above appear to be the principles behind the whole-school planning movement. Based on the mission of the school, each school department develops plans on a cyclic basis, generally over the school year. Components are run across the school—for example, the Year 7–12 Art program. On the basis of component objectives, the resources needed for its implementation are determined and placed before the school council, which has the power to agree to or amend the budget. Towards the end of the school year, an assessment of the impact of each component is carried out. While student learning outcomes are often considered, attention is also given to resource issues—for example, the need to replace or update old equipment (Caldwell & Spinks, 1988). All component evaluations are considered in the development of the whole-school plan for the following year.

### Systems analysis

The third Approach applies to a Program which is centrally specified and disseminated for implementation to a large number of sites. The Program specification includes a set of important goals. Guidelines are provided to for field staff to aid implementation. Field staff have little or no say in Program specification or implementation plans.

An evaluation scenario consistent with this design involves:

- a set of important outcomes to be defined and made operational;
- using a centralised evaluation unit to compare directly the performance of sites using the same operational criteria;
- relating differences in attainment of the outcomes to differences in Program delivery across sites. In this way, statements about the relative effectiveness of each site can be made.

Key evaluation questions are:

- Is the Program reaching the target population?
- Is it being implemented in the ways specified?
- Is it effective?

- How much does it cost?
- What are the costs relative to its effectiveness?

The systems level approach to evaluation developed in the United States in the mid- to late 1960s (Rossi & Freeman, 1989). While a central management information system would be useful for all three Approaches, it is essential for systems analysis, where it provides the basis for creating relevant indications of the relative effectiveness and efficiency of the Program at different sites. While the creation of a large-scale system which is easy to manage and responsive sounds attractive, there are few case examples which illustrate the advantages of such a system for Program management. This and associated issues are discussed in the next section.

## MONITORING EVALUATION: TRENDS AND CASE EXAMPLES

### Evaluands in Program monitoring

As we have indicated, evaluation within Program management is often associated with mega and macro Programs, as defined in Chapter 2. The focus is on evaluation within 'big P' Programs which are *ongoing* rather than smaller discrete 'one-off' social interventions.

An example of such a Program within the private sector is the Training and Development Program of a large regional bank. Training takes place at a dedicated central location, and at a range of other sites throughout the region it serves, and in response to emerging priorities of the bank. The Program can be thought of as the mission of the department responsible for training, and all the plans and activities are designed to achieve that mission.

An example with the public sector is an Intellectual Disabilities Services Program (IDS) in a State Department of Human Services. The IDS Program is planned and administered through head office. However, service provision occurs at a range of sites, including regional offices throughout the state.

While these examples are drawn from different sectors, the Programs have much in common. They:

- contain mission statements and broad objectives which are taken as a given for the purposes of determining outcomes;
- are designed to translate aspects of the policy of an organisation into tangible outcomes;
- are centrally planned and financed, but delivered at a range of locations, and/or in a range of different ways. That is, within each Program there will be individual components

('small p' Programs or projects), designed to achieve a subset of the objectives of the Program;

- are the prime responsibility of staff with the responsibility for the total Program. We will refer to staff in these positions collectively as senior management in this chapter. Senior management is, in turn dependent on others, sometimes at regional level, and field staff for Program delivery;
- are ongoing, rather than discrete, and are subject to modification due to organisational, political and fiscal factors, over which senior management has only partial control.

These are typical characteristics of mega and macro Programs. In some cases, such a Program cannot be distinguished from the organisation or department which is responsible for its delivery—for example, the Intellectual Disabilities Service. However, there is not always a one-to-one correspondence between departmental organisation and Program provision. The government in the state of Queensland, Australia once identified ten policy areas, such as education, health, transport, and mining, energy and electricity. Policies were translated into practice through 36 Program areas, an example of which was 'Law Courts and Legal Services'. Within this area, there were ten components, four of which were the responsibility of the Justice Department, two the responsibility of the Attorney-General and so on.

These structures are significant because of the emphasis on evaluation within the more general commitment to Program management at the executive level of government. All development and evaluation procedures are subsumed under the heading of Program management. Developments such as those in Queensland are a manifestation of a strong interest in Program management within governments in democratic countries, and in some organisations in the private sector.

Major reasons for this interest include:

- the need for departments and agencies to undertake systematic planning, to ensure greater control over service delivery than previously. This assumes that managers can identify a chain starting from an identification of need through to the delivery of outcomes, and are able to develop organisational systems to ensure that the outcomes are achieved;
- allowing senior managers to feel that they 'have their fingers on the pulse' of their bailiwicks—that is, to know what is happening at a given point in time and to be able to make decisions on the basis of this information;
- enabling management at all levels to account for their Program and organisational responsibilities. In the case of middle-level

managers, this means reporting to the next highest level of management. For senior managers, this means accounting to those who finance Program operations, such as the Treasury in the case of government. The fact that many Programs (and components within a given Program) are not self-funding means that their future, and that of those who manage them, are largely in the hands of others who provide funding. Thus evaluation within Program management often requires evidence about the effective utilisation of funds, for use by someone in a more senior or more powerful position.

## Elements of Program management

Elements of Program management include:

- a strategic plan for the implementation of relevant aspects of government, or head office policy. The strategic plan is the first operational step in the translation of policy into Program goals and implementation strategies. By strategic planning we mean:

  the process by which an organisation creates a vision of its future and develops the necessary structure, resources, procedures and operations to achieve that future;

- a Program structure that reflects the strategic plan and has goals and objectives in terms of desired outcomes. The Program structure directs the development of Program management frameworks and represents a systematic ordering of related management and provider activities which are consistent with the strategic plan;

- management arrangements to ensure the implementation of the structure. Generally a requirement is the development and maintenance of a management information system or systems (MIS), a coordinated data base on aspects of Program provision;

- the use of the MIS to help determine the extent to which outcomes (performance) are being achieved;

- the use of this information when considering effective existing and innovative means of achieving Program goals—in other words, MIS information is used as a basis for decisions about delivery;

- the use of MIS when considering fundamental issues about the Program—for example, its goals and relevance to the achievement of government or head office policy. This information is often considered in conjunction with other relevant factors, such as changes due to political and other non-evaluative factors.

In association with the adoption of Program management, a system of personnel management is sometimes implemented. This involves the development of position statements, including objectives, and the supervision of more junior workers by more senior ones. This is based on the assumption that the delivery of service is strongly related to the performance of individuals.

An authoritarian view of personnel management by objectives works on the assumptions that if workers have clearly defined work objectives and control processes and financial incentives are in place, then workers will have the direction and drive to be productive. On the other hand, a process view of personnel management concentrates on the development of outcomes, services and products, rather than the individual. In this approach, there is acknowledgment that at least some of the causes of non-achievement of Program goals are outside the control of the individual worker (Pall, 1987). In a process approach, personnel management attempts to identify the relative effects of worker and other factors on Program delivery. Supervision takes on a formative nature, designed to assist staff to improve their performance, rather than to use the information for appraisal purposes. An essential part of Program management is the need to manage people. Clear guidelines are needed to assist those responsible for counselling and assisting staff responsible for implementing the projects and activities within a Program.

## Large P Program evaluation

From the above discussion, it is clear that systematic Program evaluation is an essential component of Program management. There is a need at all levels of management for information:

- on which to base decisions about the Program and its components; and
- to account for funds allocated to the Program and its components.

The general principles of evaluation which have been discussed in Chapters 1 and 4 still apply. These include the need for evaluation planning, the collection and analysis of information, and the development of appropriate reporting systems. While there are similarities, there are also unique characteristics compared with other Forms. These are as follows:

- There is a strong emphasis on outcomes, and in some Programs there may be a series of linked outcomes rather than a single one (Funnell & Lenne, 1989).

- Programs are ongoing and there is a need for evaluative information over time—that is, trend data is generally required.
- Many Programs are designed to provide goods or services rather than promote changes in behaviour.
- Evaluative data are often processed and reported in simple but logical ways.
- Senior management, in particular, may require gross or aggregated information rather than, or in addition to, information about individual components.

These points imply that evaluators are likely to be insiders and may need to have a rapid response capability. While it is unlikely to be the case in schools, other government agencies have developed evaluation units to undertake evaluative aspects within Program management. Muscatello (1989), with the benefit of experience, has outlined the culture and roles of such a unit within a large state government authority.

Evaluation units within organisations are a recent innovation. A large Road and Traffic Authority (RTA) set up a Performance Evaluation Branch as an independent authority within the RTA. Harrison and Barboza (1991), reviewing the impact of the Branch after one year of operation, report that:

> the deliberate separation of the performance evaluation function from the operational and strategic functions within the authority has provided the Branch with the necessary degree of independence and impartiality to determine the nature of performance problems confronting the Authority.

The writers describe the work of the Branch as being akin to 'carrots' and 'sticks'. The former include such roles as educator, facilitator and promoter of evaluation within the organisation. The latter category includes 'performance appraisal' and checking or monitoring the role of the Authority, a process seen as vital to 'good management'. Stick-focused activities predominated over carrot-focused ones in the first year of the Evaluation Branch's existence.

By contrast, a Workcover Authority set up a Corporate and Strategic Planning Branch in which evaluators worked closely with planners. Vincent and Motbey (1991) believe that this arrangement facilitates ongoing planning through informal small-scale evaluations, as well as allowing for larger scale formal evaluations, generally conducted to prove the effectiveness of Program delivery. They say that:

> [In] our experience, the single most important factor in successfully linking planning and evaluation is placing responsibility for their promotion and co-ordination in one unit. At best, planning and evaluation units which are structurally separate will have to expend time and effort on getting and keeping their acts together. At worst they will operate in isolation and their value to the organisation will be significantly reduced.
>
> Secondly, it is important that the organisation's planning and reporting requirements and systems are integrated and that progress and performance are always evaluated by reference to objectives and targets established in a plan.
>
> Thirdly, planner-evaluators should model integration of planning and evaluation in all their activities. Evaluation should be an integral part of any planning process and document (not tacked on at the end). All evaluation reports should address the means by which implementation of findings is to be planned and achieved.

## Use of Program hierarchies

In all three Approaches described above, the selection of key evaluation issues and sound data management techniques is essential. Because of an emphasis on impact, information for management purposes is likely to focus heavily on Program outcomes.

In Program management terms, data collection and analysis processes are designed to produce *performance information*, because of the need to show that the Program is both efficient and effective.

An important and recent development in structuring the compilation of performance information is the use of outcomes hierarchies, a chain in which each successive outcome depends on the attainment of a prior one. Suchman (1967) was among the first to suggest that Program objectives and outcomes could be classified as immediate, intermediate and ultimate. In Chapter 10, we have provided some examples of outcomes hierarchies which have been developed as part of a Clarificative evaluation. Outcomes hierarchies are an essential component of Program logic, a plan which connects objectives, implementation and outcomes.

In Monitoring evaluation, all goals are fair game to be assessed. Alternatively, an evaluation can concentrate on those goals which are amenable for use as impact criteria at a given time in the life of a Program. In determining which outcomes are to be examined in a given evaluation, the information needs of the clients must be considered.

The Program logic approach has been used with some success in some public sectors. Funnell (1990) suggests that the employment of a logic approach:

> helps managers to organise the results they are trying to achieve in a cause–effect chain. It helps them to identify what considerations should enter into their interpretation of measured results. It provides a framework for taking due account of the perspectives of a range of stakeholders.

### Example 12.1 Larger than life: an evaluation of a media campaign

(This case is a summary of a paper given by Masters at the 1990 conference of the Australasian Evaluation Society.)

The New South Wales Tourism Commission conducted a major media campaign to increase visits to the state. The campaign was aimed at the domestic tourism market and included both print and TV advertisements interstate (Melbourne, Brisbane and Adelaide) and in the intrastate market (Sydney, Newcastle and Wollongong). The campaign theme was: 'New South Wales: Larger Than Life'.

In allocating the enhancement to fund the marketing Program, the New South Wales Treasury required evaluation of its impact. The Tourism Commission of New South Wales approached the New South Wales Office of Public Management to assist in the evaluation.

*The evaluation approach*

The campaign was evaluated using the Program logic methodology originally developed by the New South Wales Program Evaluation Unit (see Table 12.2). As a mass communication Program, the media campaign attempted to influence behaviour through an educational/advisory strategy. The left-hand side of Table 12.2 presents a generic outcomes hierarchy for educational/advisory Programs. This generic hierarchy was used for deriving the intended outcomes of the Tourism Commission media campaign. The right-hand side of Table 12.2 shows how the desired outcomes of the media campaign correspond to the various levels of the generic hierarchy.

The top level of the hierarchy, increased visitations to New South Wales, corresponds to a corporate objective of the Tourism Commission. To achieve this outcome:

- the advertisements had to run as planned;
- an appropriate number and type of people had to see the advertisements;
- people had to respond positively to the campaign;
- as a result of the campaign, people had to seek information about holidays in New South Wales (the TV campaign had a 008 telephone number response and the print campaign a coupon response mechanism);
- an acceptable proportion of those who sought information actually purchased holiday packages. (These packages had been produced as part of the campaign and were specifically targeted at the market segments identified through market research.)

*Issues raised by the evaluation*

The following issues arising from the use of the Program logic methodology in evaluating the media campaign were notable:

1   Evaluations of public communications Programs, such as mass media campaigns, suffer from the difficulty of disentangling the effects of the Program activities (e.g. advertisements) from external influences on the ultimate outcome (e.g. increased visitation to New South Wales). For example, in this evaluation, the impact of the Tourism Commission's media campaign was affected by an air pilots' dispute. The outcomes hierarchy approach helps overcome this problem by including a series of intermediate outcomes in a cause–effect chain. Thus the evaluation enables measurement of these intermediate outcomes as determinants of ultimate success.

    Traditionally, funding bodies ask for *direct* evidence of a Program's contributions to ultimate aims or corporate objectives without recognising the methodological problems inherent in doing so. The outcomes hierarchy in this study was successfully used by the Tourism Commission as a tool for communicating the Program logic to the Treasury.

2   There is another methodological problem in evaluating

public communications Programs and educational Programs in general: traversing the gap between knowledge/attitude/skills change on the one hand and change in behaviour on the other. This evaluation obtained information not only on people's *reaction* to the advertising campaign, but also determined whether people actually sought further information on holidays in New South Wales and whether that translated into their purchase of holiday packages.

3   In identifying a number of levels of intended outcome, the Program logic approach lends itself to an evaluation employing multiple methods and multiple sources of information.

The outcomes hierarchy enabled the Marketing Director to understand how these different information sources fit together in an evaluation context.

4   As indicated above, the evaluation of the media campaign was initially 'driven' by accountability requirements: demonstrating to Treasury how the campaign contributed to increased domestic visitation in New South Wales. However, by collecting data on a range of outcomes, the evaluation yielded information useful to the Program manager in pinpointing deficiencies in the campaign that could be redressed, and identifying successful components that could be built upon in future marketing activities. (Masters, 1990)

## ASSEMBLING EVIDENCE FOR MONITORING

To inform managers and others about the success or otherwise of a Program such as this, it is essential that evaluators use the full range of data collection and analysis techniques available to evaluators. Up until recently, most of the discussion about management evaluation has centred around data management, in particular the use of performance indicators or performance measures. These are the criteria for evaluation first encountered in Chapter 1. Because of the interest in their use, most of the remainder of this Chapter is devoted to critiques of indicators or measures, and examples of ways in which they can be deployed.

A case could be made for indicators to be at least part of the data collection and analysis in all three Approaches to Program management outlined in the previous section. However, there is now significant debate about the past usefulness of performance indicators in government agency and corporate planning. Winston

**Table 12.2    Outcomes hierarchies: advisory/educational programs in general and the media campaign**

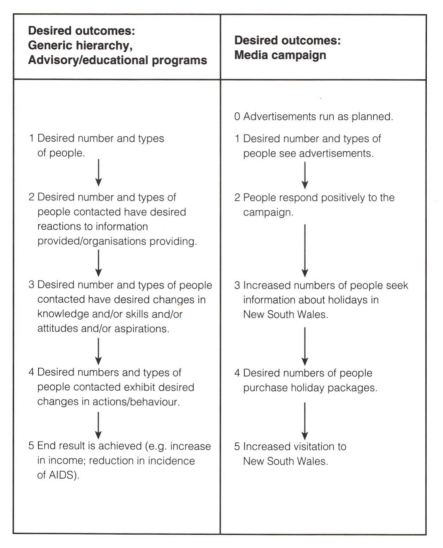

| Desired outcomes:<br>Generic hierarchy,<br>Advisory/educational programs | Desired outcomes:<br>Media campaign |
|---|---|
|  | 0 Advertisements run as planned. |
| 1 Desired number and types of people. | 1 Desired number and types of people see advertisements. |
| 2 Desired number and types of people contacted have desired reactions to information provided/organisations providing. | 2 People respond positively to the campaign. |
| 3 Desired number and types of people contacted have desired changes in knowledge and/or skills and/or attitudes and/or aspirations. | 3 Increased numbers of people seek information about holidays in New South Wales. |
| 4 Desired numbers and types of people contacted exhibit desired changes in actions/behaviour. | 4 Desired numbers of people purchase holiday packages. |
| 5 End result is achieved (e.g. increase in income; reduction in incidence of AIDS). | 5 Increased visitation to New South Wales. |

(1991) is one of the major critics of their use at national and state levels. He challenges us to find exemplary examples of use:

> It appears that there is no evidence in the literature or in the practical experience of governments that performance indicators have ever been successfully applied by governments to the evaluation of human service Programs, in the context of Program budgeting. There is evidence to the contrary, that exemplifies failures to get performance indicators to contribute as intended to management and budget cycle decision making.

Winston goes further to question the terminology, asking rhetorically:

> What does the term (performance indicator) mean? Why is some-thing a performance indicator, rather than just an indicator, rather than a *management* indicator?

This is helpful, for it moves the emphasis from the *source* of evaluation data, the measurement of performance, to one which emphasises *use* of evaluative data—that is, the management of Programs. The use of the term 'management' is preferred; it is less ambiguous than 'performance', for the latter has a range of meanings including personnel appraisal. As we have seen, this means something very different from Program evaluation.

Nevertheless, the term 'performance indicator' has assumed a life of its own in evaluation terminology. We will use the term *indicator* in the discussions within the remainder of this chapter. Readers might wish to substitute 'management indicator' or 'per-formance indicator' if they wish.

The idea that indicators could be used as tools of management was introduced about 20 years ago, and is derived from studies of private-sector organisational effectiveness. Ferguson & McIntyre 1991 comment that:

> the extent to which the use of indicators can in practice contribute to the management and quality of service in the public sector is directly related to the extent to which managers fully understand the concept, come to appreciate accurately both their uses and limitations, and learn to apply them appropriately in the context of their particular Programs.

In summary, indicators have a place within the range of possible evaluation methods within Program management. They need to be used carefully, so the next section is devoted to ways in which they should be designed and applied.

## INDICATORS AS EVIDENCE

An indicator is a simple statistic which is made up from a number of other, generally simpler, statistics. We are familiar with social indicators measuring the extent of social phenomena in our every-day life. The national balance of payments, the rate of school retention and the proportion of families below the poverty line are indicators which come to mind as examples which receive media coverage. A key feature of these indicators is that they are used continually to inform decisions designed to alter the state of the social system affecting them.

Indicators can also be used to make statements about the effectiveness of organisations or the impact of social Programs. Well-constructed indicators can provide summary information which allows Program managers and others to evaluate the effects of Programs for which they are responsible. They must be used in some form of meaningful data analysis, not as a set of statistics which have little or no meaning.

Indicators for a given Program (or component) must therefore be used in one of the following ways:

- to compare Program (component) trends at different points in time. This is known as monitoring;
- to compare the performance of a Program (or component) to an acceptable set of standards or goals. This is a competency approach to Program evaluation and can be used to determine how to modify a Program in order to attain its goals. Again this is a monitoring operation and could be used by managers or Program deliverers at a single site to help make decisions about Program directions;
- to compare the implementation of the same Program at different sites or locations. This is a comparative approach to Program evaluation and can be used in centralised systems to scrutinise sites at which there is poorer performance. This is known as a systems approach to evaluation.

### Types of indicators

A distinction has been made between three kinds of indicators:

- *appropriateness*—this refers to the match between current community and government priorities and Program objectives;
- *efficiency*—this refers to the relative cost of achieving positive impacts via the Program under consideration;
- *effectiveness*—this refers to the match between Program outcomes and Program objectives (Wells, 1986).

However, in most Program management approaches to evaluation, objectives are taken as given and indicators are designed to provide a basis from which judgments can be made about the extent to which the Program is achieving its objectives. Thus the emphasis is on efficiency and effectiveness indicators.

There are differing approaches within the area of efficiency. Economists see cost benefit analysis indicators as economic ratios (rates of return) and cost effectiveness indicators as those in which inputs are measured in money terms and outcomes in physical units. Efficiency indicators thus measure how well resources are being used within the general perspective of maximising output per unit of input.

An example is the ratio of the number of graduates from a training Program versus the cost of running the Program.

It is important to note that efficiency indicators cannot be used independently of qualitative judgments, particularly if a range of indicators are being used to assess the worth of a Program. Owen (1993) notes that:

> In assessing efficiency data, it should be recognised that all outputs may not be at the same level of quality. As an example, achieving a lower cost per unit of output at the expense of a decrease in the quality of standard of service is not a true improvement in efficiency. To address this issue, quality considerations can be built into the efficiency indicators. The indicators could show the cost of water per million litres supplied that meet minimum quality standards or the cost of handling complaints from the public and are answered within 'x' working days. In this way calculations would include only those outputs which meet certain quality standards.

Effectiveness indicators show the extent to which the objectives of a Program have been met and generally concentrate on the effects on the target population for the Program. An example is the ratio of the number of graduates who find employment from a training Program in a given time versus the number who entered the Program.

## LINKING PROGRAM PLANNING WITH THE USE OF INDICATORS

As already discussed, the use of most indicators depends on clear and specific objectives and so, before any indicators can be developed, objectives must be clearly and simply articulated. In practice, undertaking an evaluation in which indicators are to be used involves this articulation as a first step. The case study example which follows expands on this position, in which indicators are used to monitor the implementation and outcomes of service provision over time.

**Example 12.2 Home Energy Advisory Service (HEAS) program**

In reading this Program development and evaluation outline, you might consider how the suggested indicators could be made operational.

    1 *Specify Program objectives*

The objectives of HEAS are:

- to provide a free in-home energy audit and advice and a limited free retrofitting service to low-income householders to reduce their energy costs and improve their comfort;
- to contribute to the provision of targeted and integrated energy assistance schemes to low-income households;
- to provide cost-effective audit and advice services to other target groups.

The Program, by assisting low-income high energy users to reduce their energy bills, will contribute to the Social Justice objective of ensuring that people on low incomes have increased access to essential goods and services.

2 *Identify the target group(s) for the Program*

HEAS is available to holders of a Commonwealth Card who have a minimum expenditure of $100 on energy during any three-month billing period over the preceding year.

3 *Identify the resources, staff and equipment needed to run the Program*

(Sometimes these resources are called the inputs, but we prefer to regard them as costs of providing the Program.)

- *staff*: energy advisers, DITR administrators, SEC administrators;
- *capital*: energy advisers' cars, office facilities;
- *equipment/ materials*: energy advisers' personal computers, retrofitting materials;
- *non-resource*: advisers' attitudes and technical knowledge, clients' responsiveness to the service and behaviour modifications suggested.

4 *Specify the activities needed to achieve the objectives*

HEAS provides free in-home service to eligible households on the efficient and cost-effective use of appliances, thermal performance within the home and appropriate efficiency behaviour. Energy advisers visit each home and conduct an energy audit to identify the scope for improvement in energy efficiency in consultation with the householder.

The adviser can authorise expenditure by HEAS of up to $250 per month on energy-efficient home improvements such as insulation and weather stripping. The service is provided statewide and delivered under SEC management. Clients are identified through responses to HEAS letters and other marketing activities and referrals from welfare and other agencies.

5 *Establish that the outcomes are 'on stream'*

In other words, that it is reasonable to expect that the Program has been in place for a sufficient time to produce effects.

(This would be a decision made by Program providers and management.)

6 *Develop indicators and use them to monitor the Program over time*

Outcomes:

- number of referrals from welfare agencies;
- number of completed home visits;
- number of energy-saving audits conducted.

Possible indicators include:

*Efficiency*
- number of audits/cost of inputs;
- costs of retrofits/cost of inputs;
- average energy saving per household/average cost input per household;
- number of audits/administration costs;
- number of retrofits/administration costs;
- average length of time between referral and auditing/retrofit.

*Effectiveness*
- energy saving per month by clients in receipt of retrofitting;
- proportion of clients receiving retrofitting;
- proportion of assistance requests outstanding;
- number of households receiving assistance by income band;
- number of households receiving assistance by housing tenure.

An important point to make about this prescription is the emphasis on Program development and implementation. The evaluative aspect is the final step of six important processes, five of which are concerned with delivery. This is a reminder that monitoring processes should not be undertaken unless there is ample evidence that the delivery aspects have been given sufficient attention. Example 12.3 below uses these steps to detail the use of indicators.

## CREATING AND USING INDICATORS

Once key outcomes have been identified, there are technical and logical issues associated with making the indicators operational. This involves the creation of written 'measures statements' for each objective, which can be turned into a simple algorithm, and hence into an indicator.

### Example 12.3 Corrections Services evaluation

Given the paucity of examples, it may be useful to examine the following example of translating measures statements into algorithms. Day (1990) developed a set of performance indicators for discussion by a national conference on Corrections Services. The comments provided by Day in this example show the need for users to be aware of the assumptions made in the development of the indicator.

*Objective 1*: To carry out the penalties of the courts efficiently and effectively

*Indicator 1*: Daily cost of correctional Program per prisoner

*Calculation*: If 'a' is the annual cost of the Program and 'b' is the annual 'stock of prisoners'—that is, the number of prisoners in custody each day summed across 365 days—then:

$$PI(1) = a/b$$

*Comments*: Program needs to be defined. There is a problem of which cost to use, capital or recurrent. Summation of daily prisoner numbers is tedious, but copes with issue of variable duration of confinement. Assumes that stock of prisoners is calculated by summing the daily average prison population over the year.

- considering issues associated with the use of data from the management information system:
  - *validity*: Does the indicator measure a Program outcome which can be attributed solely to that Program?
  - *accuracy (reliability)*: Is each indicator a 'true' measure of the index intended? Are the measures used biased in any way—for example, are they continuously understating or overstating the value of the variable of interest?
  - *availability*: Will the data be available from all sites (in the case of a cross-site analysis), and/or will

the data be available from the one site at different periods of time (in the case of monitoring)?

- *practicality*: Can the information be collected and processed without excessive strain on the evaluation team and on others who may be involved in information retrieval?

- Checking for each indicator and the indicators as a set against the following criteria:
  - substantive considerations;
  - *significance*: Does each indicator measure some aspect of the Program which is of significance? Is the data worth collecting?
  - *uniqueness*: Does each indicator provide information not provided by any other in the set, or in any other way?
  - *comprehensiveness*: Do the indicators, taken as a set, cover the objectives as a whole?
  - comparative considerations:
  - *norms*: Are the norms on which judgments are made about the Program(s) clear? Will the indicators be used to compare measures from: the same Program at other times; other Programs at the same time; or an absolute standard?
  - utilisation considerations:
  - *interpretability*: Will decision-makers be able to make sense of the information?

## ADDRESSING CHALLENGES IN DEVELOPING AND USING INDICATORS

Organisations developing Program monitoring systems face a number of challenges. These include: identifying and clearly specifying the intended outcomes; developing appropriate measures of performance; establishing sustainable sytems for collecting and analysing data; and using comparisons and judgment to turn the performance data into performance information.

### Example 12.4 Encouraging the use of indicators

A survey of federal government agencies conducted by the US General Accounting Office found that the most difficult challenges in developing performance measures were: (a) getting beyond outputs to develop outcome measures; and (b) specifying quantifiable performance indicators. Strategies which had been used to develop outcome measures included:

- developing a measurement model that encompassed state and local activity to identify outcome measures for federal programs;
- encouraging program managers to develop different funding scenarios;
- conceptualising the outcomes of daily activities;
- planning and implementing customer satisfaction and developing multiple measures of satisfaction;
- using qualitative measures of outcomes; and
- involving stakeholders. (GAO, 1997)

## CONCLUSION

As indicated earlier, much of the literature about effective Monitoring has focused almost exclusively on the use of indicators, rather than on broader evaluation issues, of which the use of indicators is a relatively minor part. Evaluation for management purposes does require summary information for decision-making. However, an over-emphasis on the use of indicators or measures can result in a partial rather than complete description of the impact of a Program. It can also lead to a negative feedback effect on Program delivery—for example, where indicators are used to rank the effectiveness of sites in delivering a centrally developed Program, there could be strong pressure on site staff to focus their work on outcomes measured by the indicators, resulting in a neglect of important outcomes not amenable to measurement by these indicators. This is known as *goal or objective displacement*.

In most Programs, there are outcomes which can only be assessed by qualitative means and, as we have seen, there is always the possibility of unintended outcomes. If one or both of these outcomes are important, then indicators may not be useful at all, or should be used in conjunction with other forms of data collection and analysis to give an accurate overview of Program achievements.

This takes us back to the notion of management *information*, a judicious mixture of indicators and other more descriptive data. Some of this information might describe how the Program operates, and include attention to discrepancies between operational intentions and actual Program implementation. The usefulness of indicators is thus dependent on our ability to understand Program processes which influence indicator results and may be amenable to change. If information on processes is not available, on what basis do managers make changes designed to improve Program effectiveness and efficiency?

A regular and useful supply of management information cannot rely on a blind commitment to indicators. A more eclectic mixture of evaluative data will provide a more useful information base for managers. This can be achieved through management support for internal evaluation units, but it requires unit staff to be creative and flexible in response to emerging management concerns.

## REFERENCES

Caldwell, B.J. & Spinks, J.M. (1988). *The Self Managing School*. London: Falmer Press.

Day, N.A. (1990). 'Performance Indicators in Custodial and Community-based Programs'. Unpublished paper. Centre for Program Evaluation. The University of Melbourne.

Ferguson, C. & McIntyre, G. (1991). 'Using Performance Indicators to Monitor Service Delivery'. Paper prepared at the *Annual Conference of the Australasian Evaluation Society*, Adelaide, pp. 675–80.

Funnell, S. (1990). 'Developments in the Use of the NSW Approach to Analysing Program Logic'. Paper prepared at *Annual Conference of the Australasian Evaluation Society*, 2, Sydney, pp. 247–55.

Funnell, S. & Lenne, B. (1989). 'A Typology of Public Sector Programs'. Paper presented at the Annual Meeting of the American Evaluation Association, November, San Francisco, CA:

GAO (1997). *Managing for Results: Analytical Challenges in Measuring Performance*. GAO/HEHS/GGD–97–138). Washington, DC: United States of America General Accounting Office.

Harrison, C. & Barboza, E. (1991). 'Performance Evaluation: Carrot or Stick?' In *Proceedings of the National Conference of the Australasian Evaluation Society*, Adelaide.

Mangano, M.F. (1989). *Rapid Response Evaluation for Decision Makers Office of Analysis and Inspections*, Office of Inspector General, US Department of Health and Human Services, Washington DC.

Masters, G. (1990). 'Promoting NSW: An Evaluation of a Media Campaign'. Paper presented at the *Annual Conference of the Australasian Society*. Sydney, NSW, pp. 283–87.

Muscatello, D.B. (1989). 'Evaluation and the Management Process'. *Evaluation Practice*, 10 (3), 12–17.

Owen, J.M. (1993). *Program Evaluation, Forms and Approaches*. Sydney: Allen & Unwin.

Pall, G.A. (1987). *Quality Process Management*. Newark, NJ: Prentice Hall.

Rossi, P.H. & Freeman, H.E. (1989). *Evaluation: A Systematic Approach*. 4th edn. Newbury Park, CA: Sage.

Suchman, E.A. (1967). *Evaluation Research: Principles and Practice and Social Action*. New York: Russell Sage Foundation.

Telford, H. (1991). 'Responsive Evaluation for Development in Self Managing Schools'. Unpublished paper for Doctor of Education, The University of Melbourne.

Vincent, I. & Motbey, D. (1991). 'Linking Planning and Evaluation'. In *Proceedings of the National Conference of the Australasian Evaluation Society*. Adelaide, pp. 760–3.

Wells, C.H. (1986). 'The Development and Use of Performance Indicators: An Approach Being Used in the NSW Public Sector'. Paper presented at the Annual Conference of the Australasian Evaluation Society. Sydney.

Winston, J.A. (1991). 'Linking Evaluation and Performance Management'. Paper presented at the Annual Conference of the Australasian Evaluation Society. Adelaide, pp. 598–607.

# 13

## Impact Evaluation

### INTRODUCTION

Impact evaluation is predicated on the not-unreasonable assumption that citizens at large should know whether programs funded by government, or in which they have an interest, are making a difference. In times of economic stringency particularly, the public has a right to know that money spent in the public arena has been translated into effective social or educational interventions. For example, have the millions of dollars spent on making cities safer places actually led to a decrease in inner-city crime? For a given program, stakeholders have a right to expect that programs, where possible, meet their intended goals and do not lead to negative side effects. Parents at a local school are rightly interested in whether the literacy approach taken by that school is meeting the needs of their children. Likewise, those in management positions need to know whether the strategies they have selected to solve a given problem are being used and whether they work. For example, the manager of a new road safety program needs to be satisfied that the program can be implemented as planned and that it will lead to improvements in safety. All these scenarios provide a rationale for impact studies.

Impact evaluation has a strong summative emphasis in that it provides findings from which a judgment of the worth of the program can be made. Impact evaluations are retrospective in that they logically occur at an end-point, a time at which it is decided to take stock of the program. Ideally, Impact evaluations are undertaken on programs which are in a mature or settled stage and have had sufficient time to have an effect.

It is not uncommon for commissioners of an evaluation to

ask for an Impact evaluation on an immature program. Those responsible for the evaluation need to educate commissioners and clients that, by agreeing to this request, they may prematurely judge and terminate a program which, with some improvements, might become effective.

*Impact evaluation* is concerned with:

- determining the range and extent of outcomes of a program;
- determining whether the program has been implemented as planned and how implementation has affected outcomes;
- providing evidence to funders, senior managers and politicians about the extent to which resources allocated to a program have been spent wisely;
- informing decisions about replication or extension of the program.

Consider the case of a program being offered as a trial in one location. The program is sponsored by a government department, which is considering the expansion of the program to other locations. An Impact evaluation of the trial program is undertaken to inform decisions about the expansion. In this case it would be important for the Impact evaluation to focus on both the outcome and implementation phases of the program.

Key aspects of the Impact evaluation Form are summarised in Table 13.1.

As can be seen, outcomes are a major concern of Impact evaluation. What do we mean by an outcome? Based on some recent work done to assist the American-based United Way carry out evaluations of their projects (Hatry & van Houten, 1996), an outcome can be described as follows:

*Outcomes* are benefits for participants during or after their involvement with a program. Outcomes relate to knowledge, skills, attitudes, values, behaviour, condition or status. For a particular program, there may be various levels of outcomes, with one level of outcome leading to a 'higher' or longer term outcome (see Chapter 10 for a discussion of outcome hierarchies). Examples of outcomes include: increased knowledge of nutritional needs, changes in literacy levels, getting a job, having higher self-dependence. An example of a hierarchy of outcomes for a youth mentoring program could be: (a) attending school more regularly; (b) improved reading skills; (c) getting higher grades; (d) getting a job.

By comparison, *outputs* are products of the program's activities, such as the number of meals provided, classes taught, participants served or materials distributed. Outputs might be thought of as a summary of the implementation of the program.

**Table 13.1   Summary of Impact evaluation (Form E)**

| Dimensions | Properties |
|---|---|
| Orientation | Establishment of program worth<br>Justification of decisions to mount the program<br>Accountability to funders and other stakeholders |
| Typical issues | • Has the program been implemented as planned?<br>• Have the stated goals of the program been achieved?<br>• Have the needs of those served by the program been met?<br>• What are the unintended outcomes?<br>• Does the implementation strategy lead to intended outcomes?<br>• How do differences in implementation affect program outcomes?<br>• What are the benefits of the program given the costs? |
| State of program | Settled |
| Major focus | Focus on delivery and/or outcomes. Most comprehensive studies combine both delivery and outcomes known as process–outcome studies |
| Timing (vis-à-vis program delivery) | Nominally 'after' the program has completed at least one cycle with program beneficiaries. In practice, impact studies could be undertaken at any time after program is 'settled'. |
| Key Approaches | • Objectives-based<br>• Needs-based<br>• Goal-free<br>• Process-outcome studies<br>• Performance audit |
| Assembly of evidence | Traditionally required use of preordinate research designs, where possible the use of treatment and control groups, and the use of tests and other quantitative data. Studies of implementation generally require observational data. Determining all the outcomes requires use of more exploratory methods and the use of qualitative evidence. |

The implementation of the program, through its component activities, should be designed to achieve intended outcomes, as we also saw in Chapter 11.

While Impact evaluations can provide findings of direct interest to stakeholders of the program under review, they can also be a source of information for the wider community of scholars and policy-makers. Probably more than any other evaluation Form, Impact evaluation findings related to a given program may contribute to the funded knowledge about a phenomenon of which the given program is typical. Either individually, or by aggregating findings across similar programs, it is possible to arrive at some generalisations about the phenomenon. Thus, as we mentioned in a discussion of evaluation utilisation in Chapter 6, evaluation findings can contribute to the social science knowledge base. Given that most Impact evaluations are retrospective, their direct influence on the program being examined is obviously limited unless it is replicated elsewhere. But the fact that the findings might be used more broadly provides those responsible for impact studies with an incentive to carry them out with rigour. For example, Ainley (1978) undertook an extensive evaluation of the impact of a national program to provide science laboratories and facilities to schools. The study was undertaken just as the program was completed and thus could not affect the way in which the program operated. Nevertheless, the findings were of great interest, not only to the politicians who had supported the program, but to science educators at large. The findings were used often in subsequent years in debates about the importance of facilities in the teaching of science in schools and the need to maintain and upgrade them wherever possible. In fact, this study was used extensively by administrators to ensure that science in schools continued to be based on an enquiry approach to learning.

## KEY APPROACHES TO IMPACT EVALUATION

In summary, Impact evaluations are concerned with establishing what works and why. The Approaches within Impact evaluation represent the closest manifestation in the real world to the logic of evaluation which we discussed in Chapter 1. To be able to back up claims that a program is having an impact, we must translate the logic of evaluation principles into action. This involves selection of key variables, setting standards and having access to evidence from which we can determine the success or otherwise of the intervention. Impact evaluation provided the genesis of evaluation practice—in fact, for some time it was seen as the only Form of evaluation. While thinking about evaluation has progressed from this position, it is still true to say that Impact evaluation is the most practised Form of evaluation. Thus it is important for evaluators to have a thorough grasp of the essentials of this Form of evaluation. As can be seen from Table 13.1, five Approaches to Impact evaluation are included within the Form. These are:

- objectives-based;
- needs-based;
- goal-free;
- process-product studies; and
- performance audit.

These will now be discussed in turn.

## OBJECTIVES-BASED

The first Approach to Impact evaluation is based on a judgment of whether the stated goals or objectives of a program have been achieved. Tyler (1950) was the chief proponent of evaluation based on goal achievement, and is regarded as the father figure of program evaluation. In this Approach, the goals of a program are taken as a given, and decisions about the success of the program are based on the extent to which goals are achieved, according to some standard or level of achievement. In some cases, these objectives are expressed in terms of gains in attainment of program participants.

Tyler was concerned with the attainment of educational objectives, but the approach has been used in other helping professions, and in management. Management by objectives can focus on organisations (big P Programs) and/or on individuals. In the latter situation, we move into the realms of assessment or appraisal rather than program evaluation. The development of fair and valid procedures for assessing the performance of individuals is a contentious area because the results of performance appraisal have direct consequences for them. Staff can be demoted or promoted and bonuses in some public and private organisations are tied to the results of individual performance appraisals.

The translation of program goals or objectives into valid measures of outcomes is a major methodological issue. It may be possible to use previously developed instrument(s), but the evaluator must be satisfied that the instrument has face validity—that the intended audience for the evaluation will find it a credible measure of the objective(s). There is a temptation to use 'off-the-shelf' instruments, even though they do not fully measure up to this validity test. There are instances where the evaluators themselves must develop instruments which validly reflect the intentions of the program under review, so some skill in developing tests and other outcome measures is called for.

The main tasks in setting up an objectives-based evaluation are as follows:

- Determine whether a key issue for stakeholders is to check on the attainment of program outcomes. Bear in mind that the program should be 'settled' for an outcomes study to be realistic (see Table 13.1).
- Determine the 'real' objectives or goals of the program. Possible sources of information about program goals include:

    - policy documents;
    - program statements;
    - interviews with program providers;
    - a combination of more than one of the above.

- Decide on the most appropriate ways to determine whether the program has led to the attainment of the goals—for example, with relation to the design of the data management, whether a 'control group' is available, whether it is possible to use a 'before and after' design, and when one can logically collect outcome data.
- Select an appropriate measuring instrument, or write and trial a new instrument:

    - selection of appropriate instruments as discussed above. This includes the style and content of data collecting instruments, and the items to be included in the instrument;
    - the level of goal attainment acceptable as the criterion for judging the effectiveness of the program.

- Identify the sources of evidence.
- Collect and analyse the evidence.
- Draw conclusions, in some cases make judgments or recommendations, and report the findings.

## NEEDS-BASED

An alternative to an objectives-based approach is to determine impact on the basis of whether a program meets an identifiable need. Thus it is important that nature and extent of need be established as the basis of structuring an Impact evaluation when this Approach is adopted. Needs-based Impact evaluations were first suggested by Scriven (1972) within a more general discussion of the limitations of objectives-based approaches. A judgment of the worth of a program depends on the extent to which it meets the needs of the program participants. Underlying this Approach is an assumption that the objectives or goals of the program do not necessarily reflect the needs of program beneficiaries. Thus, while an objectives Approach is based on the internal consistency, a needs-based Approach adopts an external standard of reference for judging program worth. You will appreciate that, if program goals do reflect needs, then the objectives-based and needs-based findings should be similar. It is probably true that most program developers attempt to reflect the needs of participants in their program design, but there are always likely to be programs which are developed without reference to the needs of participants. In fact, if a needs assessment is not undertaken (a Form A Approach), this leaves well-intentioned program developers reliant on other sources of information for their planning. Of course, there are also instances where programs are developed without reference to participant needs—for example, if a program is 'thrown together' in order to spend unallocated resources at the end of a financial year.

## GOAL-FREE

The goal-free Approach was also a reaction to what was seen as a slavish acceptance of the objectives-based Approach to Impact evaluation. In Goal-Free evaluation, the evaluator deliberately ignores the stated or intended goals of the program. The purpose is to examine all program effects, rather than limiting the investigation to outcomes which reflect program objectives. Practically, the notion of deliberately ignoring the intentions of a programmatic intervention borders on the bizarre. Commissioners and clients are almost always interested in whether program objectives have been met, and the evaluator would need to go to extremes to ignore information about how the program is meant to operate. So, in practice, Goal-Free evaluations are rare. However, the notion of Goal-Free evaluation has led to one important aspect of the practice of Impact evaluation: examining unintended as well as intended outcomes. In almost every social or educational intervention, there are outcomes that could not have been anticipated in advance of program provision. In some cases, they can be judged as being as important as the intended outcomes. For example, a well-known physics curriculum met its stated goals of increasing deeper understanding of physics principles among senior high school students. However, as a result of the pressure placed on students by the teaching methods used, student liking for and enjoyment of physics declined over the instruction period. This was a major unintended outcome. There was evidence that students were 'turned off' physics as a result of the curriculum and this may have affected their subsequent decision to study the subject at college level.

## PROCESS-OUTCOME STUDIES

As we have seen, Impact evaluations examine mature programs to determine their outcomes. In association with outcomes determination, it may be necessary to check on the extent of program implementation in order to explain the pattern of outcomes. Thus an examination of program implementation can be an integral part of an Impact evaluation.

Implementation is also an important phenomenon in its own right for the very reason that it is an integral part of program intervention. Realisation of the importance of implementation emerged in the 1960s and 1970s, when attempts were made to reform and improve societies through social and educational provision. Examples include the design of national-level school curricula, the development and diffusion of agricultural innovations such as new strains of grain crops, and social biotechnological initiatives such as birth control programs.

Many of these change proposals were based on a Research Development and Diffusion (RD&D) model of change. RD&D relies on centrally researched and developed solutions to problems which are then disseminated to field users. The RD&D paradigm reflected an engineering perspective towards change which had been successfully used in the development and use of products by industry, particularly within Western economies of the twentieth century.

Many of the educational reforms in the period between 1960 and the late 1970s in Western countries were based on variations of RD&D. It was assumed that, if the developers 'got it right', improvements in the field would automatically follow. All that was required was for practitioners to translate the program plan into action by following specified guidelines.

Early research on the impact of these programs concentrated on measuring outcomes. For many educational innovations, the findings were not impressive. Student learning gains, compared with more traditional teaching approaches, were small or nonexistent. It was concluded that the innovative curricula were having minimal impact. They appeared to have been a waste of time and money.

However, some evaluators began to look at the implementation of these programs. Rather than make an assumption that the new curricula *were* implemented in ways which were consistent with the intentions of program developers, evaluators began to look at what was actually happening in classrooms. When observations of programs in action were made, wide variations in the degree to which teachers actually implemented these programs were noted. Analyses showed that there was a strong correlation between student learning outcomes and degree of implementation. This made an enormous difference to the conclusions about the effects of educational RD&D; the large-scale educational projects were making a difference when they *were* indeed implemented.

Studies of this kind are called process–outcome studies. The outcomes can be thought of as the 'dependent' variables and the implementation or process characteristics as the 'independent' variables. As with all Approaches in the chapter, process–outcome studies are generally undertaken within the context of a summative evaluation, examining the worth of a program for an external audience. There may be a political accountability reason for the evaluation—for example, to justify expenditure on a program. In other instances, process–outcome studies can aid policy decision-making. For example, a process–outcome study of an innovative reading program in one educational region might be commissioned with a view to making a decision to adopt the program statewide.

A standard procedure is to develop instruments that measure outcomes; another is to determine the degree to which implementation action is consistent with the intentions of the program plan. Observations by trained personnel are the preferred method of data collection for the implementation aspect of the study.

## Implementation as the dependent variable

In some circumstances, the end-point of an evaluation is the study of the extent of implementation of the program itself. There may be situations where outcomes are not considered; the focus is on implementation. In these cases, the implementation of a program becomes the 'dependent variable'.

A logical approach to measuring implementation within this scenario is to derive a series of implementation characteristics from a program plan. This assumes that the plan is sufficiently well specified to include details of the expected processes of the intervention; this is known as a *fidelity approach* to measuring implementation.

Hall and his colleagues (Hall & Loucks, 1979) designed a conceptual scheme for determining program implementation that acknowledged the importance of time as a variable. They found that staff responsible for innovative program use move through stages of understanding and action which determine the state of implementation of the program. The stages are: non-use, orientation, preparation, mechanical use, routine, refinement, integration and renewal.

In a conceptual sense, fidelity-based evaluation concentrates on mechanical and routine use to the exclusion of other implementation features. The evaluator develops measures of the essential features of the program in action. This is easier if the program has a well-defined and, in many cases, simple logic—for example, programs which emphasise skills training. In theory, it should be possible to develop a checklist which enables each of the essential elements of implementation to be monitored. While observation is the most frequently used method of data collection, there are examples of multiple measures of implementation, such as records, self-reports and interviews. Directions for the construction of schedules and for the ensuing collection of information are found in Morris & Fitzgibbon (1978).

## Adaptation

There is a large body of literature to show that a centrally developed program undergoes changes when implemented at the local level. Hall and his colleagues also found that most programs and those implementing them undergo a process of mutual adaptation during implementation. That is, the implementor alters his or her actions towards those specified by the program, but may not implement the program faithfully. The nature of the adaptation depends on local conditions and on the degree of support given by the developers for the change. Thus programs are often not implemented in the rational fashion of adopting a set of means to achieve a predetermined end. From an incrementalist point of view, a program takes shape slowly as decision-makers react to the realities of the context, with its emerging complexities. Those concerned with program design must be aware that final acceptance is never certain at the beginning, and that things change from the plan to the operation.

This has implications for assessing the extent of implementation of a program. To understand how and why programs are implemented differently in different locations, there is an argument for implementation evaluation to document variations in use and factors which lead to patterns of use at each location or site. Evaluation methods thus need to be more flexible than those used in a fidelity approach. In this situation, a combination of preordinate evaluation design and flexible data collection methods is required.

Thus an implementation evaluation may focus on factors affecting implementation—that is, the identification of conditions which encourage successful action. A motive for such a study could be the need to suggest ways of overcoming barriers to the implementation of an important social or educational intervention.

## PERFORMANCE AUDIT

The term 'audit' is well known to those familiar with the need for company and other accounts to be checked by a qualified accountant. The notion of auditing has typically been associated with a review of financial arrangements—that is, a retrospective examination of an entity's financial statements for the purpose of forming an opinion of their fairness in conformity with generally accepted accounting principles. Recently the term 'audit' has been used more widely, signifying an expansion of the roles typically undertaken by the accountants and the adoption of auditing notions within other professions. We have seen the emergence of auditing approaches which are not necessarily based on financial compliance. For example, an operational audit is designed to provide management with an objective appraisal and opinions of all the activities of the organisation and may include recommendations for action. Auditing procedures have also been used to examine the reported research output of government and university departments. For example, the administration of a large university we know of commissioned external auditors to check all the research work undertaken by staff as a means of ensuring that the research met quality standards set by university funding bodies. This example relates to the performance of individuals, but it leads us to the notion of performance auditing (PA), more generally defined as:

> a custom crafted analysis of program efficiency and effectiveness. It differs from financial auditing in that it deals with a combination of financial and non-financial measures and usually must define a unique set of measurements and standards for each audit that is undertaken. (Brown et al., 1982)

According to Davis (1990), PA involves the:

> determination of the economy, efficiency, and effectiveness of government organisations, programs, activities and functions, in addition to their compliance with laws and regulations.

More recently, PA has been defined as:

> an objective systematic examination of evidence . . . of the perfor-
> mance of a government organisation, program or activity of function
> in order to provide information to improve public accountability
> and facilitate decision making. (Wisler, 1996)

For some time, evaluation theorists have been interested in
comparing the work of program evaluators and auditors. In the
United States, a key impetus was the movement of influential
evaluators into senior positions in federal and state accounting
offices. As long ago as 1985, Eleanor Chelimsky, one of the most
impressive writers on evaluation theory, contrasted the history and
development of auditing and evaluation and compared methodologies used by practitioners in the two fields. While there was then
a relatively dormant period of writing on the topic, more recently
a spate of articles have elaborated on some of the issues first
raised by Chelimsky (see for example, Davis, 1990; Brooks, 1996
and Leeuw, 1996). These articles have been stimulated by the fact
that more and more financial auditors are also taking on performance auditing.

There has been keen interest in performance auditing as an
evaluation Approach in Great Britain and Europe, but less so in
the United States. This may be due to the fact that the evaluation
profession is dominated by social scientists in the United States.
In other countries, and in particular those in Europe, there has
been more influence on evaluation practice from practitioners who
have a grounding in areas such as accounting, economics, law and
the natural sciences.

However, most of the discussion has contrasted data management or methodologies used in performance auditing, comparing
methods used in outcomes evaluation with those of performance
auditing, and the assumptions underlying these methods (see for
example, Pollitt & Summa, 1996). We must extend this analysis
to the epistemological basis of PA as a means of fitting it into a
framework of evaluation.

The actual practice of PA has been analysed by Schwandt and
Halpern as including the following:

- a systematic process—an auditor's review and examination is
  planned, orderly and methodical;
- objectively obtaining and evaluating evidence—an audit is an
  independent empirical investigation;
- ascertaining the degree of correspondence between assertions
  and established criteria—auditing involves the exercise of professional judgment in applying a set of criteria;

- communicating the results to interested users—the outcomes of an audit examination is made public (Schwandt & Halpern, 1988).

Based on a review of current practice in Australia, we see PA within the public sector being characterised by:

- considerable power to undertake an evaluation without the permission of program providers;
- a strong emphasis on verification. The major role is to provide independent findings for accountability purposes;
- concentration on mature interventions which means that most evaluations are retrospective and *post hoc*;
- a strong focus on compliance and 'management' variables, plans and procedures.

While more attention is now given to actual program effects, there is an inclination to concentrate on easily measured variables at the expense of important ones—for example, unintended outcomes. To date, performance auditors have tended to emphasise the use of documentation and key interviews as key sources of data:

- a focus on organisations as a whole or macro programs;
- a corresponding tendency to downplay the individual influence of components within an organisation;
- an emphasis on reporting to outsiders. The primary audience is well defined and outside the program—for example, the legislature or parliament.

Comparing these characteristics with those of evaluative inquiry outlined earlier in this text, there seems to be sufficient similarities to acknowledge that PA *is* an evaluative Approach which fits within the Impact Form. We believe that it should not be treated as if it were outside the umbrella of evaluative inquiry. PA should not only be embraced by those associated with the accounting profession, but also by those engaged in investigations in the helping professions when it is appropriate. This has already begun. For example, performance auditing has been used to review the curriculum in school systems in the United States (English, 1988) and Australia (Owen et al., 1996).

In the public sector, a universal trend has been for government auditors to increase the proportion of time spent on performance audits, compared with financial audits. Government auditors-general are seen as a 'public watchdog', reporting without fear to the legislature about the effective use of public resources. While their role as independent agencies has largely gone unchallenged, there are some politicians who believe that, in adopting the more evaluative roles associated with PA, auditors-general have over-stepped the mark. This reminds us that evaluation work must take account of the political environment. Evaluation should be seen as important to any democratic society in that it should inform public policy, benefit those who make decisions about that policy, and inform citizens who have to live with those decisions, once made.

Evaluators must make objective findings available, especially in a hostile political environment, and also when relevant public groups are unaware of the facts. It is up to evaluators because they have the ability to assemble the evidence and possess a commitment to the value of knowledge in decision-making.

Chelimsky (1995) believes that improvements and changes should be made according to whatever has been proven to be good, practical, desirable and meaningful, without the arrogant assumption that evaluators and stakeholders understand every-thing about the world and thus know everything there is to know about how to change it for the better. This is consistent with the Emergent Realist paradigm regarded as a philosophi-cal basis for the conduct of evaluation (see Chapter 5). However, we should not imagine that stakeholders in any political environ-ment are all likely to be open-minded, or willing to change their value positions, or share power, except in extraordinary circumstances. Rather, the norm is that political actors never forget their agendas, and so evaluators need to work with those agendas, concentrating on securing the one thing that is most important for any evaluation in any political environment, which is the independence necessary to conduct their evaluations and state their conclusions without political interference (Chelimsky, 1995).

Professional evaluators, including performance auditors must deal with the fact that what we report in one political environment will be seen later on from the viewpoint of another. It is true that when policy is made in one environment, neither the policy nor the evidence evaluators bring to support it is likely to be perfect. Policy and evidence cannot be perfect; instead, they are iterative and should be correctable. Rather than being seen as sublime, those involved in evaluation should be serious, credible and persistent. For those working squarely in the political arena, the challenge is to understand the strengths and vulnera-bilities of both politics and evaluation and to use both of them to help us contribute to public policy in a meaningful and enduring way.

# IMPACT EVALUATION: TRENDS AND CASE EXAMPLES

## Determining outcomes in economic terms: benefit for cost analysis

At a conceptually simple level, there is appeal in constructing a simple measure or measures of program worth. This is an approach which resonates with those who subscribe to the view that a program should be evaluated in terms of its economic benefits to an individual or organisation. This effectively reduces the objectives of a program to a measure of efficiency: the more efficient the program, the more worthy it is. To employ methods consistent with this approach, outcomes must be reduced to financial units of measurement.

Key notions associated with studies with this orientation include:

- benefit to cost ratio (BCR), defined as the ratio of program benefits to program costs;
- return on investment (ROI), defined as the ratio of net program benefits to program costs.

One area in which evaluators have encouraged greater attention to benefit to cost analysis is that of training in business and industry (Brinkerhoff, 1989). In business terms, showing that training has contributed to the 'bottom line' is generally regarded by management as an imperative. The following is an example of a recent evaluation of a training program which took this approach.

### Example 13.1 A benefit for costs analysis of training

Phillips (1994) undertook an evaluation of a training program in a bank with offices across central states of the United States. The bank had a well-established loans section, which was in an expansion stage.

A training seminar on consumer lending for existing and new officers had been established within the Human Resources Department (HRD). The consumer lending seminar occupied three days. In the past, the HRD staff had always used reaction sheets for evaluation. However, senior management wished to see this program in terms of its benefit to the organisation. The trainer and the manager of the HRD decided to take up the challenge of undertaking a benefit for cost analysis. A return on investment study was undertaken to meet this requirement. This involved making estimates of the costs and benefits in dollar terms.

- Program costs were as follows:

| | |
|---|---|
| Instructors' and coordinators' salaries | $1570 |
| Admin. support | $500 |
| Facilities, food, refreshments | $1800 |
| Participants' salaries (n=20) | $7200 |
| Development costs (pro rata) | $300 |
| Training materials | $400 |
| Travel, lodgings, meals, etc. | $5250 |
| Other costs | $490 |
| **Total cost of seminar** | $17 510 |

To calculate the impact of training, the evaluators:
- determined changes in the work effectiveness of the loans officers;
- allowed for changes by factors other than training which also affected the change in results.

Changes in effectiveness were obtained by collecting data on the 'before' and 'after' performance of each loans officer for a period of one year following the training. Where the officers were new, their performance in their previous job was traced. Where the officer had not been employed this way before, the average level of performance across the organisation was assigned.

Factors other than training which influenced the effectiveness of the officers were reduction in interest rates during the year, and natural improvement—that which would have been likely to have occurred without the training. Corrections for these factors were made on the basis of data obtained from the bank. The key finding was that the loans officers finalised an increase of six loans per month after training, corrected for the above factors.

From the bank's records, it was possible to assemble the following information:

| | |
|---|---|
| Average loan yield | 9.75 per cent |

| | |
|---|---|
| Average cost of funds | 5.50 per cent |
| Direct costs for consumer lending | 0.82 per cent |
| Corporate overhead | 1.61 per cent |
| Net profit per loan | 1.82 per cent |
| Average loan size | $15 500 |
| Average monthly increase in loans per participant (corrected for other factors) | 6 |
| Number of participants in training seminar | 18 |
| Total amount of increased loans (15500*6*18) | $1 674 000 |
| Annual improvement in loan values (*12) | $20 088 000 |

**Profit from improvement(*1.82)**
$20 088 000*1.82
**$365 601**
**Return on investment (ROI)**
**= net benefits/costs**
365 601 – 17501/17501
**19.88**

This is almost a 2000 per cent return on the training investment! Not surprisingly, this was regarded as extremely high by the HRD and the senior management of the bank, and ensured that the training seminar remained an integral part of the work of the Human Relations Department.

## Treatment and control groups: Using variations in program provision to determine program worth

While some clients are content with the reduction of outcomes to cost benefit terms, others want more detailed information about the effects of a program.

One way to determine, with a high degree of certainty, whether a program has an effect is to invoke the use of what is known as an *experimental design*. Borrowing from a traditional scientific paradigm, this involves the random assignment of subjects to two groups. One group undertakes the program (or treatment), while the other group, the control group, is not subjected to the treatment. By comparing the outcomes of the two groups, it is possible to reach a conclusion about the impact of the program. Sometimes such studies are known as *laboratory studies*, because the conditions under which the program is evaluated are tightly controlled—in particular the implementation of the program. They also rely on the availability of a population of subjects from which the treatment and control groups can be drawn.

It is sometimes possible to find situations 'outside the laboratory' where such principles can be used to evaluate a program. These are naturally occurring situations which approximate to an experiment, as defined above.

## Example 13.2 Evaluating alternative modes of learning college physics

A tertiary-level Physics Department became dissatisfied with courses provided for potential teachers at the first-year university level. Several members of the staff became convinced that a 'traditional' course was no longer sufficient to meet the needs of the society, the schools and the teachers. What was required of science teacher preparation courses was a shift in basic philosophy and approach. A revised first-year course was outlined which gave attention not only to physics knowledge and skills, but also—by its content, structure and presentation—to the nature of science in its social and historical context and to the professional orientation of physics teachers. It was decided that a pilot version of the new course should be offered to an 'experimental' group of students, whose response and achievement would be compared with a control group taking the traditional course. Key evaluation questions were:

- Will the time given to the additional aims interfere to an intolerable extent with the students' acquisition of basic knowledge and skills?
- Can the new course be presented well enough that students perceive and develop towards the new goals?
- Will the students value the new approach in relation to their own perceptions of their personal and career futures?

The course presented to the control group was aimed at

an understanding of the basic laws and theories of physics, an appreciation of their explanatory power, and skill in their application to solving physics problems. The course structure emphasised the logical structure of physics and was spiced with demonstrations and examples to help achieve these aims.

The course presented to the experimental group had three strands which ran side by side: one, the knowledge and skills of physics; another, discussions about physics; and a third, personal development and professional orientation through discussions about teaching physics.

Even though the two courses differed markedly in approach, their 'basic physics' aspects were similar in coverage and level of treatment. In this sense, the new course was an evolutionary development from the old, with many of the existing resources and ideas adapted to suit the new approach.

The evaluators compared the previous achievement in the areas of math and physics and found that the groups were similar.

After the courses were taught, it was found that the experimental group did no worse on achievement than the control group, despite the fact that they spent less time on basic concepts.

Both groups were also tested on a set of other scales which measured laboratory skills, the ability to link physics with real-world problems, and a test of 'personal' skills, such as persistence in study. It was found that the experimental group performed considerably better on the first two of these additional tests.

The findings of this study were a key factor in having the new course adopted for all students. (Hirst et al., 1980)

## The need to establish real program objectives

Sometimes when an evaluator is asked to undertake an objectives-based evaluation in the field, the objectives are not explicit. They have to be determined by the evaluators before investigations of outcomes can be pursued. This is not an uncommon situation, for often developers do not provide well-developed objectives in program documentation.

### Example 13.3 Evaluation of a Community Agency Human Development Program

For several years, the Richmond Community Health Centre (RCHC) has offered a unique program devoted to the discussion of issues such as contraception and the impact of drugs, aimed mainly at students in Year 11 (15–16-year-olds). Instruction was carried out by nurses and gynaecologists at RCHC. The material covered and resources used in the program are not normally included in school curricula (see Chapter 4).

When the management of the RCHC found funds for the evaluation, the program providers (two nurses and a doctor) set the direction for the evaluation. A major topic in initial provider–evaluator discussions was the potential use of the information from the study. It became clear that the providers had an agenda to produce information which could be used in negotiations at the RCHC and with funding agents to expand the influence of their program.

On this basis, it was considered essential to include a strong outcomes component and to spend less evaluation energy on an examination of program processes. In this case, the key outcomes issue was to determine whether the program was having an impact on students in terms of their knowledge and skills related to pre-pregnancy.

While there was extensive documentation on the program, there was no clear statement of objectives. To develop this, the evaluators interviewed the providers about their intentions and attended two program sessions. A member of staff no longer working on the program was asked to check trial items for their consistency with the intentions of the program. Thus the development of the final instrument relied more on interviews than on formal documentation of program objectives.

The need to convince outsiders of program worth led the evaluators to recommend the use of a simple pre–post achievement test design and the collection of testimonials from students and teachers involved. The fact that there was time for evaluation planning in advance of program delivery enabled careful matching of data management to the list of issues raised by the providers.

It was agreed that the providers would administer a simple instrument to students before and after each program session to measure achievement and to collect student opinions about the sessions. Further, it was decided that the evaluators would analyse these data, collect additional information about demand for the program over recent years from RCHC records, and design and carry out interviews with teachers responsible for the classes which attended the RCHC.

Data-collecting instruments were designed by the evaluators, who also undertook analysis for all phases of the study. The data collection methods and results included:

- an analysis of demand for the program over several years. This showed that more schools came from outside the educational region in which the Centre was located than from within it, and that up to 15 per cent were country schools;
- the development and administration of a validated test of content covered in the program, included here as Figure 13.1. This was administered immediately before and directly after the one-day course.

**Figure 13.1   Richmond community program content test**

Your ID Number ☐☐☐

**RICHMOND COMMUNITY HEALTH CENTRE**
**PROGRAM REVIEW**
*Form Two*

First, write your ID number, given to you on Form One, in the box above.

In this second questionnaire we would like you to answer the 'true/false' questions again and to give us some information about how the session was conducted. This will help us to make decisions about how good the course is and how to improve it.

Again, please answer every question even if you are uncertain or don't know.

1. A baby's estimated date of birth depends on the date of ovulation.

☐ True
☐ False
☐ Don't know

2. The major period of growth of the fetus (baby) is during the first months of pregnancy.

☐ True
☐ False
☐ Don't know

283

3. Most fetal organs develop in the first two months after conception.

☐ True
☐ False
☐ Don't know

4. The only signs of pregnancy are a missed period and morning sickness.

☐ True
☐ False
☐ Don't know

5. A baby's heart doesn't start to beat until at least 3 months into pregnancy.

☐ True
☐ False
☐ Don't know

6. Most problems in the formation of a baby occur either at conception or in the next few weeks.

☐ True
☐ False
☐ Don't know

7. A woman need not be concerned about drinking alcohol or taking other drugs until she finds out that she is pregnant.

☐ True
☐ False
☐ Don't know

8. Most problems in the formation of a baby are caused by cigarette smoking.

☐ True
☐ False
☐ Don't know

9. The only function of the placenta is to channel nourishment from the mother to the baby.

☐ True
☐ False
☐ Don't know

10. A baby has little chance of survival if born before the 22nd week of pregnancy.

☐ True
☐ False
☐ Don't know

11. Babies can be born small and undernourished if the mother smokes heavily during pregnancy.

☐ True
☐ False
☐ Don't know

12. Babies can be born deaf or blind if the mother suffers from rubella (german measles) in early pregnancy.

☐ True
☐ False
☐ Don't know

13. Babies of drug addicts suffer withdrawal symptoms after birth.

☐ True
☐ False
☐ Don't know

Now, we would value *your* opinions of the session.

14. What is the most important thing you have learnt from today's session?

_____

_____

_____

_____

15. What was the best aspect of the session? Why?

(You might like to think about the content, presentation or the organisation of the morning.)

_____

_____

_____

_____

16. What was the worst aspect of the session? Why?

(You might like to think about the content, presentation or the organisation of the morning.)

_____

_____

_____

_____

17. Have you any comments to make about the video(s) you saw? Please write them below.

_____

_____

_____

_____

18. If you wish, please suggest one way in which the session could have been improved.

(You might like to think about the content, presentation or the organisation of the morning.)

_____

_____

_____

_____

**Before you hand this second questionnaire in be sure that you have written your ID number on the top of this questionnaire and that you have answered every question.**

The results showed that:

- the average gain scores of the participants was statistically significant;
- increased scores occurred for students from all schools;

- almost equal gains were made by male and female students;
- there were variations in gains between items on the test, which suggested that some sections of the course had been more successful than others;
- some items were answered well on the pre-test which indicated that they need not be included in any future course.

Opinions about the program were sought from students and their teachers, focusing on the 'best' and 'worst' aspects of the program. The most frequent student response in the first category was an appreciation of the style of presentation. Students liked the friendly, informal atmosphere of the classes and straightforward manner with which issues were dealt.

A follow-up interview with all participating teachers found that information about the program most frequently came from other teachers, that the program was used to complement and reinforce what was being done at school, and that the visit was treated as an adjunct to subjects taken at Year 11 level in areas such as Home Economics, Human Development and Society, and Human Studies.

Besides presenting these results, the evaluation also made recommendations relating to the development of more appropriate videotape support material, the criticisms being that the imported tapes used were not entirely appropriate for Australian audiences, and that they were factually incorrect and out of date (Hurworth et al., 1988). This issue emerged early in the teacher interview phase, and its exploration required follow-up by cross-checking with health centre staff.

In this case, the findings were used to argue a case for the introduction of this course in other health centres. The evaluators agreed to join providers in presentations of findings to various health agencies. The extent of evaluator commitment to this phase was determined by the strength of the findings. If the impact of the program had been small or negative, the evaluators may not have adopted a strong dissemination role.

This example shows one approach to an evaluation in which the implied goals of a program were important as the basis for a major aspect of the evaluation. It is evident from the description that additional data were collected in order to provide comprehensive information for decision-making. It is also notable that data were collected in a variety of ways and in different forms.

### Surrogate measures of outcomes

As indicated earlier, a standard procedure in outcomes-based evaluation is to develop outcomes measures which have strong face validity. However, there are situations where one has to compromise; it is sometimes necessary to use surrogate measures, those which substitute, or stand in place of preferred or ideal measures. If one uses such surrogate measures, an argument must be made in terms of their validity when presenting the evaluation findings. This was the case in the following example in which an outcome indicator was used as a surrogate for direct learning to evaluate the impact of a health education program.

---

**Example 13.4 Evaluation of the impact of a health education program for ethnic mothers**

Among staff at an inner-city health centre, there was concern about the quality of nourishment provided within local non-English-speaking households. After extensive consultation with these families, the centre implemented a program aimed specifically at women with small children from an ethnic group. The program, offered in two-hour evening sessions, was intended to:

- promote a return to eating traditional food of the ethnic group;
- promote breast-feeding (all participants had at least one child under two years of age);
- reduce the extent of obesity among children in the families.

Over the eight weeks of the program, the ten participants were given information, through an interpreter, designed to change existing approaches to feeding their children.

A short time after the program had been completed, the health centre decided to commission a small-scale evaluation of the impact of the intervention. As for the previous example, the roles of the external evaluator, described earlier in the unit, are used as anchor points to describe how this evaluation was undertaken.

Assisting providers to identify key evaluation issues was a prerequisite to detailed evaluation design. The major audience was the administration of the centre. In this case, a genuine need emerged to discover whether this pilot program had led to a change in the nutrition intake. In identifying

---

this issue, the evaluators recommended the collection of simple indicators of impact.

*Developing the evaluation design in conjunction with the providers.*

In negotiations between the evaluators and the primary audience on design, the major issue revolved around significant problems in choosing and collecting the most appropriate data on program impact. The problems were caused by the limited resources for the study and its timing vis-à-vis program delivery; in this case, the evaluation was *post-hoc* in nature.

One suggestion was to follow up the participants using an interview or a questionnaire. There were difficulties envisaged in using either of these approaches. These included negotiating access to the women within the context of traditional ethnic households, problems of language translation, and finally—even if these difficulties were overcome—issues relating to accurate and open recall of information about the program needed to be addressed.

Doubts about the reliability of the data collected by these means led the evaluators to consider alternative data sources. The evaluators became aware that it is an almost universal procedure in Australia for mothers to take their babies to local health centres for periodic check-ups. Contact with the Centre revealed that all mothers who attended the nutrition program used these check-ups.

Documentation at the Health Centre includes a running record of infant physical development, including weight charts. Given that a major aim of the program was to reduce the obesity of children in the families, the evaluators decided to use changes in weight of children as indicators of the impact of the program. The Health Centre was assured of confidentiality in the use of these records. The availability of the charts allowed the evaluators to follow two lines of investigation.

The first involved variations in mass (weight) of the ten young children born before the program began. The analysis charted variations from birth through the period of the program, and subsequently during the ten months following its conclusion. Inspection of the charts, included as Figure 13.2, showed that the weight of children in these families was consistently above the median before the program, that it fell during its duration and then maintained a trend close to the median after program conclusion.

**Figure 13.2   Variations in baby weights over time**

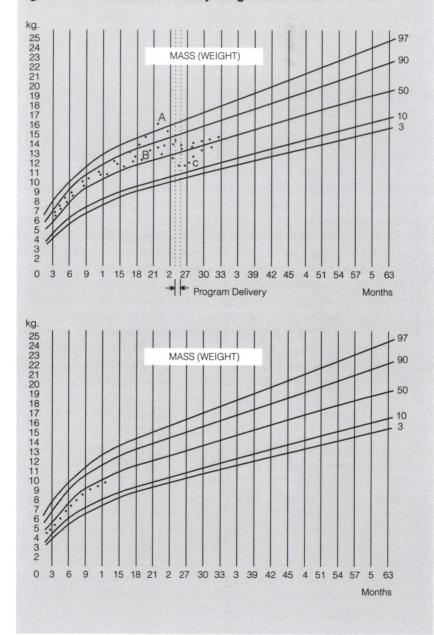

On the basis of this analysis, the evaluators were prepared to conclude that the program had been a success, at least on the grounds of reducing obesity among the children.

However, it was felt that further information should be collected for us to be more sure of the conclusion that the program had a lasting impact. Through discussion with program staff it was found that three of the families had produced an additional child subsequent to the program. As before, charts were investigated and showed that the weights of these children followed the median from birth. We were thus more certain that the program had left a lasting impact on these families.

The evaluators prepared a 'user-friendly' report and ensured that all members of the Health Centre became aware of the findings through seminars and discussion. Despite the problems inherent in the *post-hoc* nature of the evaluation, the findings were seen by the audience as strong grounds for the Centre staff to be confident that their program had a lasting impact on the participants. Subsequent to the findings of the study becoming known, the evaluators encouraged the Health Centre to apply for funding to conduct the program again. This application was successful and the program ran again the following year. (Hick, 1988)

This case illustrates the need for evaluators to explore possibilities within evaluations which have difficult methodological and ethical dimensions. Some commentators say that a good evaluation has a touch of artistry and creativity and this is a case in point. Hard and fast rules did not apply here, even though the approach was consistent with a goal-based outcomes approach.

### Needs-based impact: Finding a suitable external criterion for judgment

As indicated earlier, needs-based Impact evaluations are rare. This is due in part to the fact that few needs assessments are actually carried out in advance of program planning and development. It is also true that program providers base their planning decisions on other factors than empirical data, relying more on their 'local knowledge', on the way they prefer to deliver their programs, or on an ideology or view of the world. This provides a challenge for an evaluator to establish a framework from which an assessment of impact can be made which refers to need. The following example employed a creative solution to this dilemma.

## Example 13.5 An evaluation of alternative courses within a teacher education program

A large College of Advanced Education offered five alternative courses within a one-year preservice teacher education program. The extent of variation in the program was based on an argument that there was no 'best way' to educate a prospective teacher. However, dwindling resources and other factors led the course committee to a view that the range of choice and diversity was no longer acceptable. An evaluation was undertaken to inform course committee debate about which courses should remain and which might be discontinued.

The key issue which underpinned the evaluation was to determine the relative effectiveness of the courses in preparing students for their first years as school teachers. It was therefore necessary to develop outcome measures of effectiveness, and to develop ways of determining the effectiveness of the alternative courses in preparing students to be effective beginning teachers. These issues were a focus of discussion within the course committee.

There was a concern to develop procedures for fairly judging the relative worth of the alternative courses, not on their own terms (that is, relative to their objectives), but on grounds which allowed the courses to be compared.

The issue was solved satisfactorily by reference to a recently completed national enquiry into teacher education. The enquiry recommended a core of learning experiences which should be required of all students and was effectively a policy statement about teacher education for Australia. The availability of these guidelines provided a set of common criteria for making comparisons between courses. The course committee endorsed this approach and decided that beginning teachers should be a major source of information, given that they had participated in one of the courses and most of them were now working in schools.

A survey, included as Figure 13.3, was sent to all graduates eight months after they had completed the program.

## Figure 13.3    Diploma in Education course evaluation

**Diploma in Education course evaluation**
Melbourne College of Advanced Education
Diploma in Education course evaluation

1. What team did you belong to in the Diploma in Education course at the
Melbourne State College?
(Tick one)

☐ A        ☐ B        ☐ C        ☐ D        ☐ E        ☐ F
(part-time)  (core-     (school-   (contract- (elective- (community-
             elective)  based)     based)     based)     based)

2. Please list your method studies

_____ , _____ , _____

3. Which of the following activities applies to you in 1983? (Tick one or more)

☐ Teaching    ☐ Teaching    ☐ Student    ☐ Other    ☐ Unem-
  full-time       part-time                    job         ployed

*If you are teaching (full- or part-time) go to QUESTION 5 and complete the
remainder of the checklist.*

4. *IF YOU ARE NOT TEACHING AT ALL* please state briefly the reason why you are
not teaching this year (be as specific as possible).

THIS COMPLETES THE CHECKLIST FOR THOSE NOT TEACHING THIS YEAR.
THANK YOU FOR YOUR ASSISTANCE.

5. Listed below is a series of items which describes aspects of teaching. On
the left-hand side indicate the emphasis each was given during your teacher
education year. On the right-hand side we would like you to evaluate each aspect
according to its current *importance to you in your present position (as a teacher).*
PLEASE RESPOND TO EVERY QUESTION.

*Emphasis in my teacher
education year (tick one)*                          *Importance to my present
                                                    position (tick one)*

Little/None ☐    i) An ability to control      ☐ Not Important
Small       ☐    classes which I teach         ☐ Slightly Important
Moderate    ☐                                  ☐ Moderately Important
High        ☐                                  ☐ Very Important

Little/None ☐    ii) An ability to translate a ☐ Not Important
Small       ☐    curriculum plan into action   ☐ Slightly Important
Moderate    ☐                                  ☐ Moderately Important
High        ☐                                  ☐ Very Important

Little/None ☐    iii) An ability to evaluate my ☐ Not Important
Small       ☐    own teaching performance       ☐ Slightly Important
Moderate    ☐                                   ☐ Moderately Important
High        ☐                                   ☐ Very Important

| Emphasis in my teacher education year (tick one) | | Importance to my present position (tick one) |
|---|---|---|
| Little/None ☐<br>Small ☐<br>Moderate ☐<br>High ☐ | iv) An ability to plan a curriculum unit which I will teach | ☐ Not Important<br>☐ Slightly Important<br>☐ Moderately Important<br>☐ Very Important |
| Little/None ☐<br>Small ☐<br>Moderate ☐<br>High ☐ | v) An awareness of the ways schools can develop closer relations with the community | ☐ Not Important<br>☐ Slightly Important<br>☐ Moderately Important<br>☐ Very Important |
| Little/None ☐<br>Small ☐<br>Moderate ☐<br>High ☐ | vi) A knowledge of factors affecting the intellectual development of adolescents | ☐ Not Important<br>☐ Slightly Important<br>☐ Moderately Important<br>☐ Very Important |
| Little/None ☐<br>Small ☐<br>Moderate ☐<br>High ☐ | vii) Insights into the interconnections between subjects offered in the school curriculum | ☐ Not Important<br>☐ Slightly Important<br>☐ Moderately Important<br>☐ Very Important |
| Little/None ☐<br>Small ☐<br>Moderate ☐<br>High ☐ | viii) Sensitivity to the range of disadvantages students might face in schools (on the bases of ethnicity, gender, socio-economic background or physical handicap | ☐ Not Important<br>☐ Slightly Important<br>☐ Moderately Important<br>☐ Very Important |
| Little/None ☐<br>Small ☐<br>Moderate ☐<br>High ☐ | ix) A knowledge of factors affecting the emotional and social development of adolescents | ☐ Not Important<br>☐ Slightly Important<br>☐ Moderately Important<br>☐ Very Important |
| Little/None ☐<br>Small ☐<br>Moderate ☐<br>High ☐ | x) A knowledge of recent developments in 'method' areas related to my subject specialisations | ☐ Not Important<br>☐ Slightly Important<br>☐ Moderately Important<br>☐ Very Important |
| Little/None ☐<br>Small ☐<br>Moderate ☐<br>High ☐ | xi) An ability to cater for the strengths and weaknesses of individual students | ☐ Not Important<br>☐ Slightly Important<br>☐ Moderately Important<br>☐ Very Important |
| Little/None ☐<br>Small ☐<br>Moderate ☐<br>High ☐ | xii) An awareness of the relationship between schools and the broader social/political context | ☐ Not Important<br>☐ Slightly Important<br>☐ Moderately Important<br>☐ Very Important |

| Emphasis in my teacher education year (tick one) | | Importance to my present position (tick one) | |
|---|---|---|---|
| Little/None ☐<br>Small ☐<br>Moderate ☐<br>High ☐ | xiii) An ability to work with students in different settings (classroom, excursions, camps etc.) | ☐ Not Important<br>☐ Slightly Important<br>☐ Moderately Important<br>☐ Very Important | |
| Little/None ☐<br>Small ☐<br>Moderate ☐<br>High ☐ | xiv) An understanding of the organisation and structure of education in Victoria | ☐ Not Important<br>☐ Slightly Important<br>☐ Moderately Important<br>☐ Very Important | |

6. Now, please use the space provided below to make any comments on your *teacher education year*, in the light of your subsequent experiences. *Please be as specific as possible.*

i) Strengths:

_____

_____

_____

_____

ii) Weaknesses:

_____

_____

_____

_____

iii) What changes would you recommend to the teacher education year you undertook?

_____

_____

_____

_____

7. Finally, could you tell us how satisfied you are with your present teaching position?

☐ Very satisfied    ☐ Moderately satisfied    ☐ Slightly satisfied    ☐ Not at all satisfied

Write a note to explain your response if you wish:

_____

_____

295

Information was sought about, first, the degree to which core learning experiences were covered in the course they undertook at college; and, second, the degree to which each of these were perceived as important to them as beginning teachers. Fourteen items were written to cover the core learning experiences. From the replies (N= 165, 80 per cent response after telephone follow-up), it was possible to determine the discrepancy between importance and emphasis for all items on the survey and the relative degree to which the program as a whole emphasised each core learning experience, as indicated in Figure 13.4a. This information enabled comparisons to be made between items, and allowed high discrepancies between importance and emphasis to be identified. Figure 13.4b compares the emphasis of each course on all items. Open-ended responses supported the statistical information that showed Course C was the most effective in preparing teachers for the workplace.

**Figure 13.4a  Evaluation of college teacher education programs**

|  | none | small | moderate | high |
|---|---|---|---|---|
| i) An ability to control classes which I teach | | DC EB | | |
| ii) An ability to translate a curriculum plan into action | | DCB E | | |
| iii) An ability to evaluate my own teaching performance | | | BE C D | |
| iv) An ability to plan a curriculum unit which I teach | | | CD B E | |
| v) An awareness of the ways schools can develop closer relations with the community | BDE | C | | |
| vi) A knowledge of factors affecting the intellectual development of adolescents | | CD EB | | |
| vii) Insights into the interconnections between subjects offered in the school curriculum | D EB C | | | |
| viii) Sensitivity to the range of disadvantages students might face in schools (on the bases of ethnicity, gender, socioeconomic background or physical handicap) | | E B C D | | |
| ix) A knowledge of the factors affecting the emotional and social development of adolescents | D ECB | | | |
| x) A knowledge of recent developments in 'method' areas related to my subject specializations | E | | | |
| xi) An ability to cater for the strengths and weaknesses of individual students | B D C E | | | |
| xii) An awareness of the relationship between schools and the broader social/political context | EBD C | | | |
| xiii) An ability to work with students in different settings (classroom, excursions, camps etc) | D BE C | | | |
| xiv) An understanding of the organisation and structure of education in Victoria | B D E | | | |

KEY:  
• results with high statistical between-team significance  
↑ Grand mean (all in together)  
B Core elective program  
C School-based program  
D Contract-based program  
E Elective-based program

296

**Figure 13.4b   Evaluation of college teacher education programs**

| | none | small/ slight | moderate | high/ very |
|---|---|---|---|---|
| i) An ability to control classes which I teach | | | ○ · | |
| ii) An ability to translate a curriculum plan into action | | | ○ · | |
| iii) An ability to evaluate my own teaching performance | | | ○——· | |
| iv) An ability to plan a curriculum unit which I teach | | | ○—· | |
| v) An awareness of the ways schools can develop closer relations with the community | | ○——· | | |
| vi) A knowledge of factors affecting the intellectual development of adolescents | | | ○——· | |
| vii) Insights into the interconnections between subjects offered in the school curriculum | | ○——· | | |
| viii) Sensitivity to the range of disadvantages students might face in schools (on the bases of ethnicity, gender, socioeconomic background or physical handicap) | | | ○· | |
| ix) A knowledge of the factors affecting the emotional and social development of adolescents | | | ○——· | |
| x) A knowledge of recent developments in 'method' areas related to my subject specializations | | | ○· | |
| xi) An ability to cater for the strengths and weaknesses of individual students | | | ○———· | |
| xii) An awareness of the relationship between schools and the broader social/political context | | ○—· | | |
| An ability to work with students in different settings (classroom, excursions, camps etc) | | ○———· | | |
| xiv) An understanding of the organisation and structure of education in Victoria | | ○——· | | |

KEY:   ○ emphasis   · importance

A short paper was sent to the Program Course Committee in which findings, *not* recommendations were highlighted. The information provided compelling reasons to retain Course C, the so-called 'school-based' course which was judged to be superior to the other courses within the program. The information became the focus for decision-making by the committee, in which one of the evaluation team was involved. They effectively saved this course which was about to be scrapped on other bases, such as it was too demanding of staff to be in the field rather than in the institution for most of the week.

This was a case of a study making an immediate and identifiable difference to decision-makers. The example above relied on a strategy of examining the effects of a program in terms of the way it prepared participants to function effectively in employment subsequent to its delivery. This is analogous to evaluating goods and services in terms of effective usefulness criteria, an approach used in consumer magazines.

The general point is that programs must meet a clearly nominated level of social or educational need in order to be judged to be of value. The approach has an undeniable logic and is highly appealing as a basis for undertaking impact studies. The difficulty of translating these principles into action, however, is testified to by the paucity of needs-based impact studies in the literature.

## Managing impact studies of big P Programs

Federal agencies responsible for the delivery of big P Programs often have an evaluation component built in to the funding agreement which finances their operations. The size and breadth of big P Programs provides a challenge for evaluators, in particular when they are asked to undertake Impact evaluations. This is because big P Programs are often delivered at many sites, at different locations often widely spread across geographical areas. Individual programs can also be delivered at different times. In addition, the intentions of individual small p programs offered within the umbrella of the big P Program have different objectives. There is also the problem of encouraging local staff to cooperate with the large-scale evaluation effort. Many cannot see a pay-off for collecting the data and at some sites, there may be difficulties in obtaining useful data due to such factors as problems of language. The study described below managed to surmount most of these problems. By adopting some generic outcomes, and using a range of person-intensive procedures, a good quality data base was developed from which aggregated findings were assembled.

### Example 13.6 Evaluation of training programs of the Center for Substance Abuse Prevention

The Center for Substance Abuse Prevention (CSAP) leads a major effort in the United States, to prevent substance abuse which has been linked to concerns about increased community violence, rising need for health care, teenage pregnancy and decreased work productivity. CSAP administers a range of programs by contract. Training is a key program on the CSAP agenda.

Due to the interest in the impact of training, a large-scale five-year longitudinal study of the CSAP Training System (CTS) was undertaken by Judith Ottoson (1994) and her colleagues. CTS training focus on building the capacity of individuals and community organisations to plan and carry out prevention programs. During 1994 and 1995, about 9500 participants participated in CTS training across America. Training ranged in length from half a day to five days. The evaluation represented a major effort to tap the opinions and intentions of all participants in almost 250 separate interventions. The findings of the study enabled decision-makers to judge the effect of each program and, by aggregation, the total training Program. In addition to evidence collected immediately after training, 2100 respondents were followed up two months after training was completed. Generally, respondents reported positive reactions immediately post-training. On a ten-point scale, used to indicate the extent to which participants were disposed to apply learning from the sessions, the mean score was 7.7. The follow-up data showed that the respondents were engaged in a broad range of selected prevention activities. A feature of the reporting was the classification of open-ended responses into seven categories of intervention. These were: learning; information dissemination; education; providing healthy alternatives; problem identification and referral; involvement in community-based processes; and influencing the environment. These categories had been developed by the parent agency of CSAP, the Substance Abuse and Mental Health Services Administration (SAMSHA). (Ottoson, 1994)

This study has a similarity to the previous one outlined in Example 13.5 in that a set of 'generic' outcomes was used to collect data which enabled aggregation across all individual program sites. In this case, the criteria were drawn from common expected features of all programs and from the literature on effective training. While not adopting a strict adherence to a needs-based approach, it could be argued that the training literature does reflect a needs-based position.

### Process–product studies

Process-product studies are hard to find, which may be due to the fact that few studies of this kind are carried out, and even fewer appear as public documents. These studies require measurement of implementation, an assessment of outcomes and, if possible, evidence which links assessment to outcomes. In practice, describing and measuring implementation are complex and time-consuming tasks, almost always involving the evaluator in intensive observation of program delivery. This means that, in most practical instances, studies involving implementation can only involve a small number of sites unless there is a large team of observers available. Having only a small number of sites also affects the way we make an inference about cause and effect. If there were a large number of sites, we could use a between-site correlation to see whether there was a link between implementation and outcomes. This is not possible when we have only a small number of sites or indeed just one site. We must then fall back on logic of a different kind, which does not rely on statistical inference. The following is an example of this situation.

### Example 13.7 Implementing Roadsmart

Roadsmart is an educational package designed to improve the safety of road behaviour of students. During early 1996, the section of Roadsmart designed for Years 2 and 3 students in elementary schools was trialled in two classrooms in a suburban school.

This program consisted of approximately twelve hours of in-class teaching to students, tuition outside which included practice in road crossing, and the education of parents on major issues of road safety. Two teachers were trained to deliver the program. The evaluation involved intensive recording of the road-crossing behaviour of all students in the two classes before the program began, using hidden video recorders. Data were then collected two weeks after the program had been completed.

In addition, the evaluator also spent time at the school watching the delivery of the program and the teachers kept notes on how they taught each session. Outcome evaluation focused on student behaviour.

The evaluator found that students adopted far more effective crossing behaviour after the program, watching more closely and spending less time on crossing. It was found that both teachers implemented most of the activities suggested by the program designers; however, one teacher spent much less time on most of the activities. There was no difference in the behaviour of the students in the two classes, which suggested that the quality of student experience was more important than the length of time taken to complete the program. Justification of the link between implementation was made with recourse to the fact that changed behaviour of the students was unlikely to have been due to any environmental effect in the period in which the program was taught. (Leadbetter, 1998)

It should be noted that the above example employed a pre-ordinate design. The approach to studying implementation was based on the intentions of the program, which formed the basis of the observation schedule used by the evaluator. In the following example, a more open-ended approach was used to assess implementation.

**Example 13.8 Evaluation of the Job and Course Explorer (JAC)**

Job and Course Explorer (JAC) is a multi-faceted program designed to improve the quality of careers education in a range of sites: schools, employment offices, community houses, public libraries and others. A key element of JAC is the provision of a comprehensive interactive computer data base which is designed to be 'user friendly'. In addition, JAC contains written materials to aid careers advisers and the 'end users', students and others for whom the information is ultimately intended.

JAC was one response to the need to increase the skills and employment opportunities of the Australian workforce. While aimed primarily at young people making the transition from school to college and university, and from school to work, it was also seen to be an aid to the re-education and training of more mature people.

JAC was developed in the mid-1980s and made available to sites for a nominal sum. By the early 1990s, adoption of JAC was high, with over 800 sites across the state having purchased the program. There was also interstate and national interest in increasing its availability. At this stage, those supporting JAC—the development team and representatives from government departments who had supported its use (from portfolios such as Labour and Education)—committed funds to an evaluation.

A major purpose of an evaluation of JAC was to identify variations in the impact of JAC across the range of sites described above. The evaluation became a study of implementation. However, a fidelity approach was not appropriate in this case. First, given the variations in the nature of site types, it would have been difficult—if not impossible—to specify the full range of dimensions of JAC use across site types. Second, the evaluation was asked to identify variations in the use of JAC within one site type—for example, public libraries, in response to local need. Third, the JAC program was not in itself the major focus of the evaluation. The major focus was the use of JAC within the broader framework of careers advice.

The study used a variety of data-collection methods, including the use of a specifically designed computer screen capture method in conjunction with actual use of the JAC data base, a questionnaire to careers advisers which focused on variations in use of the program, and focus group interviews designed to explore variations in patterns of careers advice within and between site types.

The second major purpose of the evaluation was to determine factors which affected the use of JAC. In this aspect of the study, there was a focus on factors which affected use in educational institutions.

The analyses showed that there were major differences in use across site types. For example, in public libraries, JAC was treated as a stand-alone facility which library patrons used without assistance from staff. In schools, use was more varied: for individual student course advice; as a resource for classroom teachers; and as a resource for parents. The variety of use in schools varied, and was shown to be dependent on the 'stock of knowledge' of the careers adviser. This was treated as a 'dependent' variable in the analysis of school use.

Four groups of variables affecting the knowledge of these careers teachers were the:

- characteristics of the JAC program;
- facilities in schools devoted to careers education;
- support from other staff especially the Principal; and
- ongoing professional development about careers programs and resources such as JAC.

A feature of the evaluation was the strong links between a steering committee and the evaluation team. This facilitated the collection of data—for example, the program staff worked with the evaluators to set up the on-screen capture data, and organised the focus groups.

Towards the conclusion of the evaluation, a draft report was developed and recommendations included. A seminar was held at the conclusion of the study during which stakeholders considered the implications of the findings for the improved use of JAC in their agencies.

A final summary of the findings was produced which made a feature of the distinction between implementation of JAC and factors which affected its implementation. The evaluation team made some specific recommendations for shifting the locus of professional development from a centrally organised focus to one in which highly skilled careers advisers would play a central role. (Owen et al., 1991)

This case shows that, in some instances, local needs promote a diversity of uses of an innovation. The focus of the evaluation effort moved away from fidelity concerns to a broader focus in which individual user creativity became a pivotal factor for the investigation.

There is sometimes a naivety about implementation among program funders and senior management. Some senior bureaucrats believe that, once resources have been allocated to a given social intervention policy, the program can be assumed to be in place. A not-uncommon scenario is one in which senior management, often under political pressures, expects program staff to plan and implement a program within extreme time constraints. The reality is that working through an idea or policy to develop implementation guidelines is often complex. The consequent step of translating guidelines into action then requires support and time to ensure that the program makes an impact in the field. Without these steps, incomplete or partial implementation is a real possibility.

In summary, implementation studies have a strong place in the evaluation literature, and they reflect the need to find out what is actually taking place during program delivery. This applies whether or not the program is disseminated from a central agency or is developed locally.

### Establishing performance auditing as an approach to evaluation

As indicated earlier, government auditors-general in most Western nations have increasingly become involved in performance audits over the last decade. The fact that we have included performance auditing as an Approach to the Impact Form of evaluation is consistent with trends within professional evaluation associations to acknowledge that there is an emerging congruence between evaluation and auditing (Wisler, 1996). Also, auditors in the public and private sectors are increasingly using staff trained in evaluation or using the consultancy services of trained evaluators in their performance auditing work.

---

**Example 13.9 The Office of the Victorian Auditor General in Australia**

This Office has increasingly devoted its resources to undertaking performance audits over the past decade. While staff in the Office once had predominantly accounting qualifications, there has been an increase in the proportion holding other tertiary degrees with components in social science techniques. From 1985/86, when the first performance audits began, the situation in 1996/97 was that 30 out of a staff of 140 were fully involved in performance auditing. In the period 1992–96, the Office undertook 34 performance audits. The major target of performance audits was government agencies and large-scale programs conducted by these agencies. While the Office continues to see its primary reporting role as providing information to the parliament, it has also developed processes for feeding back its findings to the agencies under review. In performance audits, the objectives of the program are a given. Thus the audit concentrates on the implementation and outcomes—or the lack of achievement of them. The Office of the Auditor General's reports in recent times have included some strong criticism of the lack of achievement of the implementation and outcomes of government programs and wastage of funds by government departments. There has been some implied criticism of government policy associated with some of these reports. The present conservative government in Victoria is currently reviewing the status of the Office in the light of these criticisms.

---

## CONCLUSION

Within the scope of Approaches within Impact evaluation, and indeed within any evaluation Approach, there is room for the evaluator to use a range of data-management methods. The evaluator is involved in a chain of decisions throughout each evaluation. These are open to challenge by interested observers and critics. We believe that an evaluator must be able to defend the decisions made, and that this will encourage observers and critics to accept the findings within the provisos of the adopted evaluation design, and in particular the data management or evidence assembly aspect of the design.

While there is often a high commitment to elaborate experimental designs in the conduct of research, those undertaking evaluations are often in the situation where selection from a limited range of data options must be made. Even where there is a large amount of 'front-end' planning in an evaluation, and where some form of experimental design can be used, decisions about the specifics of data management are always made on an ongoing basis after fieldwork commences.

The data analyst must make a series of 'micro' decisions about what data is most relevant to the issue. Whether the information is qualitative or quantitative in nature, evaluators make day-to-day judgments about aspects such as what data to collect, what kinds of analysis are appropriate and how they should be interpreted. These decisions influence the findings and ultimately any conclusions which flow from the exercise.

Decisions about data management must also take into account limitations imposed by the availability of data sources. For example, while it might be more appropriate to carry out a representative sample survey, the situation might be such that a grab sample is the only feasible action due to the fact that a population from which the sample is to be drawn is hard to identify or difficult to contact. Resources available for the evaluation, the need to provide information under time constraints, and the amount of staff time to be given to the exercise all influence the boundaries drawn around data management.

These aspects of evaluation in practice are illustrated in the cases described above. For example, in one of the examples described in this chapter (Example 13.4), the selection of baby mass records rather than other sources of data involved the evaluators in micro decision-making about the validity of the information available from that source compared with other sources. In framing conclusions about the effects of the nourishment program, the assumption was that this indicator reflected the achievement of all objectives of that program.

In summary, data management can be tricky. On reflection, this seems to be the area of program evaluation where there is the most need for advice and input from external evaluators in order for small-scale studies to have maximum impact.

No evaluation is totally objective: it is subject to a series of linked decisions. Evaluation can be thought of as a point of view rather than a statement of absolute truth about a program. Findings must be considered by decision-makers within the context of the decisions made by the evaluator in undertaking the translation of issues into data collection tools and the subsequent data analysis and interpretation.

## REFERENCES

Ainley, J.G. (1978). *The Impact of the Science Facilities Program*. Hawthorn: Australian Council for Educational Research.

Brinkerhoff, R. (1989). 'Evaluating Training in Business and Industry'. *New Directions in Program Evaluation*, 44, 5–19.

Brooks, R.A. (1996). 'Blending Two Cultures: State Legislative Auditing and Evaluation'. *New Directions in Program Evaluation*, 71, 15–28.

Brown, R.E., Gallagher, T.P. & Williams, M.C. (1982). *Auditing Performance in Government*. New York: John Wiley.

Chelimsky, E. (1995). 'The Political Environment and What it Means for the Development of the Field'. *Evaluation Practice*, 16 (3), 215–25.

Davis, D.F. (1990). 'Do You Want a Performance Audit or a Program Evaluation?' *Public Administration Review*, 50 (1), 35–41.

English, F.W. (1988). *Curriculum Auditing*. Educational Resources Information Centre (ERIC) Microfiche ED 302 912.

Hall, G.E. & Loucks, S.F. (1979). *Innovation Configuration: Analysing the Adaptations of Innovations*. Austin, TX: Research and Development Center for Teacher Education.

Hatry, H.P. & van Houten, T. (1996). *Measuring Program Outcomes*. A Practical Approach, Washington, DC: United Way of America.

Hick, P. (1988). 'An Evaluation of a Nutrition Program for Young Turkish Mothers'. Unpublished paper for the Graduate Diploma in Adult and Continuing Education, Melbourne College of Advanced Education.

Hirst, R., Malcolm, C. & Owen, J.M. (1980). 'An Example of Evaluation in the Development of a Tertiary Physics Program'. *Research in Science Education*, 10, 151–7.

Hurworth, R.E., Owen, J.M. & Griffin, L.D. (1988). *The Impact of the Richmond Community Health Centre Pre-Pregnancy Program*. Melbourne: Centre for Program Evaluation, The University of Melbourne.

Leadbetter, C. (1998). 'Roadsmart—An Evaluation'. Unpublished Master of Education Thesis, The University of Melbourne.

Leeuw, F.L. (1996). 'Auditing and Evaluation: Bridging a Gap, Worlds to Meet?' *New Directions in Program Evaluation*, 71, 51–60.

Morris, L.L. & Fitzgibbon, C.T. (1978). *How to Measure Program Implementation*. Beverly Hills, CA: Sage.

Ottoson, J. (1994). *Training Evaluation Report of 1994 Profile, Feedback and Follow-up Data*. Vancouver, BC: Prepared for The Training and Evaluation Branch, Division of Community Prevention and Abuse Prevention, Center for Substance Abuse Prevention.

Owen, J.M., Day, N.A. & Jouce, C. (1991). *Informing Decisions about Jobs and Courses*. Melbourne: Centre for Program Evaluation, The University of Melbourne.

Owen, J.M., Meyer, H. & Livingston, J. (1996). *School Responses to the Curriculum and Standards Framework*. Carlton: Victorian Board of Studies.

Phillips, J.J. (ed.) (1994). *In Action: Measuring Return on Investment*. Alexandria, VA: American Society for Training and Development.

Pollitt, C. & Summa, H. (1996). 'Performance Audit and Evaluation: Similar Tools, Different Relationships?' *New Directions in Program Evaluation, 71*, 29–50.

Schwandt, T.A. & Halpern, E.S. (1988). *Linking Auditing and Metaevaluation*. Beverly Hills, CA: Sage.

Scriven, M. (1972). 'Goal Free Evaluation'. In E.R. House (ed.), *School Evaluation: The Politics and the Process*. Berkeley, CA: McCutchan.

Tyler, R. (1950). *Basic Principles of Curriculum and Instruction: Syllabus for Education 360*. Chicago, IL: University of Chicago Press.

Wisler, C. (1996). 'Evaluation and Auditing: Prospects for Convergence'. *New Directions in Program Evaluation, 71*, 1–5.

# Index

308